I Am Not Your Enemy

I Am Not Your Enemy

A Memoir

Reality Winner

Spiegel and Grau

S&G

Spiegel & Grau, New York
www.spiegelandgrau.com

Copyright © 2025 by Reality Winner

All rights reserved. No portion of this book may be reproduced, stored in a retrieval system, or transmitted in any form or by any means—electronic, mechanical, photocopy, recording, scanning, or other—except for brief quotations in critical reviews or articles, without the prior written permission of the publisher.

Interior design by Meighan Cavanaugh

Library of Congress Cataloging-in-Publication Data Available Upon Request

ISBN 978-1-954118-84-3 (hardcover)
ISBN 978-1-954118-85-0 (ebook)

Printed in the United States

First Edition
10 9 8 7 6 5 4 3 2 1

I would not be here if it were not for my mother, Billie.

I Am Not Your Enemy

Introduction

> The only security of all is in a free press. The force of public opinion cannot be resisted, when permitted freely to be expressed.
>
> —Thomas Jefferson

> Arrest the reporter, publisher, editor—you'll get your answer fast. Stop playing games and wasting time!
>
> —Donald Trump

It began like any other day for me. I woke around 4:30 a.m., took Mickey outside for a few minutes, and, no later than 5:30, drove to work from my rental house in Augusta, Georgia, while listening to a podcast about national security called *Intercepted*. I arrived at work around 6:00, and several hours later, I had a coffee mixed with protein powder. It was my usual morning routine. But on this day, I took fateful steps to share some of America's classified national security secrets with the public.

Why *that* day? Why *that* document? I spent years in a prison cell asking myself that question. And the truth is, I don't know. Everything that has happened because of and since that action, the trauma and upheaval and melodrama, has merged to make some of my reasoning mysterious to me. A blank spot exists where my precise motivations should be. I wish I could say that my actions were grandly deliberate and thoughtfully strategic. But my plan wasn't even really a plan. My actions were more spontaneous and poorly organized than your average trip to the grocery store.

That's one of the many sad ironies of the government's portrayal of me as a calculating criminal mastermind, intent on doing whatever she could to reveal America's most vital information to the Taliban and al-Qaeda. If only I had been that careful and farsighted! Rather, my crime proceeded in disconnected stages. I took small actions, each one seemingly harmless on its own, that added up to something appearing coherent and dramatic—and that was irreversible when all the elements were combined, like ingredients that only when mixed in exact quantities can produce a bomb. Except that my explosion never endangered, let alone hurt, anyone but myself. Not even close.

Before that day, I had not planned to leak a classified report or do anything else out of the ordinary. I was working as a contractor for the National Security Agency, the Defense Department's arm tasked with monitoring and processing information for foreign and domestic intelligence purposes. The NSA is a behemoth that vacuums email, text, and phone conversations from around the world. Its budget is so big, its eavesdropping capabilities so vast, that if it were a corporation, it would be one of the biggest in the world, up there with Apple, Microsoft, Walmart, and Amazon. As with those businesses, hundreds of millions of Americans come into frequent contact with the NSA. Unlike with those companies, Americans don't much know when, how, and why the NSA is involved in their lives.

I liked getting to work early, and on the morning of May 9, 2017, I enjoyed the quiet and solitude. Then I opened a news website, the top-secret one available to people working in intelligence, and found a bombshell: a five-page document, listed as the most read "article" on the site, about an enormously controversial subject of public interest. The document contained newly uncovered details about events that had taken place a year earlier. I stared at it, stunned that such a thing existed. By that point, I was jaded about many things, but this jolted me out of my seat. *This will be leaked by Friday*, I thought. *It's too damning to stay secret. Everything leaks.*

The media then was filled with leaks, as though the American government was a broken pipe and information was dripping right to newspapers and journalists. Soon, then–attorney general Jeff Sessions would say in a press briefing that "in the first six months of this administration, [the Department of Justice] has already received nearly as many criminal referrals involving unauthorized disclosures of classified information as we received in the last three years combined." A study by the Federation of American Scientists found that the astounding numbers of secrets being published in the press showed that "leaks of classified information are a 'normal,' predictable occurrence." And the *New York Times* observed, "Journalism in the Trump era has featured a staggering number of leaks from sources across the federal government."

A July 2017 report by the Senate Committee on Homeland Security and Governmental Affairs found that a majority of the leaks "concerned the Russia probes, with many revealing closely-held information such as intelligence community intercepts, FBI interviews and intelligence, grand jury subpoenas, and even the workings of a secret surveillance court. Other leaks disclosed potentially sensitive intelligence on U.S. adversaries or possible military plans against them. One leak, about the investigation of a terrorist attack, caused a diplomatic incident between the United States and a close ally."

I believed that these leaks were an inevitable response to an undeniable crisis: American institutions were collapsing. I was twenty-five years old at the time and had already spent five years of my life at the NSA in various roles, and I angrily wondered why the agency had not delivered any public response in the first four months of the Trump administration, which had been constantly disparaging us. When he wasn't ignoring our work, the president denigrated the intelligence community as being part of "the deep state" intent on subverting the will of the public. Far worse, the administration lied daily with impunity, and the heads of our institutions responded publicly with only silence. Public life then was surreal. Just hours later that day, Trump would fire FBI director James Comey, who was heading the investigation into Russia's interference in the 2016 election. It seemed like an attempt to silence anyone looking into what had happened. The *New Yorker* called Trump's move "an attack on American democracy." Laurence Tribe, a Harvard University constitutional scholar, wrote in the *Washington Post* that "the time has come for Congress to launch an impeachment investigation of President Trump for obstruction of justice." Trump seemed capable of virtually anything. Envisioning him ordering that an NSA report be disappeared was not difficult. If it vanished, I thought, people would wonder whether it had existed at all, or if they had just imagined it, an example of the Mandela effect, a phenomenon in which false memories are shared by large groups of people. I decided to print the article so that at least one copy would be preserved, even if Trump's henchmen otherwise eliminated its existence.

But when I went to print it, my nonexistent tech skills proved problematic. This was one of the many ways in which I differed from Edward Snowden, the NSA employee who had handed over thousands of pages of documents to reporters at the *Guardian*, a news website specializing in national security issues. "If you see something," the publication posted on their web page detailing how to contact them, "leak something." Later, Snowden and I were often grouped together, but our motivations, our methods, and the consequences of our actions were very different. He planned his leaking months and possibly a year in advance. He contacted journalists before he leaked anything, to gain their assurances, guidance, and cooperation. He was a tech wizard who used encrypted emails and a code name. He was intent on bringing down the out-of-control national security state. He saved an estimated 1.5 *million* documents on a thumb drive.

By contrast, I spontaneously tapped the print button on a five-page document involving intelligence from the previous year without giving the whole thing much thought. And, like an actor in some slapstick comedy, I immediately realized that I didn't know where in the office the report would be printed out. I began a frantic search of the entire office space, from one twenty-foot break room (where the printers were located) to the next, hoping to hear some noises reassuringly indicating that a printer was spitting out the pages. There was no legitimate work reason for me to be looking at that document, let alone printing it out. It's an open secret in intelligence that people routinely peruse information beyond what they need to know professionally, but printing that information in hard copy is much less common. The only reason anyone would print a document would be to circulate it to people or to keep it, both of which are illegal. If someone discovered that I had printed it, they might ask questions I didn't have answers to. If I got caught, I might have to take another security training, or I could even be fired. As boring as my job was, I didn't want to lose it. If a security supervisor grilled me, I would not be able to explain the reasons for my actions, because even I was unsure of them. Despite what the FBI would later claim, I am a terrible liar, unskilled in the arts of deception. My anxiety usually leads me to drop my poker face, after which someone takes all my chips.

Before I was unable to locate the printer, I had not been nervous about what I was doing. At the time, I was emotionally numb to most things, mourning my father's recent death and suffering from general loneliness and spiraling despair about the state of the country and the world. Trump had been sworn into office in January and already was wreaking havoc. He severely restricted immigration from seven

Muslim-majority countries. His national security adviser, Michael Flynn, stepped down after just twenty-two days when it was revealed that he had lied about his paid lobbying work on behalf of Turkey. Trump also was threatening to destroy North Korea. And that's just a short list.

Or perhaps I wasn't nervous simply because I knew that the NSA was filled with other bored introverts who spent much of the time goofing off—we weren't going around glancing at one another's computer screens. The office had not seemed like a place where intellectual curiosity aroused suspicion.

But I didn't want to test that belief.

With faux casualness, I walked from printer to printer looking for my papers. *Nope, not that one. Nope, not that one either. Jesus, I'm an idiot.* After checking three printers, I returned to the first one and found the report lying there. This was the first time I had printed anything out, and I hadn't even known that the printers took a while before releasing a document! I snatched up the pages, placed them face down on my desk, and reassured myself that the problem had been averted.

And with that, I went on with my day. Nobody would know or care that the report was on my desk. I left it there when work ended and I departed for the gym. That evening, I checked the news to see if the report had been leaked, if any policymakers were talking about its contents—it was, I believed, crucial information that could further illuminate the accumulating understanding of the president's ties to Russia. Everyone at work had been discussing it, saying it would pop up in the news sooner rather than later. But no, the country was apparently obsessed only with Trump's shocking abuse of democracy in firing James Comey. The next morning, I checked the news, and again it wasn't mentioned.

The reader should know that my plea deal prevents me from verifying the report's contents. But you can easily find the entire thing online with a simple Google search, and it was later summarized by the *New York Times* as "describ[ing] two cyberattacks by Russia's military intelligence unit, the G.R.U.—one in August against a company that sells voter registration-related software and another, a few days before the election, against 122 local election officials."

To be honest, I don't think I knew what I was going to do with the document before I did it. But around 2:00 p.m. on the day after I printed it out, I folded it in half and placed it in my lunch box. At the time, I was a vegan, so my lunch box was packed with pounds of kale; I would eat two or three meals of it at work to fill up on protein and clean carbs before heading to the gym. I took my lunch box into the bathroom and went into a stall. I was wearing a ruby-red cardigan sweater, a flowy green Goodwill dress, and tight pantyhose—my outfits were always stylistically questionable yet nice; I purchased my clothes at thrift shops and swapped them out weekly in order never to repeat an outfit. I was still in my first year out of the military—I had been in the air force for six years, working my way up to senior airman before being honorably discharged—and I was extremely self-conscious about my appearance. I took the folded document from my lunch box and slipped it into my pantyhose.

Normally, at the end of my shift, getting out of the building through security wasn't hard. It still usually made me alternately apprehensive or annoyed, since they always checked my lunch box, bag, or purse. But they never patted me down or anything—this was supposed to be the NSA, but it wasn't even the TSA. And sure enough, that afternoon was no different: they let me leave through the door after doing the routine bag checks. I walked straight to my car, relieved. My common sense was strong enough to discourage me from removing the document from my pantyhose in the parking lot. Instead, I drove to the gym, parked, took out the pages, and wedged them between the seat and the center console. I went to exercise and thought more about the guy I was breaking up with than the top-secret document in my car.

Two days later, I bought a white envelope, scribbled the *Intercept*'s New York City address on it, placed the report inside, and stuck a stamp on it. I drove to yoga, where I taught a class as a substitute teacher, after which I dropped the envelope into a mailbox across the street. No return address anywhere, no name or any other identifying details. What mattered were the contents. *This is going to be big. Maybe help save this country. And nobody will ever know it was me. Or if they do find out, everyone will be grateful to me for sharing facts the public should know.*

Things didn't go exactly as I had hoped. Instead of being the public's anonymous good Samaritan, I spent more time in prison than any whistle-blower in American history.

THERE IS NO TYPICAL WHISTLE-BLOWER. Sometimes people like to group me with other individuals who have leaked classified national security information to the media: Daniel Ellsberg, Edward Snowden, John Kiriakou, Thomas Drake, and Chelsea Manning are the best known. Often, these comparisons are unflattering. According to analyst Tom Nichols at the *Atlantic*, "All of these cases . . . are bound by the thread of narcissism," the product of "a protracted epidemic," which "is on the rise, in the United States and around the world." Diagnosing people with personality disorders on the basis of their portrayals in the press is a curious thing. Actual mental health professionals refrain from such diagnoses because they understand that any person is far more complicated than a context-free sound bite. But that doesn't stop armchair psychiatrists like Nichols, who are more than happy to caricature vastly different human beings in service of the argument that we are all "menaces to national security."

Unlike Nichols and uncurious keyboard psychologists like him, I have spoken with Ellsberg, Drake, Manning, and other whistle-blowers at various points in my post-leak life. You'll hear from them. My aim in sharing their words is for you, the reader, to comprehend our motivations and actions, and to see how we are alike and how we are different. I have come to believe that far more separates us than unites us. The leakers I have spoken with have different personality types and come from radically diverse backgrounds. There are only two things we have in common. The first is that we revealed secrets, but we have plenty of company in that. The other thing uniting us, which is far less common, is that we got caught.

One of the first whistle-blowers to step forward in support, and introduce himself to my family, was Thomas Drake, who had been a top official at the NSA and served in the air force and navy. Like him, I deeply believed in America's national security system; I never wanted to destroy it. Following my six years in the military, I received the Air Force Commendation Medal for "provid[ing] over 1,900 hours of enemy intelligence exploitation and assist[ing] in geolocating 120 enemy combatants during 734 airborne sorties [air missions]." Exactly what I did to earn that commendation is something I am unable to reveal for legal reasons. I can only quote this NSA-approved Commendation Medal certificate and leave the rest to interpretation.

My commendation goes on to say: "She facilitated 816 intelligence missions, 3,236 time sensitive reports, and removing more than 100 enemies from the battlefield. Furthermore, while deployed to support Combatant Commander's requirements, Airman Winner was appointed as the lead deployment language analyst, producing 2,500 reports, aiding in 650 enemy captures, 600 enemies killed in action and identifying 900 high value targets."

That's a lot of military-speak, so I'll translate: I helped kill a lot of human beings. Hundreds, possibly thousands. I developed post-traumatic stress disorder doing it. As a child and young adult, I dreamed of receiving awards for helping people, or saving them. But that wasn't how it turned out. I helped the United States government kill people. I was good at it. So good that they gave me an award for it.

But then I shared some information with the American people, and the US government felt that was a much worse thing to do than killing scores of people. They decided I was an enemy of the country. My Pokémon-loving, yoga-practicing, vegetable-subsisting complex personality got erased. To quote my mother's sardonic comment to a reporter about the chasm separating who I really am from the traitor the government claimed I was: "The world's biggest terrorist has a Pikachu bedspread." Well put, Momface.

One

It ain't what they call you, it's what you answer to.
—Commonly attributed to W. C. Fields

Traitor. Turncoat. Terrorist. Dangerous. Enemy. Anti-American.

These are some of the names the United States government, far-right activists, and prominent media figures called me after I was arrested and charged under the Espionage Act. (Other insults they hurled at me were less family friendly.) My six years as a linguist in the air force, my love of family and faith and viral dog videos, my lifelong commitment to defending and serving my community and country—none of it seemed to register in the eyes and words of those defining my reputation for the public. As I lay on my mat in the small jail cell in rural Georgia that I shared with twelve other women, some of whom slept on the floor for lack of beds, I would watch these self-appointed jurors trying me in the media, screaming that I was dangerous to all Americans. News anchors would gravely nod in agreement and repeat that I was undoubtedly a threat to the security of this nation and its citizens. Meanwhile, I needed permission to go outside my cell or walk in a circle in a fenced-in basketball court.

It's strange to see incriminating lies spouted about you by high-ranking officials with impressive résumés, expensive suits, and well-styled haircuts. It's even more bizarre when some of those people are leaders in the same industry where you worked before they stuffed you into a dank, dirty cell. Alas, I have come to learn in the hardest of ways that the nation's most powerful people hate nothing so much as when a mid-ranking or junior individual in the vast national security state goes rogue.

That's not just speculation. According to his published memos, when he was FBI director, James Comey told then-President Donald Trump that individuals who leaked government information to the public were "terrible" and declared himself "eager to find leakers and would like to nail one to the door as a message." He proposed "putting a head on a pike as a message." According to Comey's recollection, Trump said reporters who receive and publish leaked information—a constitutionally protected right—should be placed in jail so they are forced to reveal their sources. "They spend a couple days in jail, make a new friend, and they are ready to talk," Trump said, essentially recommending that journalists get raped in jail. In response, Comey laughed.

In 2022, Trump made the same hideous "joke" at a rally in Texas. He stood on stage and told his supporters how he would handle journalists who published classified information—which, again, the Supreme Court decades ago concluded is protected under the First Amendment: "You take the writer and/or the publisher of the paper . . . and you say, 'Who is the leaker? National security.' And they say, 'We're not gonna tell you.' They say, 'That's okay, you're going to jail.' And when this person realizes that he is going to be the bride of another prisoner very shortly, he will say, 'I'd very much like to tell you exactly who that leaker is!'" The crowd applauded and roared in approval at this suggestion of rape.

But I didn't need to be jailed or raped to disclose my identity as a leaker. Soon after the FBI showed up on my driveway, I confessed everything I did, the same confession I have already made to you, right up front: in May 2017, I mailed a copy of a five-page intelligence summary to investigative reporters at the *Intercept*, an online news source. Given the fierce controversy involving Trump and Russia that was tearing apart the country in the spring of 2017, and the widespread fear of the demise of American democracy, I felt obligated to release the information to the public. If I didn't do so, and the country crumbled, how could I live with myself? But my action was illegal, and it was wrong. I regret it. I will not hide from those hard truths.

And yet those are not the only hard truths that I believe must be acknowledged. Not by a long shot. Few understand that America's harshest national security laws do little to protect the country but much to destroy the lives of our citizens. In most cases, you would have to fall on the other side of the law and be labeled a threat ever to care how such laws are misused. You must be jailed yourself, or have a loved one locked up, to see how our prisons and jails are frequently cruel places, consigning human beings to inhumane conditions for years while making it impossible for justice to prevail. For my crime, I was given a five-year sentence in federal prison. As we'll see, the punishment for leakers is highly selective, brutalizing low-level personnel with harsh sentences while more powerful leakers are given wrist slaps. I wish I could tell you that I handled the punishment well, gaining wisdom and building real-world skills. But that wasn't the case. Like most people in America's mammoth prison-industrial complex, I came out in far worse shape than I went in. The cruelty was the point.

My years behind bars taught me that the Espionage Act—the draconian law they charged me with, even though they never even claimed I was committing espionage—is not unique in its obese scope, vindictiveness, and usefulness as a political tool. Thousands of people are similarly in jails and prisons on trumped-up conspiracy charges. Nor were my conditions on the inside especially bad—they're equally terrible for the other two million Americans behind bars.

And yet, as you read this book, I hope you will also learn how it is possible to survive all this and more, from assault to mental illness. Despite everything I have endured, I can tell you that even the hardest reality can be confronted and managed. Survival is always a choice. It was mine, and it can be yours.

That's true even if, like me, you grew up under bizarre and sometimes traumatic conditions.

Two

> Names, once they are in common use, quickly become mere sounds, their etymology being buried, like so many of the earth's marvels, beneath the dust of habit.
> —Salman Rushdie, *The Satanic Verses*

"Reality. Like the word. Winner. Like the word. Uh-huh, n-n-e-r. Yes, that is my real, legal name." Every time I introduce myself to someone, I have to repeat the same spiel. My friends and family, however, call me Re or ReeRee. And to save time, my local barista knows me as Starbucks Sara—no *h*.

Reality Winner is not a name anyone sane or sober would choose as their own. I have my father, Ronald Lawrence Winner, to thank, or blame. Mom got naming rights to their firstborn and she wanted a BMW, so she went with Brittany Michele Winner for my older sister. That's a normal enough name. It's elegant, even. The type of name that a girl can be proud of, or at least ignore. But Dad insisted that he get to name me, their only other child together. He had a favorite T-shirt from a Lamaze class that read "I Coached a Real Winner," which somehow inspired his leap to Reality. Through some superstitious calculation known only to him and the gods, he thought that affixing the bizarre name to his kid would increase the odds that they'd *be* a real winner. He also insisted that my middle name start with *L*, so that he and I would have the same initials. My mother chose Leigh, even if she couldn't have the full Vivien Leigh, after the *Gone with the Wind* actress. Reality Leigh Winner. That shared middle initial set me apart from my two sisters—Dad intended me to be of his own mind. It might sound nice, like a father-daughter bonding experiment. But my father had extensive experience in the drug world, as both a dealer and an addict, served time in prison, rarely worked at his job as a sports memorabilia dealer, and beat me when I was five years old for not letting him sleep after he took us to the movies. I'd rather take after my mother, the rock of our family, thank you very much!

So my distinctive name, the one that delighted many headline writers and late-night comics when I got arrested (looking at you, Stephen Colbert and Bill Maher), was inspired by a ridiculous T-shirt and not, as many people assumed, fashioned by yours truly as some profound symbolic statement. It's undeniably amusing, I admit, but when your weird given name appears in national headlines, it's easier for the public and the prosecution to portray you as a little unhinged. As someone a little less *human* than the rest of us, and therefore a lot more dangerous.

That seems to be part of a pattern in my life: people make assumptions about me, but the truth is far different from what they imagine. It's so much more mundane.

My father badly wanted his kid to be a winner because he was very much not one. Growing up in Wisconsin, his life chances were severely limited by his own father, a severely abusive man. As a teenager, Dad, a promising baseball prospect, attended tryouts for the New York Yankees. But his father—my biological grandfather—didn't want him to play ball for a living. So he deliberately broke his son's ankle.

That fucked-up story, at least, is what my dad told me. But Dad told a lot of stories, and distinguishing his truths from his fictions is beyond even the most talented fact-checker. There weren't a lot of sources around to corroborate his tales. I never got to meet my grandfather, or any of his side of the family, despite his living the last few years of his life in the same city in which Brittany and I spent every other weekend with our dad. I didn't even learn his name until I did some research for this book: Robert Neal Winner was part of a Winner family tree that stretches from Ohio to New York, extending as far back as the early 1800s, or possibly originating from Pennsylvania in the mid-1700s.

The last time my father saw his father alive was at his home in Harlingen, Texas. After his father had reached out and asked him to visit, pleaded, even, Dad went to his house and rang the doorbell. His father answered in a wheelchair, having had a stroke. "I wanted to hit him right there," Dad told me. "I didn't care that he was sick and weak, because I was weak when that son of a bitch beat me and your grandma Betty."

My father never got over his own childhood mistreatment. Maybe none of us does totally. We always carry the past with us. It's as inescapable as the DNA that runs through our bloodstream. But as I've mentioned, I have come to believe, to *know*, that it's possible to prevail through pain, indeed to thrive, while still being burdened with the thick scars of the past. All of it, it's all survivable and surmountable. Even childhood physical abuse. Even mental illness. Even drug addiction. Even an unjust prison sentence.

My dad never realized that trauma could be overcome, and that failure led him to make up lies. I can't be too sure about his exact circumstances. The stuff that isn't murky was likely fabricated. Long before he met my mother, he told us, he was studying theology at a university (he never named it), and the school rejected his undergraduate thesis, which proposed that Judas was the most important disciple. (I never learned if he had read Nikos Kazantzakis's 1955 book, *The Last Temptation of Christ*, which likewise suggests the Judas idea.) After dropping out, Dad went to a reservation for indigenous tribes in Canada for a few years. I assume that he was really there, since he had framed needlework that on the back named the reservation, and Canada, and the year 1967. But I have no idea why he went to a reservation in particular.

Other things might also be true, things he never said but that would explain some of his life choices and whereabouts. After leaving school, Dad was probably drafted into the Vietnam War and promptly took off for other pastures. He denied that to me, saying he was in college and therefore exempt from the draft. But he didn't complete his degree until years later, by his own account, and he spent a lot of time in Canada, of all places, immediately after leaving school. In the late 1960s, young American men who departed for Canada were going for one reason: to avoid the war. More than fifty-seven thousand Americans died in Vietnam, and hundreds of thousands were wounded. I would understand if Dad didn't want to be one of them. But I think he was always ashamed to have left the US to escape the war, and so he lied about it.

My father told legends about himself, myths he wanted us and himself to believe because they were preferable to the sad truths. By the time he returned to the United States in the early 1970s, he was approaching thirty. Angry about his father's treatment of him, his school failures, and maybe his status as a draft dodger, he began a life of petty crime. He did two years at the Ohio State Penitentiary, possibly for stealing a vehicle from the cemetery where he worked. He had ridiculous stories of what could go wrong at a cemetery, of arms spilling through holes broken in the cement sarcophagi in the adjacent plots when mistakes were made with the heavy machinery. He had a daughter, Sarah "Nikki" Nicole, with his first wife in 1974. When that marriage dissolved, he went to Wisconsin to complete his degree.

That's where he connected with my mother, a bright and pretty redhead with lovely green eyes. She, too, had grown up with abusive, mentally ill parents, and in severe poverty to boot. But she had managed to get to university and was determined to make a decent life for herself by helping kids. The choices my mother made in response to her own crappy circumstances were very different from my father's decisions, and they established precedents that I would cite to myself decades later.

My mother was about to graduate from the University of Wisconsin–Eau Claire, where she was studying sociology, when she met my father. Mom was attracted to Dad's indisputable intelligence, and she began an affair with this smart, tall man who was twenty-one years her senior. They married when my mother got pregnant with Brittany in 1990 and decided to move to the Lone Star State. My mother had always wanted to escape her own state, and Texas's family services agency was easier to work for than Wisconsin's. Their move to the Rio Grande Valley effectively launched her career in child protective services, the field she worked in for decades. Even when my parents' marriage soured, and my father blamed my mother for nearly every aspect of their separation and everything else wrong with his miserable life, he never denigrated her profession—he valued anyone working to save kids from abuse.

Mom soon gave birth to Brittany. They were all supposed to live happily ever after. But sometimes life has other ideas.

The week after Brittany was born in the hospital in Harlingen, my father was driving her around in his mother's old Chrysler. My father was at the wheel, with my sister in a car seat in the back, when a drunk driver T-boned them at an intersection. The Chrysler spun around a full 360 degrees. Dad felt a violent pain in his back, which had already been seriously damaged in a car accident earlier that year. His lower back was shattered, and my sister's umbilical cord stump (which remains in infants for a few weeks after birth) ruptured. The doctors kept my father in the hospital but cleared Brittany to go home. Within a few days, however, her intestines pushed through her navel, and she needed surgery to repair the hernia.

My father's prospects for living a stable life were always slim, but the accident destroyed them. Though my sister's hernia healed, he never recovered from the tragedy. In some ways, he tried to put it past him: a year and three months after Brittany, I came along in December 1991 (no car accidents that week). After a year in Alice, Texas, we settled in Ricardo, a small, majority-Latino town—with a population of about one thousand, it doesn't count as a town—just outside the city of Kingsville. Kingsville, while in a constant state of expansion over my lifetime, still has under thirty thousand people and retains a small-town Texan feel. My parents bought thirty acres, and Dad promised us horses to ride.

But he never worked on that, or on anything legitimate, really. The year after I was born, he endured more than ten surgeries to replace and bolster his spine with computerized disks. In 1995, a new form of pain management—a miracle drug—was approved, and my father was promptly prescribed OxyContin. This became an addiction that lasted the remainder of his life. He was sick and bedridden for most of my childhood.

Fuck the Sackler family criminals, the architects of the opioid crisis. Fuck every single one of them. I believe my dad to be one of their many victims. They ruined whatever shot he had at a normal life, with consequences that I live with every day.

The car crash is imprinted in my mind as one of those stories that makes you aware of life's randomness and grateful for your good fortune. You're lucky if fate hasn't severely impaired you in an auto accident. To hear my dad tell it, though, you'd think what mattered was the settlement money they got from the insurance company. When she turned eighteen, Brittany would receive $20,000 each year, for four years. This was to be her college tuition money. He thought she was set! He ignored his Oxy addiction and somehow never connected his excruciating back pain to the accident. In his mind, the accident had been a lucky break. The money was all that counted.

Opioid addiction is common knowledge now, but as kids, we didn't know what caused my father's chronic fatigue and occasional delusions. For years, Britty just thought he was sick with some undetermined illness. Me, I knew something else was afoot; I didn't know what exactly, but I knew he was doing something to himself beyond your traditional malady. Maybe my intuition came from seeing what my father was like when he was up and about; he was a vastly different man when he was on his feet, but he still wasn't a normal parent.

From my infancy, my father took us on "errands" to Mexico or to shady pharmacies across Texas. We accompanied him to a particular doctor Dad said was the only person with the proper medication for him. Only years later did we realize that this doctor was giving him meds to sell, which is how my dad got his nickname, Doc, which he wore proudly on his billiards jersey. We thought he got that name because he was so smart! But the truth was that our cool father with the earring and ponytail was a drug dealer, and he brought us along while he sold his illegal pills. When I consider my odds for having an ordinary life, given my childhood, the first image that pops into my head is my draft-dodging, drug-dealing, opioid-addicted father, who named me after a T-shirt.

Dad and I always had a difficult relationship, but I'll admit that I wasn't the easiest kid to deal with. I've always had trouble controlling my anger. My mother said that even at two years of age, I could be calm one minute and screaming with rage the next. Growing up, I routinely smashed my parents' telephones, and I continued to smash the occasional phone even as an adult. In rural Texas in the '90s, no one ever investigated the sources of my fury; my mother knew from her job what happened to children diagnosed with behavioral disorders at early ages. Instead of being relegated to special education classes I was left festering in school, but also with access to a normal education. Most importantly to my mother, I was left unmedicated.

My mother's way of dealing with my anger was shrewd: she walked away, to avoid feeding into it. That calmed me down. My father took the opposite approach and screamed back at me. His method escalated situations, pouring gasoline on my fire. Then, a few years later, my father took us to see the film *The Prince of Egypt,* paying for our tickets with my birthday cash from Grandma Betty. Later that day, he paid me back, using five-dollar bills instead of ones. I was too young to understand that this smaller stack of bills was almost all my magical birthday money being returned to me. I yelled at him about it while he was trying to sleep after the movie, and he whipped my back with a belt. As far as abuse goes, this hardly seems worth mentioning, but my parents were both against spanking, and my mother wanted him to leave for that alone. It wasn't the beginning of the end, nor the end of the end, but it was a huge red flag signaling the deterioration of our father's lucidity and his increased dependence on painkillers. He never mentioned the incident again, and he swore up and down for years that he had never laid a hand on us.

By the time I was six, my parents had divorced. Dad migrated into a two-bedroom trailer owned by his parents in Harlingen, a bigger city about an hour and a half south of Kingsville. After he moved, he picked us up every other weekend and on the occasional weeknight for a movie and dinner. But he couldn't manage anything resembling normal parenthood, partly because he had never known it himself. He'd never had any friends or family members to spend time with. Outside of his customers and my half sister Nikki, during the years she lived in Harlingen with her three children, we were the only people in his life.

The visits were bizarre. One Christmas, when I was eight or so, my father picked us up after church. Brittany and I assumed we would go back to his home to decorate a tree or open presents. Instead, he took us to a bar "to do some business." Needless to say, Santa didn't show up.

If he had, he probably would have been drunk off his ass. We almost got used to Dad taking us to bars, as though those were normal places for kids to be.

For years, we never had a bedroom set up for us at the trailer. Sometimes Brittany and I shared our grandfather's old bed; other times I slept on the couch or crashed on the floor of the computer room, wedged between old Macintosh screens and countless boxes of baseball, football, and basketball cards. One morning waking up there, I discovered I had spent two weekends sleeping three feet from the memorial urns containing my grandparents' ashes.

More adventurously, sometimes we spent weekends procuring drugs in Progreso, Mexico, although my sister and I didn't realize that was what we were doing. Those Saturday afternoon trips south of the border were both a lifeline and a chore. They broke up the monotony and loneliness of the trailer park, but anxiety always accompanied them because the trip back home was never guaranteed. Once, our dad mixed pills and alcohol, and so his equally elderly, equally drunk cohort, Bernard DuFabrique—a friend of my father's who was in even worse health than he was, but whom I always liked because he kept a bunch of copies of *National Geographic* at his house and collected African art—took over the driving, navigating all four of us across the Progreso International Bridge, through customs, and back into San Benito, Texas, where he lived.

On the hottest summer days, we crossed the fertile Rio Grande Valley to the dust and clay of Progreso, where temperatures soared. Then we headed to an auto shop, where my father handed over money to someone to watch the car. Our next stop was an art and jewelry store in something called the Arizona Building, painted with murals of the Grand Canyon and western American landscapes. In the potted plants in the lobby were thirsty horned lizards with whom we were always excited to share our water. Britty and I took the stairs to the third floor to see all the paintings on the way up, while our father took the elevator.

In the store, more money changed hands, and we waited to see the orthodontist, who drove in from Matamoros every month for us. He had green eyes and would pronounce the word "teeth" as "tits," which is how I say it to this day. Afterward, we would head upstairs to the bar, which was nearly empty at that time of day but sometimes had live music. Even the ceiling there was painted, with clouds, prompting Dad to lecture about how Michelangelo painted the Sistine Chapel by hoisting himself onto a platform and lying on his back, toxic paints dripping into his eyes.

By 2004, Dad had suffered several overdoses that I later realized were not accidental. It was a profoundly dark period, but since he was paying for my and Brittany's braces—I was thirteen and Britty is fifteen months older—we still saw him on the regular. On another trip to Mexico to get our orthodontic work done, he passed out in the bar upstairs for hours, and Brittany and I were stranded. Even now, I have recurring nightmares about those times, desperately trying in my dreams to find a way to the highway to return home.

In 2006, the final year we went to Progreso, the violence spurred by the drug cartels was spiking. When we reached the intersection where we turned to find parking, we saw a tank. Young soldiers walked the streets carrying their AK-47s. We had heard rumors that they opened fire on a hair salon from the opposite rooftop for target practice. That day my father handed the receptionist a large wad of cash and our braces were taken off. Small metal retainers were cemented behind our teeth instead of the removable kind. Mine broke off in three days, but we never returned to Mexico for repairs.

On another memorable trip with Dad, we visited a flat furnished only with a mattress, a television, and a Nintendo 64. Brittany and I played video games while Dad haggled with the young couple who lived there. They couldn't pay cash for the goods, which led Dad to notice how entertained we were by the video game console. We went home with it that night, and that was my introduction to the iconic *Super Mario World 64* and *The Legend of Zelda: Ocarina of Time*.

Britty and I never felt maltreated or deprived on these visits because on the last day of our stays, Dad would treat us to huge shopping sprees. He'd drop us off at a shopping mall and give us $300 each—an incredible amount of money for kids our age. It's difficult to see that your father is a bad parent when he's showering you with money or teaching you how to gamble at poker like a professional.

The intoxicating effect of these shopping excursions soon wore off, however. Instead, what lasted were the feelings of dread that flooded me when my father would pick us up from Kingsville. With the visits to bleak lands full of suspicious people engaged in unsavory activities, time with our father became a regular source of familiar horror. A head-spinning contrast existed between the noisiness and festiveness of our family home in Kingsville where, after our mom remarried (more on that soon), we had stepsiblings visiting and laughing loudly and loving one another, and the emptiness of our dad's life. In his trailer, Dad just lay in bed, so Brittany and I escaped into Harry Potter books and spent hundreds of hours playing *Pokémon Stadium* on the Nintendo 64. It was always just Brittany and me, and we didn't always get along, so the overall feeling of isolation was real and devastating. Sometimes we wandered outside in separate directions and approached the elderly people living in the trailer park. A kind woman once invited me in to play with her ornate Chinese checkers set. Other times, we went door to door singing or trying to sell the canned goods from our father's pantry. We once got a quarter for a leaking can of sauerkraut.

Sometimes I wonder if my sister and I should have clued into the nature of my father's activities. But we had no frame of reference to understand the drug world. As kids, we were mostly forbidden from consuming popular culture with adult themes like violence or sex, which meant we relied on Disney movies and fantasy novels well into high school. You know those weird kids in school who miss all their classmates' references to pop songs and television shows? That was us. We didn't spend much time with other kids because our house was in the middle of nowhere. There wasn't any neighborhood near our home in the proper sense, the closest house being more than a football field's length away. At home, it was quiet and secluded. Even though our father was an emotionally distant drug addict and cross-border dealer, we were sheltered, secure at our family home.

Dad brainwashed us into believing that the divorce was Mom's choice, Mom's fault, and that only he did right by us. It was bullshit, but he had a naive, captive audience and a marvelous ability to speak, to lecture, to persuade. We had no counterinfluence then, so we mostly believed him, until we got older and wiser.

Compounding our confusion, ironically, was my father's disdain for people who used drugs. Dad always talked about his first daughter, my half sister Nikki, as if she were a missed opportunity, defined by her unused potential. He suggested she was a lost cause, saying, "Well, she used to be so beautiful and good at school, but now she's on drugs." While *he* was on drugs and dealing them! And he was a poor parent to her, leaving her to grow unsupervised and making her feel unloved, which is what led her to take drugs in the first place and end up in prison for stealing from him. Nikki always pushed back on Dad's accusations, saying that he wasn't perfect either. And if I had known the truth of his addiction—known that he, too, had gone to prison during key years in Nikki's youth—I never would have held a grudge against my half sister. Instead, I treated her shabbily, convinced by my father that she deserved our scorn.

My father's claims about Nikki not living up to her potential were of course projections about his squandering of his own potential to be a father to her. Shortly after coming back into her life following his release from prison, he officially left his first wife, her mother, for my mother, who insisted he finalize his divorce and marry her before Brittany was born. Legend has it that even though Nikki was excited to have Brittany as a baby sister, she drew the line at me. Supposedly, when my parents told her that I would be born, her teenage response was, "Y'all did it *again*?!"

Nikki took Brittany for joy rides in her car and listened to music with her. My father would remark on how similar they looked, with their straight blond hair. Conversely, with my curly hair, chubby face, and fiery temper, I was the ugly duckling of the trio. Being left out shielded me from the tensions between the other two, who were always vying to be Dad's golden child. Only when our father's physical and mental health declined did Nikki and I become close, trying to take care of him together. She was unconditional in bringing Dad into her home for his final year and during his hospice decline, despite how badly he had treated her. He died in her home, in 2016. To me, Nikki was the smartest of all of us, the only one who knew what was going on and saw through Dad's bullshit. I try not to have regrets in life because they are unproductive, only pulling you down like weights in water. But I do regret buying my father's narrative about who Nikki was and her capabilities. She embraced life, stayed sober, and is there for her grandchildren in a way our father was not.

And yet, even though Dad was a complete fuckup in most areas, and despite the physical, moral, and behavioral distances that opened between us, I loved my father deeply. Some subjects I could discuss in meaningful ways only with him. For all his waywardness, he was something of a genius, earning multiple master's degrees. He always used to boast about getting into Mensa and then quitting because he disliked the people, a believable tale because he was so intelligent. During the ninety-minute drive to his house from Kingsville, he would quiz us with the Mensa test questions he remembered, and trivia and word games. He was unmotivated to achieve anything, but he was deeply curious, always reading, watching, and listening to interesting things and opining on them.

So that's what I did. We watched history documentaries together and discussed ancient civilizations and aliens. His favorite topic was the Mayans, their staggering scientific discoveries and calculations providing endless fascination. His knowledge was immense on these subjects, and his lectures filled long hours on the road. Other times, he would tell ghost stories, one after another, with him always at the center of the experience. Everything seemed real and possible when it came from his imagination. At one point, he led me to believe he *was* L. Ron Hubbard, the Scientology founder. He knew too much about the subject and teased me that he was the man himself after he saw me reading *Battlefield Earth*. He asked me, "Why do you *think* I know all about this?" And he said, "They think I died on my houseboat twenty years ago." Then he winked at me. He would quote a line Hubbard reportedly said: "If you want to get rich, start your own religion." Why, then, weren't we rich? Or maybe I believed this was what rich looked like.

The September 11 tragedy had united us. He was the only person who talked to me directly about the events. Despite being ten years old, I was mesmerized by the horrific attacks, which marked the awakening of my curiosity about political events. Over the years that followed, Dad encouraged me to learn more; he was on the same intellectual journey, analyzing the landmark event, questioning it, seeking to understand it. He didn't parrot headlines or the president's rhetoric but instead pored over statements made by Osama bin Laden, seeking to discern the terrorist leader's justifications. And he told me that bin Laden did not represent Islam but was misusing the faith. He explained the difference between a world religion and a murderous sect, saying I shouldn't be misled just because a terrorist decided to cloak his actions in the sanctity of "faith."

Sometimes he took me to the library after school, and when I pulled the *A* volume of the encyclopedia, he would trace maps of Afghanistan. The same volume had the Arabic alphabet in it. It didn't show all the language's different forms, just the alphabet, and I wrote it out (from right to left as Arabic is written, like Hebrew). Years later, the government would absurdly, repulsively portray this teenage curiosity and parental bonding as evidence that I sympathized with terrorists even before I graduated from high school. But I learned about Arabic and Islam to show my father that I was studying what he was discussing. It was the only reason we would talk, the only common language we had. Maybe that's why intellectual curiosity became so fundamental to my personality; it was what glued me to Dad.

In the few years before Dad moved out, we had a flimsy gold bookcase in the living room that seemed to be supported by Stephen King hardcovers—big, heavy, thick books with yellowed pages and macabre graphic art on the covers. Claws came through the grate on the cover of *It*, wild cat eyes watched from *Pet Sematary*, and the duel froze in place on *The Stand*. But what held my attention most was a novel on the bottom shelf: *The Satanic Verses*, by Salman Rushdie, with its serious red jacket featuring mysterious tribal artwork on the cover. Whenever my dad saw me looking at it, he would point and say, "People died for that book." He never elaborated. But how could someone die for a work of fiction? Who had died, and how had they done so? It was a tantalizing idea for an imaginative child. From the day I comprehended full sentences until I finally read the entire book at age eleven, I tried to decipher the mystery of the first page: "'To be born again,' sang Gibreel Farishta tumbling from the heavens, 'first you have to die. Ho ji!'" Even though Rushdie spells out for readers what those words mean in the introductory paragraph, for many years I didn't understand. Though

I consumed *The Hobbit* and waited in line for the next Harry Potter, I was most focused on wanting to solve this intellectual mystery and someday getting past this first paragraph. My fascination with *The Satanic Verses* came full circle in 2017, when a passage I wrote as the beginning of a novel in response to Rushdie's landed me in hot water with the US government (we'll address that later).

Dad and I also bonded through guns. For my family, guns weren't weapons; they were sporting tools. (Left-leaning journalists and podcast hosts have asked me how a vegetarian do-gooder like me could own guns. The answer: It's my culture! I grew up with them.) When I was seven or eight, my sister and I got our first Red Ryder BB guns. Brittany and I loved shooting spiders in the pasture—Texas spiders are so big that you can actually shoot a hole through them. When we were little, our father enjoyed hunting on nearby King Ranch, and one of his regular errands was to the dusty warehouse of a meat-processing and taxidermy shop on the north side of Kingsville. I have pictures of Dad dwarfed by a nilgai (antelope) he had shot, hanging from hooks. He would use the meat he hunted in Hamburger Helper meals. (Dad loved the way we pronounced it, asking for "Nilly Guy" in our cheese noodles.) Later, our stepfather, Gary, taught us gun safety, which we took seriously. My first and only experience shooting an AK-47 was using my stepbrother's out back in the cow pasture, which had been converted into a shooting range immediately after some cows we had wandered off one day and never came back during a drought. Our stepdad loaded all his guns and ammo into a wagon behind the riding lawn mower and told us to hop on and hang on or walk. It was my first time shooting what felt like an immensely heavy revolver, and the kickback made me cry.

As I progressed from one year of high school to the next, my father got sucked deeper into the whirlpool of addiction. He became sicker, suffering frequent delusions, and depended on daily nursing. Late one night, a kind couple found him wandering the streets and called the hospital. While they were waiting with him in their house for the ambulance to arrive, he tore up their curtains and pillows; he told them he was a Union soldier and that his battle buddy had gotten shot—he needed to get back to the battlefield to make a tourniquet. He suffered a full Civil War delusion. At least he fought on the right side: my great-great-grandfather was named Abraham Lincoln Winner.

Shortly after I graduated from high school, I got a phone call from Dad's live-in nurse that he was at the hospital, possibly dying. My mom drove me to the hospital, and I went up to his room. He was awake and said, "Hey, I know you're sixteen, and I know yesterday was your birthday, but you're never too old to call your dad on your birthday."

I looked at him and said, "Well, it's September, and I'm already eighteen." So, yeah, he was completely out of it. I didn't stay longer than fifteen minutes before I went downstairs and we left. He lived on for years after that, and we occasionally talked on the phone, but I found every excuse not to see him after that. His curiosity and ability to parse the truth from the noise were qualities I hoped to claim for myself. Even though he never managed to buy us horses, he did give me something much more valuable: a bigger way of thinking.

Three

Reality is merely an illusion, albeit a very persistent one.
　　　　　—Commonly attributed to Albert Einstein

For Mother's Day once, I bought a little glass plaque from a cheesy catalog that lets you customize gifts. It began, "Moth´-er," like a dictionary entry, then proceeded through five affectionate definitions of what a mother is and can do. Such as: "4. One who is giving, nurturing, caring and kind." Finally, at the bottom, there was an "i.e." I used every character space available to write, "i.e.: You, Momface!" Normal kids would have put their mother's actual name, Billie.

If I was unlucky in being born to a brilliant yet dysfunctional and disappointing father, I was incredibly fortunate in being born to a wise, caring, strong mother, one with an extreme tolerance for nonsense. I'll say it outright: I would not be alive today if not for Momface's loyalty and resilience. When I was in decrepit jails and prison for years and wanted to end my life, she wouldn't let me. When I was hoping she would leave town and go home so she could resume something of a normal life while her daughter was an incarcerated, shameful walking global scandal, she refused. And because she wouldn't give up, I couldn't either. To this day, she remains the person most unwaveringly dedicated to, and hopeful about, my receiving a full pardon from the president of the United States, which would enable me and my family to resume something of a normal life.

And even beyond being the hero I needed at my most vulnerable and desperate, my mother has been our family's backbone for the day-to-day stuff. Always. My mother was forced to make up for Dad's failings. With no financial contributions from him, Mom worked twice as hard as most parents to ensure that Brittany and I were taken care of. For some time, all we knew of her was glimpses of a figure going to and from work, wearing a power suit with shoulder pads and high heels. That's the image we had—the working woman of the 1990s. Everyone always assumed my mom was some badass lawyer because she carried herself that way.

Somehow we were never late for school. Somehow Britty and I never missed a sports practice. We never missed a game. Mom magically got us where we needed to go, by herself. And on holidays, she went all out, all the time. On Easter, baby-powder bunny tracks in the blue-gray carpet led us to toys and oversized chocolate bunnies. During the Christmas season, anywhere from two hundred to three hundred little snowmen made of plastic, ceramics, or cotton resided in our home. One three-foot stuffed snowman was named Martha, and even though each room in the house had its own Christmas tree, Martha got a private forest with extra trees just for herself. Although Martha had a wide stuffed-snowball base, shoddy construction meant she couldn't stand up by herself, so my mom told us that Martha had had too much to drink. My sister and I got stockings the size of garbage bags, each weighing around twenty-five pounds, filled with trinkets, candy, perfume, and makeup. My first Hanukkah home postprison—I converted to Judaism as an adult, which I'll say more about later—Momface picked up where she left off, giving me a necklace, a candle, and perfume for eight nights. It was never about the monetary or material value, of course. Acknowledging holidays is just *how she loves*.

Under Momface's benevolent oversight, our home also did Halloween the way other families do Christmas, by decorating the house to the nines, dressing up, and baking cookies. She even let us make black frosting for the bat-shaped cookies, icing that I managed to spill everywhere. She loved elaborate costumes, once going to work dressed as Harry Potter, complete with the giant white snowy owl. And she liked the owl so much that the bird joined the good snow-people in colonizing our home during Christmas.

Mom made miracles come birthday times. We had our parties at kids' restaurants with arcade games, like Peter Piper Pizza one year, where a whole long table was set aside for the celebration. I felt like royalty. The next year, I had the back game room at Pizza Parlor on King Avenue.

Mom's work ethic meant that my sister and I stayed above the poverty line despite the odds. We never felt financially strapped, mostly because, as my father put it, our prefabricated mobile home was not only a double-wide but a double-long! It stood on its own land, and not in a trailer park. Even though we were in fact hanging on to the middle class by our fingertips, my sister thought we had more toys than any other kids. All because of my mother's efforts. She did this all while dealing with a deadbeat, drug-addicted husband, two unruly children, and endless work at a demanding, thankless, yet important job that benefited the entire community.

Momface's job was her everything, especially outside of work hours; all her friends were her coworkers at Child Protective Services. When they got together, the conversation began with a brain dump of work events. Despite the heavy subject matter, I preferred hanging out with Mom and her friends to socializing with my peers. Mom's crew always had Important Things to discuss. Their lives were filled with moral urgency and complex dilemmas. Their work was serious, which made me preciously hyperaware of how tragic the world was. In our family, to put it bluntly, we're used to talking about dead babies at the dinner table.

As a supervisor in a small town like Kingsville, my mom was prominent. She was the one who had to answer questions when CPS got it wrong. As I got older, I started to understand why CPS is the last government agency that you want to show up on your doorstep (well, except for the FBI—trust me on that), since they might take your kids away. My mother had a job that required, yet rarely rewarded, constant vigilance. Her commitment to helping others, to the point that she worked herself to exhaustion, had strong, lasting effects on me. I never heard the word "feminist" as a kid, but I always knew how a woman with an education and a professional career lived, worked, and guided a family at the same time.

Mom's rigorous work schedule meant that, whether at Dad's or at home, Brittany and I were often alone in our adolescent worlds, reenacting cartoons and reading Dragonlance and Lord of the Rings novels. We built the wooden swords we saw in Disney movies (hard-learned fact: it hurts when they hit you in real life). It was just the two of us out on the expansive Texas land, and Brittany and I grew very close, the way siblings dependent on each other in bad situations usually do. We were different: she was quiet, I was loud; she was skinny, I was fat; she was in band, I played sports. And Britty was always pretty, always funny, always more popular than me. (She was also honest about it in the way sisters can be: "I always had friends and boyfriends from an embarrassingly young age, and you just didn't have much going on," she told me recently.) Luckily though, she let me tag along on her social adventures and encouraged my own, even driving me and my first boyfriend around once while he flicked her head from the back seat. I was the annoying younger sibling, and I harassed her poor boyfriends, even calling one a "communist" for no reason.

Dad was obsessed with making us into geniuses, and he succeeded with my sister. Sometimes Britty intimidates people because she's so smart—she eventually obtained two doctorates, one in toxicology and the other in molecular neuroscience, and she was so brilliant that I wasn't even surprised at her incredible accomplishments. When she moved away for college in 2008, she left a vacuum in the family. Still, though, her departure changed the dynamic between my mother and me in positive ways. Suddenly, Momface was no longer just an overworked chauffeur driving to and from school and tennis. For the first time, I was the front-seat child and no longer needed to shut the world out with my headphones and books. We started a nightly schedule: watching *Dancing with the Stars* to start the week, tuning into *America's Next Top Model* and *Grey's Anatomy* to get through Wednesday and Thursday nights, and meeting up with her friends at a restaurant on Friday nights. We cooked together, usually from recipes I found online. We have similar driving-related anxiety, and we like to reminisce about the autumn afternoon she and I drove over four hours to visit my sister in college, listening to the same Trans-Siberian Orchestra Christmas album on a loop to ease the stress.

One of the best things Mom did was marry my stepdad, Gary, in 2000, when I was nine. They both worked for CPS, but in different regions. The day she met him, Momface said to a friend, "I'm going to marry him someday." Gary apparently had no choice in the matter! When he joined our family, it felt like we rejoined the world. He moved in shortly before the wedding, and for the wedding, his children from a previous marriage visited. The youngest was slightly older than my sister, but they were far more independent and worldly than we were. We got actual peers to socialize with! Sophisticated ones at that, who had lived in a place bigger than Kingsville! We had the usual drama of a blended family; it was like the Will Ferrell movie *Step Brothers* (a brilliant piece of cinema if ever one existed), where two inarticulate, hypersensitive, and profoundly juvenile stepsiblings engage in civil warfare before eventually coming together in harmony, sometimes with DIY building projects our parents really wished we hadn't engaged in. My stepbrother Ross and I were very much like that. Having Gary and his family in our lives was a saving grace—they gave us a wonderful family life we hadn't known before. Whatever sense of normality sneaked into my childhood is due to them. Though Gary was not my first father figure, and though I never stopped trying to capture my own dad's intellectual attention, he became the conventional father in my life. He was a disciplinarian, and my temper was no longer tolerated.

With Gary, I had my first real experience of paternal comfort when he picked me up and held me after my sisters flipped me out of the hammock onto the concrete patio. I wouldn't have played soccer for the first time at age nine if he hadn't stepped up and coached. Not that he volunteered or knew anything about soccer—I just signed him up and came home and told him. He built a wall for me to practice tennis against. And most importantly, when I or any of our animals got hurt—you'll learn about them in the next chapter—he was the only person who knew what to do. He still fixes everything he can. That's always been so helpful, because I need a lot of fixing.

Four

Curiosity killed the cat, but satisfaction brought her back.
—Ronald Lawrence Winner,
my father, repeating a saying he loved

When I was born, my parents had a pair of bobcats. I don't remember them except in stories I've been told because they ran away when I was little. But I know that they were a problem because they jumped on my mom when she was pregnant with us girls. Taking in stray and damaged animals unconditionally is something that runs in the family.

The bobcats were definitely the beginning of *something*. As far back as I can remember, I have been infatuated with animals. With their innocence, their vulnerability, their instinct to protect. Humans have made a pact with dogs and cats in particular by domesticating them, requiring them to depend on us for their survival, and we must hold up our end of the bargain. Even while they are gentle and follow us around, dogs are stronger than we are. Despite their power, they admirably opt to restrain themselves. It's something I have always wanted to emulate—to be savage but kind. Plus, I enjoy having something to take care of, a small piece of the world to save, nurture, and cherish. Focusing on my pets' needs is a distraction from my own internal struggles. It allows me to put my issues aside and selflessly obsess over their every discomfort. I can suffer vicariously through them without having to face my own unhappiness and anxiety.

Let's examine my résumé. When I was little, we had two white ducks. I have a vague recollection of them, as if in an old Kodak photo. I don't recall what happened to them, but they likely died tragically (RIP Crackers and Waddles). At another point, my dad brought two raccoons that had been trapped at Nikki's house to our house for several days before releasing them. Their cages were poorly positioned, and the afternoon sun came in at a particular angle, so that one day their hands got sunburned and needed lotion. I remember those poor little sunburned hands grabbing the carrots we fed them through the cages. Magnificent creatures.

In fifth grade, I read fantasy books about mice fighting pirate rats and really wanted a rodent, so I brought home a rat from science class. We named him Halfchop, a character in one of the books. He was a good fella, always calm and willing to be carried everywhere, even when we jumped on the trampoline. However, he ate too much people food and had health problems (flaws I can relate to). A while later, my sister won an iguana at a fair. Once my sister lost interest in this uncuddly being, I trained Harley to sit on my lap and eat tomatoes and lettuce from my hand. Rats, iguanas, ducks—my mother was patient and indulged my passion for unusual and broken creatures. She still does.

But there were also unforgettably sad experiences involving animals. Just before Christmas when I was four, my mother was getting groceries when she saw an adorable stray dog being shooed out of the store. Being the person she is, Momface brought the canine home. Angel was a black dachshund mix with a black body and brown eyebrows. We had her for about six years, until Christmas in 2001. Down the street lived a white horse who was always getting out of his pasture, and on this Christmas, when I went out after dinner to play kickball, he was standing just across from our house. I started walking toward him out of curiosity, and of course, Angel came running to bark at him. A car came speeding down the road and hit Angel right in front of me. I screamed, and Gary ran out of the house, scooped up Angel, and held her as she died. I cried every day through New Year's. There have been other incidents of animal deaths over the years since then, but that was one of the hardest.

My first chance to rescue an animal by myself came the summer before senior year, but unfortunately, that didn't turn out so well either. I was watching television one night when I heard squeaks from the backyard. It took me a while to realize that kittens were caught up in the pool filter. I have no idea how they got there, but there they were. After pulling the kitties out, I wrapped them in a towel and held them overnight. They were really scared, so I let them back out to find their mother, whom I had never seen. The cats wandered around for a couple of days. Then the white one disappeared, so I grabbed the other one, a rag doll with Siamese coloring and sky-blue eyes, and tried to domesticate him and keep him safe, naming him Pookie. He did okay for a while, coming and going from the house. He was affectionate one moment, wild and scared the next. (Again, I can relate.) But the last morning of school before Christmas break, I heard him howl. I ran outside barefoot, but it was too late: some half-feral dogs that we were temporarily looking after had gotten to him. Pookie died in my stepdad's arms while I wailed. (Now that I think about it, Gary has had some traumatic animal-related situations alongside me.)

My mom and I were devastated. The week after Pookie was killed, we went to the animal rescue place in Kingsville. For my mother's birthday, someone had given her a gift certificate covering the adoption fee for an animal. My mom spotted a black cat with gold eyes and opened his crate, and he put his long arms around her. That was it. This plain old boring cat named Cricket was ours. That evening, I had Cricket—soon to be renamed Felix—in my bedroom with me. Days before, I had begun painting a portrait of Pookie for Mom, and Felix seemed to enjoy the sound of the brush on the canvas. Our bond solidified that night. That spring, the animated movie *How to Train Your Dragon* was released, and the sweet dragon in the film looked just like Felix. In fact, he looked *so* much like Felix that my mom and I cried in the theater, and I held Felix up to watch the previews of the movie when they appeared on television. I even went to McDonald's to get the Happy Meal with the dragon toy. It's still in my car today, with Felix's teeth marks on the wing where he chewed it.

But the anxiety that would become a fixture in my life worsened when I was taking care of Felix. Before leaving for school, I had to confirm three, four, five times that the front door was closed. But no matter how often I checked the door, I didn't feel *sure* I had locked it. After leaving for school, I would panic, turn around, and drive home to make sure it was locked. I was inevitably late to school, and my mental health problem became a disciplinary issue at home because when it came to Felix, I was demanding, pushy, and disrespectful. Sleep was impossible unless I knew he was safe. What if my parents let him out accidentally? No one talked about my exaggerated fears as trauma resulting from the fates of Pookie and Angel, but I believe that's what they were. My need for constant reassurance about his safety was textbook obsessive-compulsive disorder.

That anxiety could sometimes be channeled productively: my high school years were largely spent learning languages and playing sports. Between books, tennis, school, and soccer, I didn't really have time for a social life. I wasn't very good at sports, which is why I insisted on playing them often and intensely. That's how I do things. In soccer, being a goalie is considered a lazy position, a spot for whoever can't run or dribble the ball but still wants to play. That didn't fly with me. I took my goalie duties seriously, aiming to be faster than anyone else on the field. I was also an extremely aggressive goalkeeper. Once I broke someone's leg (accidentally), by lying down in front of her. My mom told me I'd gone after the girl like a bowling ball, and I must confess she was right, although it was more Sonic the Hedgehog. Sports was a frustrating world; I could work endlessly at something and not improve. That didn't stop me from trying, however. I have never been afraid of quixotic quests. Maybe I am even attracted to them.

For a profile in *New York* magazine, the writer Kerry Howley spoke with my friends and family members. She concluded that I was an "almost comically mature adolescent, intellectually adept, impatient with her peers, with a compulsive drive to improve herself she would eventually channel into an obsession with nutrition and exercise." It's funny to see yourself summarized that way, but her account sounds right, I must admit. Parties and drinking and drugs never appealed to me. On Friday nights, I'd go out for dinner with my parents and their friends—the adults and me. On Saturdays, my mom and I watched a movie, pouring cheap red wine over frozen pineapple chunks. We went through an Alan Rickman phase—he was the villain from *Die Hard* and, most importantly, Professor Snape from the Harry Potter movies. I can safely say I've seen every movie Alan Rickman ever made. Not something I can put on my résumé, unfortunately, but it's still pretty impressive.

In early 2008, I began experiencing stress pains. I shook frequently and ground my teeth. When I ate, I felt nauseous and vomited, so I stopped eating before my tennis practices and matches. I got into the terrible habit of not eating until late at night, when I would binge, eating a day's worth of calories in one sitting. At first, I didn't make myself throw up—that happened on its own. Gradually I started to feel the curse of bulimia: I enjoyed the feeling of vomiting. The rituals of fasting, bingeing, and purging became a part of my life, and it has never stopped rearing its ugly head when I am intensely stressed.

For obsessive people, for women surviving a world that judges and fixates on their bodies, for anyone with unlucky genetics, and for many other people, eating disorders can strike anywhere, anytime. It happens to the unlikeliest and toughest of people and is no sign of weakness. In his memoir *Undisputed Truth*, Mike Tyson writes of his years in boxing school: "I was always struggling with my weight. In my mind, I was a fat pig even though nobody would know by looking at me. When I trained, I would put Albolene over my pores and wear a plastic suit for a week or two and only take it off at nighttime when I was taking a hot bath so I could sweat some more weight off. Then I'd go to bed and wake up the next morning and put it on and go run and wear it the whole day." That's not bulimia, but it's a similar mindset, in which you are always trying to get rid of something, always trying to be two steps ahead of what you might see on that scale.

Still, beyond the obsessions, there was joy in my life. Besides the birthday parties and holiday extravaganzas, my fondest memory might be the only major crime I committed besides the felony that landed me in jail.

Eighth grade is a big year. And the graduation ceremony is a big deal, in my case marking the transition from small Ricardo Middle School to the high school in Kingsville proper. The cap, the gown, the whole thing. My grades were top-notch, and I was slated to be either valedictorian or salutatorian. Either way, I was running shit there. And so, in my wisdom, I decided to do the only honorable thing: gather my fellow seniors into the cafeteria and initiate a food fight. It was an epic brawl, but not worth the consequences: I was suspended and prevented from speaking at graduation.

Aside from that discreditable incident, I was well-behaved. But I was not a rule follower, even then. Around the time I was seventeen,

I began questioning religion. Despite my father's strong foundations in Catholicism, he always told my sister and me that everything the Christians were doing wasn't what Jesus has taught, that their politics and aggressive behavior violated the teachings of the Old Testament. Starting when I was seven or so, Dad would send me on covert missions at Episcopalian Sunday school to teach the staff that, as he had learned studying for his graduate degree in theology, Jesus was born in the spring and not in December, despite what they thought. I also told them that most of the holidays bore little resemblance to the actual historical events they were supposedly based on. Yes, I was *that* kid. He always framed religious dogma as a political stance as well as a spiritual one. Every time he made pork chops, for example, the meal came with a dinner table discussion of the history of kosher eating, and whether the practice was divine in its origins or based on health and hygiene standards. When I read about Judaism in high school, my reading seemed to confirm what he had taught us. More than that, Judaism *felt* right to me. It felt more appropriate than being Christian, a religion I had always felt detached from. In addition to learning the Hebrew alphabet alongside the Arabic, I began slowly trying to understand the Hebrew calendar and ritual obligations, and to transition to a kosher diet. Mostly, I just kept reading and following light in my life where I could find it.

Alongside my faith, I discovered my other intellectual passion in high school. I became enthralled by Latin's intricate grammar and history. To comprehend the different Latin phrases, you had to understand the language in the historical context of ancient Rome. It was a different universe, and language was a key to accessing it. If everybody were to study languages, let alone Latin, with history and culture in mind, I think everybody would be interested in linguistics (the study of languages).

My small high school offered Latin, but they certainly didn't offer Arabic. When I expressed interest, my Turkish-born art teacher set me up with a young Somalian woman taking classes at nearby Texas A&M University–Kingsville. She taught me how to read the first page of the Quran, mostly because that was the only Arabic she knew, and helped me through a few Arabic children's books I had found on Amazon. I met with her at the university library once a week, and she taught me the alphabet, the vowels, how to pronounce certain things, how the words and sentences flowed, how they sounded, all the parts that composed language. At the time, I didn't realize that studying non-Western languages in your spare time was not a normal teenage activity; I just knew it gripped me.

I had some other projects in my youth: the boys and girls I dated. "Reality takes in a lot of strays," my mother sighed to Kerry Howley, "and I don't mean just animals." Guilty as charged, I guess. In my freshman year, I dated a guy named Carlos. My mother was familiar with family situations like his through her work; CPS once opened a file on Carlos's mother because she tried to kill him with a glass bottle. He needed a job in high school but didn't even have money for khaki pants from Walmart to start working at the local movie theater. Enter my mom to buy pants for him. Mom was kind to Carlos and empathetic toward his situation, but she understandably would have preferred her daughter to date someone in a more stable situation, if at all. Most of my relationships have been fixer-uppers, and somehow my mom and stepdad have always been dragged along for the ride.

The truth is that I have an impulse to save the world, just like Mom always has. She attended events with us in tow all the time to volunteer for foster kids, and CPS was such a massive part of her life that it was inevitably a massive part of *my* life. This missionary passion I inherited sometimes gets me into trouble, and I sometimes become overzealous with it, as you'll see down the road. But it's intrinsic to who I am. In 2015, the journalist Larissa MacFarquhar wrote a relevant book chronicling the experiences of people like me, people who are fanatical altruists or obsessive do-gooders, called *Strangers Drowning: Grappling with Impossible Idealism, Drastic Choices, and the Overpowering Urge to Help*. She profiles people who donate their kidneys to strangers, adopt twenty-two children, or give away 90 percent of their wealth. The individuals MacFarquhar covers frequently make other people uncomfortable with their righteousness and annoyed with their rigidity. "The people in this book are extreme in their commitment, but they are not crazy," she writes. "Their lives aren't easy, but they are galvanized by strong beliefs and a sense of purpose." I can be guilty of these charges, too, I suppose. But I have also been chastened in my commitment to try to fix the world; I have seen that the world doesn't always react well to that sort of thing.

Approaching high school graduation, I had some decisions to make. Brittany and I knew our parents couldn't pay for college, so we had to get scholarships if we wanted to attend. Getting financial aid just seemed unwise, a recipe for mountains of debt. The free kind of financial aid lay just outside our reach, the penalty for our parents' stability in keeping us in the lower-middle class. Getting paid to go to school seemed like a better hustle. My father had encouraged me to appreciate the complexities behind global affairs. My mother demonstrated how challenging and rewarding public service could be. And I now had a burning love of languages that I wanted to put to good use. So I looked to the military.

People on the left forget it was like this after 9/11, but in my home, it was more than possible to be simultaneously pro-military and pro-humanitarianism. Being so was almost taken for granted. In an era when terrorists had killed scores of innocent people, defeating al-Qaeda and other violent extremists seemed like a major human-rights priority. My thinking about terrorism and its causes was: if you could just go and help people survive day to day, they wouldn't be fighting or killing; people fight because they don't have the means to survive otherwise. "What could be more humanitarian," my mother asked Kerry Howley much later, "than protecting your country and innocent victims of war and terrorism?"

I decided to find a college that would help me become fluent in Arabic or whatever language al-Qaeda was speaking. Without telling Momface, I also secretly applied to Texas A&M–Kingsville's engineering school. And I not only got accepted, I got offered a full scholarship, as part of a program supporting girls in engineering and math. But I was intent on the military. In my senior year, I spoke to recruiters from the armed forces, insisting that I would be a linguist in Middle Eastern and African languages. By doing that, I could help work for peace in some of the most tortured parts of the world.

I was leaning toward the army, but my parents thought it was for idiots and staged an intervention. They told me to talk to my stepbrother Cole, who was then almost eight years into his air force enlistment as a Russian linguist. I didn't have a good feeling about the air force. They were the elite, but they knew it and acted like it, like the snobby popular kids in school. They were also an hour's drive away from where I lived, in Corpus Christi, and I wasn't excited about the long commute. Eventually, though, my parents convinced me to give the air force another look. Sure, the army might accept me more readily, but I would have no specified job once I completed basic training. They could send me anywhere, for any job, regardless of my test scores. The air force, conversely, would keep me waiting and preparing for basic training until the unique position they'd recruited me for became available, plus give me a signing bonus if I signed up for six years as a linguist.

I took the language aptitude test and scored high enough to be what's called a "crypto-linguist"—someone who eavesdrops on people speaking non-English languages and translates the contents into English. It sounded amazing. I'd be getting paid to study non-English words and sentences and then using the fruits of my study to improve the world a tiny bit. Incredible. I was game.

It didn't take me long to realize how little other Americans really think of the military they claim to love, however. I remember sitting though my high school graduation ceremony as school officials complimented all the top students going to prominent colleges. They announced the kids' names, asked for applause, and mentioned the students' future plans. When the principal got to my name, even though I had some of the best grades in the graduating class, he mentioned that I was going into the US military, and then he moved on immediately. No pause for applause for me! It was like they were embarrassed for me, as though joining up was shameful when others were heading to Ivy League and Texas state flagship schools. I felt awful, like I was a failure for choosing something other than the traditional career path. But I reminded myself that I would be getting paid to learn languages and would be basically guaranteed a job while others would take out loans only to graduate into a shitty economy.

Six months later, I left for the air force's basic training. It was the hardest time of my life. Many recruits dropped out or were "rolled back" to redo weeks of training. But I knew I had made the right decision.

Five

That's right: you're all angry, sick people. But over these next eight hours, you will be broken down to the level of infants, then rebuilt as functional members of society, then broken down again. Then lunch. Then, if there's time, rebuilt once more.

—Police Chief Wiggum instructing a room of adults taking an anger management class, *The Simpsons*

Patience is a virtue, the saying goes, but it's never been *my* virtue. Now that I was headed for the United States military, my new life stage became all I could think about. This would be more than a language I would be learning, more than a job I would be training to perform. It felt like a calling, a vocation I had been born to pursue. As part of the generation that came of age in the wake of the 9/11 attacks, I was eager to don the uniform and serve my country, to be part of something larger than myself. Corny as it may seem, I was bursting with patriotism.

But first, I had to wait. Every branch of the military has what's called a delayed entry program (DEP). It's usually for folks who join up but are too young to start basic training, or for those who don't yet have the requisite skills. But the air force uses the program because bringing on anyone they won't use immediately is too expensive. In my case, the air force had a long wait list for spots in various language classes at the Defense Language Institute. So I waited for six months until a slot opened.

In the meantime, I met with my recruiter every other weekend to do physical conditioning. She needed to confirm that I would pass the first physical test once I got to basic training. And to ensure I would keep my nose clean and avoid trouble. The last thing the military wants is to accept someone into the service and then have them instantly become a reckless douchebag who gets a DUI or something. They needn't have worried about that part: there was no way I was letting anything come between me and my dream job. Anyway, I wasn't much of a partyer. Even at nineteen years old, my idea of a good time was an evening of movie watching on the couch, cuddled up with my furry friends.

Anyone in the DEP bonds with their recruiter, just because they spend so much time together. Mine was a tech sergeant in her early forties, and I instantly admired her, so polished, well traveled, and professional was she. She walked me through some things about basic military training (commonly known as boot camp, but referred to as BMT, since everything in the military must be an abbreviation). Things like the importance of following orders. Like how to endure the experience of getting yelled at by an overbearing man without yelling back. Like ways to interpret my superiors' intentionally vague commands. Like the importance of not standing out. Of course, these were all variations on the same theme—surviving a shitty environment—but they proved to be deeply helpful instructions.

The recruiter explained that BMT would be very stressful, but in a safe way. They called it "controlled stress." The drill sergeants would scream in my face, humiliate me, insult me, and call me degrading names, but they wouldn't physically endanger me. They wouldn't even touch me. They would force me to do burpees until I wanted to pass out and make me do more push-ups than someone in a prison movie, but I would not actually drop dead. If I kept my cool, I would be okay. For me, though, keeping cool is the hardest thing in the world. Anger issues and disordered eating mix poorly with insecurity, uncertainty, and fear. But maybe I would be too busy at BMT to be preoccupied with my bulimia? It was all still new to me, this impulse to control my surroundings and my psyche by vomiting. Nobody in my life knew what I was doing in the bathrooms I retreated to after eating, and I wasn't about to tell them, let alone my recruiter. Instead, I hoped that BMT activities would distract me from my compulsions, perhaps even cure them. Sometimes life's problems disappear with time.

Sometimes they don't.

I reported at the recruiting station in Corpus Christi and arrived at BMT around 8:00 p.m. We were among the first ones in the building. It was one giant room, with two long rows of twenty-five bunk beds each in the middle and big lockers on the walls. The floor had generic white tiles, like in supermarkets. In fact, everything was white, sterile, hospital-like. We didn't know if we should just pick a bunk, or if they were assigned.

We figured it out quickly. A skinny, short, uniformed guy screamed at us to grab a bunk. Hoisting my black duffel bag filled with clothes and toiletries, I randomly went over to one bed.

"No, dumbass," the sergeant said to me. "The next one, take the next one." So I did as told and then stood erect and kept quiet, which worked for the moment.

The only thought in my head was my reporting statement. My recruiter had drilled six simple words into my head for me to use when addressed by a superior at BMT: "Sir (or Ma'am), Trainee Winner reports as ordered." That was all I needed to say. Any more was going to attract trouble. Any less would do the same. I was warned that the military training instructors (a.k.a. sergeants) would play gotcha and ask trick questions to catch trainees off guard. *Always start with the reporting statement, no matter how ridiculous it seems.*

Other trainees lacked such helpful recruiters. A sergeant would bark orders at them, and they would respond by saying, "Yes, sir."

"What did you say? Are you fucking stupid?"

"Sorry, sir. I meant, sir, Trainee Jones reports as ordered."

"That's better. Don't fucking do it again." But they would, because the correct statement hadn't been instilled into them.

Trainees: that's what we were for the next eight weeks. After graduating, we would be airmen. The title change was small but significant; it meant the difference between being horseshit and being a horse, between being a peon and being a person. Over the next sixty days, we learned nothing about fighting enemies but much about making beds, keeping lockers organized, standing in formation, and performing marching drills. More than anything, we learned how to handle the constant stress of being late for wherever we needed to be, being told we were doing everything wrong and obviously not understanding anything—and being screamed at and insulted the entire time. *That's the training for the United States military.*

It wasn't all bad. Among the best parts of BMT was getting fitted for our fatigues, called the battle dress uniform (BDU). I loved their comfort, and not having to worry about choosing clothes every day. I felt proud in them too. Knowing my mother had considered going into the air force, understanding my family wanted me in the service, being part of the giant institution that protected the country, and eventually being able to help to reduce extremism in the Middle East—the fatigues seemed to embody all that for me. And they were baggy enough to hide my heavier frame.

But the rest was hard. Not everyone succeeded: about 15 percent of our class dropped out, and I gather that rate is similar for every class. Either the physical demands or (more often) the mental tensions are too much for some. A good number of trainees develop autoimmune disorders such as lupus at BMT—something about the stress triggers them. The air force didn't mind the dropout rate; they expected it and didn't want anyone who couldn't cut it, I suppose.

Everyone got a nickname, picked by a sergeant, to fuck with you and show you who was in charge: *You don't even get to control your name.* My recruiter had warned me to "wear a pair of jeans that don't have any design on them. Dark denim, no low-cuts, wear a belt with the jeans, and then wear a plain gray T-shirt." Because if you wore something displaying the words, say, "American Eagle," those two words would be your name for the next two months. My nickname was Winnie-the-Pooh. Someone had trouble saying my last name once, so Winner became Winnie. It could have been worse. Another trainee brought hot-pink floral flip-flops to use as shower shoes, and she was given various names, starting with Flip-Flops, Floppy, Flippy Longstocking, and South Padre. Every new MTI on our floor stopped to admire her shoes and ask her about the surf and weather conditions at the beach. She was even denied permission to buy plain black flip-flops at the base commissary to replace the ones that defined her.

Occasionally the ridicule got darker. Simply to be jerks and assert power, sergeants declared certain items off-limits to trainees at mealtimes: cereal, pastries, cakes, and pies. These tasty treats were beckoning to us from behind glass cases, but nobody wanted to be the person seen eating them—you'd get a higher-up blaring in your face for that, mocking you when you took bites. As a result, trainees avoided even looking at the glass cases. Sometimes the only other breakfast options were unkosher meat products. Because I didn't want to violate my growing religious beliefs, I opted for a biscuit or toast. A sergeant who caught me doing that reprimanded me for eating a forbidden food and ordered me to the back of the food line. It was petty shit, but it was a real problem. For someone with an eating disorder, being hazed at mealtimes is no small thing. Often, I didn't eat much. Other times, I was so grateful to have food I could eat that I devoured too much of it, like the time I had five whole minutes to inhale a plate of spaghetti. I threw that up shortly after.

It turned out that constant motion, unceasing action, and never-ending strain did not, in fact, translate into a healthy relationship with eating and my body. Despite being busy, surrounded by other people, and deprived of privacy, I found spaces to make myself vomit even in the crowded, filthy bathrooms, as I huddled around the toilet with feet facing forward so as not to arouse suspicion. For those of us with eating disorders, I have come to see, the urges arrive in our lives as mysterious creatures. The disorder often first appears to us as manageable or vanquishable, a cold rather than a disability or disease. We imagine we can wrestle the problem to the ground on our own, strangle its breath until it taps out and we raise our arms in ecstatic triumph. We convince ourselves that being in a different environment will be the solution, as though the problem were external and circumstantial and not inside our own minds. That delusion can persist for years, decades, sometimes until only death itself disabuses us of our magical thinking. Other times, it is the means to an escape. Bulimia is, after all, a disease of survival. When life is out of control, it is the last remaining source of control. At the heights of my bingeing and purging, I was fighting to survive my life itself, not the disease I was hiding within to cope.

Truthfully though, much of BMT was a blur—literally. My vision has been terrible since childhood, but with just six sinks between sixty women, and hygiene often going to the wayside when there was an inspection looming, it was against regulations to wear contact lenses. My recruiter had warned me about that going in. So, having worn contacts since I was a kid, I switched to glasses for the next eight weeks. But I hadn't worn glasses since, well, ever. In elementary school, I refused to wear them because they never fit my face right, and I hated being able to see the outline of where vision ended and blurriness began. I also had always thought glasses made me look even fatter than I felt. Although I could see through my frames at BMT, everything was out of focus. It was disorienting in a way that seemed an extension of the chaos of the place somehow.

But then, mercifully, after eight weeks, it was all over, like a rash that disappears one day. BMT was miserable, too intense and stressful to enjoy, and it didn't prepare us for anything other than taking shit from angry people in charge of us. But I had made it, with as much (or as little) sanity as I had possessed when I began. And I felt proud that I was one step closer to putting on the air force uniform with an actual rank. Annoying as it was, the chickenshit that trainees were forced to endure didn't dilute my desire to be part of the service. What I wanted to devote my life to helping wasn't any single institution or branch—it was the United States, and the ideas I believed it represented. Four years of college? Say hello to eight weeks of basic military training, and on to the real mission. Much better.

Or so I thought.

Six

> Years after the war started, the U.S. military still had almost no uniformed personnel who could speak Dari or Pashto fluently. Few troops possessed even a remote grasp of Afghanistan's history, its religious customs or tribal dynamics.
>
> —Craig Whitlock, *The Afghanistan Papers*

Right after graduation, the real preparation began: language school. Finally, at the Defense Language Institute, I would be doing what I wanted, what I felt in my bones I *should* be doing. The DLI is located at the Presidio of Monterey, a military base on a mountain about 120 miles south of San Francisco. An auditorium lies at the bottom of the mountain. That's where, during orientation, a senior officer got up on stage and did something nobody had done during my military training thus far: he explained why our work mattered.

He introduced himself as a former commander of a unit that had been in Afghanistan during the early years of the war, which began in 2001. His unit had been unaware of which language the local people were speaking because it wasn't Arabic, the only non-English language with which they had capabilities. And they could not foresee the calamity that would occur because of this lapse in communication. His men were helping with the construction of a school, transporting supplies and getting along well with the locals as they shared their hard work. That was why it surprised the officer when elders from the village suddenly appeared with automatic rifles, ready to run off the American troops. The locals fired shots into the air. Barrels were leveled at each other. Angry words, indiscernible to each group, were exchanged. The Americans were utterly perplexed by the eruption of violence, especially as they were building something they thought would benefit the entire community.

Finally, a young man from the village who spoke rudimentary English told them about pictures of women an American soldier had shared with the villagers. The photos were pornographic—though it wouldn't have mattered if they were women pictured in shampoo advertisements. This culture and society strictly forbade such images. The Americans had absolutely no cultural appreciation of this difference. But honoring these mores was essential, a prerequisite to good relations. These Afghan villagers had just emerged from seven years of Taliban rule, where a woman couldn't walk around without the head-to-toe covering of the burqa, only to be slapped in the face with the pornographic litter of frat-boy Western soldiers. The construction of the school stopped immediately. The village no longer wanted American help, and they demanded that the Americans leave.

The officer cited this experience as an example of why our work as translators was indispensable. We were learning the language to understand the cultures of foreign lands, since only by understanding the cultures could America succeed in its efforts at state building and peace building. Hearing that our job wasn't simply to master language mechanics but to develop expertise in societies, I knew my work would be meaningful. I felt as if I had arrived at the Hogwarts of linguistics. I felt I might finally be at home somewhere, a place where my command of languages would become a weapon of choice in the battle for hearts and minds in sorrowful lands.

Unfortunately, the air force didn't feel quite the same way. They had us rank the languages we wanted to learn in order of preference. I chose Pashto, one of the major languages spoken in Afghanistan that is also popular in neighboring Pakistan. Anyone who worked to reduce regional conflict would need to speak Pashto. My second choice was Arabic, since I was already pretty good with it. And Arabic was the lingua franca of al-Qaeda, since many natives of Persian Gulf countries had relocated to Afghanistan during the Soviet invasion.

But they assigned Farsi to me, a huge letdown because it's spoken almost exclusively in Iran. Which . . . Iran is great. A glorious civilization and one of the world's first empires. No shade. But it's a medium-income country with a very educated populace and a large military. They didn't need my help. Plus, nobody from Iran had attacked us on 9/11. My fellow students' practice clips were of farmers in poor, rural, war-torn Afghanistan. That seemed much more attractive to me than glamorous Iran, where women reportedly outnumbered men in their medical colleges. My aim was to help the world's most struggling people, to resolve the world's most problematic conflicts. Assisting middle-class Iranians didn't fit the bill. And it seemed like the US had been at odds with Iran forever (well, since 1979), so I would be unlikely to have much impact on such an intractable clash. Even worse was discovering that Farsi was categorized as a language easier to learn than Pashto or Arabic—I wanted the challenge of mastering something crazy hard. Iran is supposed to be a beautiful country, so I wanted to visit it. But to make it my life's work? Hard pass.

Of course, the air force wasn't interested in what its trainees *wished* we could study. The military was spending large amounts of money over years to educate us in languages they determined were necessary for national security purposes. We were just numbers to them, warm bodies to fill a need.

Some people had a decisive problem with that reality. I knew someone who had studied Middle East history and had college-level Arabic skills. He could not only read Arabic fluently but also converse at the colloquial level (learning to speak a language is much harder than learning to read it). But he hadn't completed his degree, so he couldn't apply to be an officer. He wanted to be an Arabic linguist for the military, mastering this language that was vital to the United States and helping them for decades to come. He had told them that from the outset.

They assigned him... Chinese. He failed and was discharged from the air force. It seemed like such a waste of a smart young man's skills and passion, and of the military's resources. But when you enlist, you lose all your power. You lose everything you've ever done or accomplished. Nobody cares about your previous work experiences. This guy found that out the hard way. Maybe I didn't want Farsi, but there was no way I was dropping out of anything. Instead, I just set my mind to learning Pashto and Farsi simultaneously, on the down-low.

The Farsi designation was the bad news. But there was good news. The mountain home of DLI has amazing views. They call it the most beautiful military assignment you never get to enjoy, however, because language school is busy and stressful. I found that to be true. But it was at DLI that I discovered that I love to wander alone. I didn't have a car and disliked the bus system. So I would walk down to the harbor, where you can jump off the pier and get to the beach. And if you go about two miles all the way around to the other side of Monterey Bay, climb up the sand dunes, and cross under the highway, provided you can handle the chilly weather and fog, you're at the shopping center. This was the first place I had ever lived outside of South Texas, and I was in for a shock to find myself living in a place where the temperature hovered between fifty and seventy-five degrees Fahrenheit year-round. That year was my first experience of actual autumn, with trees that went through the proper color spectrum of yellows and reds instead of going from green to brown overnight.

Wandering around without any purpose or anywhere to be was delightful. Before language school, I had never had that opportunity, and now it's a fixture of who I am. I bought a Canon DSLR with lenses I never learned how to use and took shot after shot, adjusting for the light without knowing the first thing about photography, hoping, as with other forms of art, that I could fake it till I made it. Every foreign restaurant became an opportunity to talk to someone new, collect stories, and try new foods, my own version of *No Reservations*. If I went a certain way, or out a certain gate into Monterey, it required a series of pit stops along the way at the various shops and eateries, just to check in, see how business was, or ask what was new. After doing this a few times, suddenly I was in the back room of a rug store on Lighthouse Avenue, being invited to touch a rug stolen from one of Saddam's palaces worth eighty grand!

Language school also encouraged camaraderie. After basic training, they put thirty of us on a bus, after which we caught a plane to California. Then we got on another bus for two hours and arrived at language school together. Even though we were assigned different languages and lived apart, we language students formed a bond, and those goofy bastards became my family. For the first time in my life, I had a group of friends. Very few linguists are extroverts. We are socially awkward, borderline-autistic people who love nothing more than huddling over textbooks, studying foreign words and sentences. Now we could enjoy being among our own kind.

Even though we were college-age students, the stakes were high for the few of us who would go out and get shit-faced on the weekend. One time, we were all on a 2100 curfew, seven nights a week for three weeks straight, because our unit had had three drunken incidents with police before 2300 on a Saturday night. By the third time the police let our squadron know someone was cited, we were all receiving texts to return to base, get into uniform—service dress blues—and be in formation by midnight. We were there until 0200 and were then required to be in formation by 0800 the next morning for a day of marching drills and picking up trash. The following weekend, someone from my own Farsi class decided, curfew or not, he was getting shit-faced. Drinking started in the morning, and by 2030, staggering through the woods to return to the barracks for curfew and head count, he was so drunk that he shat himself, and in crawling back to his room, he seriously jeopardized the unit again; fortunately, some brave element leaders on his floor managed to clear his shit up by the time the sergeants made their way through at 2130 for inspection. Nevertheless, these were my people.

Most airmen lived in college dorm–type facilities on base, but for the airmen who were married with families, off-base residence was approved. A couple of my friends lived across from each other in a cul-de-sac on Fort Ord, a ten-minute walk from the shopping center. On Saturdays, I would walk over, often staying overnight in one friend's spare bedroom after game nights across the way at the other house. It felt like a mini-vacation every week with people I loved.

And then there was Alex. The first night that our bus arrived at the Presidio of Monterey, we were given folders containing all the necessary information about the base and our living situation. I looked over at the lanky, handsome guy with glasses and (obviously) a military haircut sitting next to me, and written on his folder was his name: Alexander Harris. For my readers who have tragically not watched *Buffy the Vampire Slayer*, the main character has a best friend/sidekick named Xander Harris. I began laughing at Alex's name and said, "So what, do people call you Xander?"

He was not having it. "No, that's not funny," he said. "I hate that." He'd clearly been the butt of that unoriginal joke an infinite number of times, creative wit though I thought I was. And then he looked over at my folder and had a comparable reaction. "What the fuck is *that* name?" he said. How hadn't I anticipated him doing that? So we were making fun of each other from day one. And isn't that how all good relationships begin?

Alongside his name, Xander had another sterling quality I found attractive: he was studying Pashto. Come to think of it, that was probably the main thing I liked about him. I mean, we enjoyed walking around Monterey together, and I loved watching him hilariously flail around on ice skates at the rink we went to too. But the Pashto thing counted for a lot. Once we began dating, I started stealing his textbooks, but I didn't slack on my own schoolwork. In fact, I excelled at Farsi because, in a very distant way, Farsi and Latin are slightly similar. The easiest way for me to understand Farsi grammatical concepts was to translate Farsi sentences into Latin and then back into English. I had three different notebooks in front of me at all times in class, since I would bring my Pashto and Latin textbooks to Farsi school, working with three languages simultaneously instead of concentrating on the one they were teaching us.

This caused friction with the military personnel. An air force sergeant who came into our class to teach us told me that I couldn't work on multiple languages during class. Well, I put the extra books away, since he'd be gone the next hour, and then I went right back to doing it. More problematically, one of my fellow students was older, already an army sergeant. Just as I have trouble learning chemistry, she had a harder time picking up languages. She did not take kindly to my answering too many questions or peppering the instructors with advanced questions, nor did she appreciate the teachers who delighted in bringing me extra assignments (and the occasional succulent for my collection). When a teacher wanted to walk me around the schoolhouse to speak in Farsi about the Iranian art posters that lined the hallways, this student would try to stop me, saying, "You have to stay and participate in the class," yet she would say, in the same breath, that I was hogging the class. "Nobody gets to answer anything," she told me once. "This isn't *Jeopardy!*, there's no game to win." But I felt that either I was going to be my overachieving self and do my best, or else I would completely detach and do my own thing. I had no in-between. They had to remove me from her class because even the teachers felt it was personal between us. I'll admit it: I was a cocky nineteen-year-old asshole who felt I had just given up a full-ride engineering scholarship only to be treated like a child again, and the moment I could excel at something, I was quick to rub it in people's faces and be Hermione Granger about it.

Much of the time, that is how they treated us at DLI: like children. Hell, they *called* us children. Not students, or recruits, but children. *Salaam, bache-haaaa.* The Farsi group's class was at the top of the mountain; a bus drove back and forth, but when you missed it, you were walking a mile straight up a mountain, racing to get to school on time with your backpack and laptop, like in middle school. They gave us children's books to learn the language—not books for beginners but books written for children. At other times, even though we were in school to join the military, our curriculum was very unmilitary. We translated news and lifestyle articles from BBC Persian, practiced the right way to ask to use the bathroom and get a taxi and how to give someone road directions.

The teachers were civilians, mostly people who had no experience with the military and couldn't tell us anything about what kind of work we would be doing with our careers. There was no accreditation to become an instructor, so two of our aged teachers were senile. A third would sit down in front of the class and fall asleep on the regular. Yet another gem of an instructor refused to follow the curriculum. He said to us, "You guys need to understand what you're going to be listening to"—meaning, as eavesdroppers. He pointed to the textbook and said, "You're never going to see words like that. You're never going to hear that." He said he wanted us to understand how human beings speak in real life. So in front of the class, this teacher regularly phoned his brother, who lived in Los Angeles, and put him on speakerphone. And he and his brother would talk in Farsi for hours about finding women, cocaine, heroin, and hashish, and where to get guns. They would then plan their upcoming weekends. All on speakerphone, so we could listen in on their shenanigans. (I enjoyed this class.) But then, in the following class, our next teacher would be stern and serious, asking us how far we'd gotten in the textbooks that day. We told him the truth. Of course we hadn't completed the curriculum—the first teacher had slept the whole hour, the second teacher was senile, and the third teacher wanted to talk about opium with his brother. The by-the-book teacher was not pleased, but he couldn't do much—the Defense Language Institute ran on incompetence.

There was one way in which a few instructors treated us like adults, however. Some of the Farsi instructors would say openly that the United States had caused the hostility between our country and Iran. In 1953, the CIA had helped overthrow the democratically elected government of Iran, because it was not solidly pro-Western in the Cold War. The shah came to power, and the US loaded him up with arms for decades. His repressive rule caused Iranians to resent his American benefactors, and when there was a revolution in 1979, the Islamists that gained power acted on that anger, and relations between Iran and the US had been bad ever since. It was shocking to hear that we were not always the good guys in the Middle East, or anywhere else, for that matter. In this telling, we weren't solving extremism or resolving conflicts; we were fueling it and creating them. And the instructors were telling *us*, newly minted American soldiers! In military school! For someone like me, curious but somewhat sheltered, the teachers' words were intellectual crowbars, prying open a door to my mind that I hadn't even known was shut. Slowly I began reading more about history and foreign policy on my own time and considering alternative viewpoints. But at the time, just the idea of my country causing harm was an uncomfortable revelation. I was wearing the country's uniform, after all, and came from a family that revered military service.

Some Afghan instructors gave us truths too. After one year of Farsi, we took the "Dari conversion course," a sixteen-week course in the Persian dialect some people speak in Afghanistan. Picking up Dari sounded terrific because we would learn things pertaining to an actual war, unlike with Farsi, and I thought being fluent might help me get a mission to Afghanistan. We went to the Pashto schoolhouse to meet our Afghan instructors, who had survived years under the rule of the Taliban in the 1990s.

But they were not just disdainful of the Taliban—they were ruthlessly realistic about the war the US had committed itself to more than a decade earlier, the same war the military was training us to fight. "The Taliban has never gone away, and they're going to outlast the US," they said, one after another. They clarified that the US presence in Afghanistan would end eventually, but the Taliban would survive.

We had a very charming, younger teacher who had us on the edge of our seats with a story from his childhood in the southern city of Kandahar, at the height of Taliban rule. His brother was arguing with a friend over which of them would marry a girl from the village, so his brother played a trick on his friend. He bought the good *charras* (hashish) to get his friend stoned, so he could cut his beard off. The next day, the friend had to leave home for work and was immediately picked up by the Taliban for violating the beard-length law. They beat him and held him in jail for three days. We were aghast. Our teacher, still chuckling, knowing he had us enthralled, glibly finished the story, "So on the third day, they took my brother's friend out behind the jail and shot him dead." He waited a little too long while we sat there in silent horror before he laughed and said he was joking. Once the beard grew a little longer, he assured us, the friend was free to go, no worse for wear.

We barely learned our teachers' names but instead used nicknames based on their appearance or character when they weren't around, to avoid fumbling on their foreign-sounding names. We called one of our teachers Khanome Culture, or Ms. Culture, because she would follow up everything with the comment, "It's the culture, ya?" It was perhaps a nervous tic that helped her explain where she came from to so many American military students. For example, she told us that in the southern province of Helmand, women were beaten for wearing white shoes, because the Taliban flag is white. So the white sandals the women had worn for years now earned them harsh beatings. This story was followed up with a nervous laugh and a "It's the culture, ya?" Over time, parroting that remark became *our* culture.

Another teacher kicked me out of class over mixing up two words. At the end of a lesson, he would usually ask if it was *kifayat*, or "sufficient." He once asked me how the textbook was, and I mixed up that word with *kesafat*, or "garbage." I was in the principal's office with no idea why until it was explained. He never forgave me.

The Afghan instructors would give us controversial news articles to translate, articles covering Afghanistan's forty years of constant warfare, which detailed how the United States was giving millions of dollars annually to Pakistan, which was handing over some of that money to the Pakistani Taliban. So the United States was funding its own enemy.

Keep in mind that these defeatist lessons were occurring and being sponsored by the American military at a military base in the continental United States while the war was underway. Tens of thousands of American troops were occupying Afghanistan. But we students mostly did not resent these subversive lessons. We appreciated the straight talk, which served as a welcome counterpoint to the usual bullshit about the indestructibility of the United States. When the US finally pulled out of Afghanistan in 2021 after a futile twenty-year war that accomplished little but cost a lot, leaving the Taliban to regain power over the whole country, we linguists were unsurprised and prepared because we had been taught well by knowledgeable experts. I just wish the military always gave its trainees and new service members this kind of historically and locally informed honesty.

Inspired by our instructors, I read a work called *Taliban: Militant Islam, Oil, and Fundamentalism in Central Asia* by the distinguished Pakistani journalist Ahmed Rashid. The book details the history of the militant Islamist movement, showing how it fed off the misery of Afghans in the wake of the long, bloody war following the Soviet Union's invasion of the country in 1979. In Rashid's telling, the US had recklessly funneled planeloads of weapons to the anti-Soviet insurgency, which helped form the Taliban after the war. The Taliban were not just a group supporting al-Qaeda and other international terrorists; they were a national movement with deep roots in Afghanistan, overpowering all others. The book had a profound effect on my thinking, leading me to take another step in the gradual process away from my immature assumption that my country was always a force for good in the world. But I also stubbornly thought that with better intelligence and more sensitivity to local cultures and societies, the US could correct its mistakes and use its enormous power to help the world's most suffering people. Some of the news articles our Afghan instructors distributed showed how much better life had become for women once the US and its allies overthrew the Taliban. Girls attended school; water and electricity poured through the towns. I wanted to be a part of that. And also, I just wanted to stop people from destroying towers in New York. Wasn't that the whole point of this?

It took us only about two weeks to comprehend the new Dari accent and pick up vocabulary that came from Pashto, and we spent the next three and a half months dying from boredom. It was then that I found myself going down various internet rabbit holes during class. I watched all seventy-two hours of gameplay for the newly released *Legend of Zelda: Skyward Sword* on YouTube. I became obsessed with lists: "10 Most Creepy Audios Ever Recorded," "10 Worst Methods of Torture in Human History," you know, light reading. Each list item could inspire a week's worth of morbid fascination. A recording of a doomed cosmonaut reentering Earth's atmosphere, for example, could lead to a week of reading about every known gruesome casualty of the Russian space program, and decades-long cover-ups in which their very existence was intended to be wiped from history. It was a dark three months, paired with an equally frustrating classroom experience. During the Farsi course, my friend Sadie saw that I was struggling out of the classroom. Sometimes, astute, sensitive women who have encountered people with disordered eating will notice other women having difficulties. They recognize the telltale signs: perfectionism, secrecy, unusual behavior around meals and foods. Sadie suggested I go running with her. Before then, cardio was a chore I endured to better myself at team sports, or to pass physical tests demanded by coaches or the military. But Sadie asked me to join her jogging just to be healthy, which had never occurred to me. I loved it. This was the beginning of my workout fixation, my efforts to channel my obsessiveness and anxiety productively and positively into a healthy activity.

Finally, after more than a year of studying Farsi and Dari, I graduated from the DLI. We were ready. Difficult though it might be to believe, most jobs in the air force require only six weeks to four months of training, so we linguists were desperate to move on, just as our counterparts already had. At the graduation ceremony, they gave us a paperback guidebook to Iran. It included instructions and information on everything from common greetings to dangerous snakes to the structure of Iran's military. It was complicated—Iran and the United States had not had official diplomatic relations since 1979. Imagine an outsider with limited English trying to understand the bewildering structure and culture of the United States military. It's even harder with Iran, which is large and powerful but far less transparent than modern developed nations. All countries have their secrets, but Iran has more than most: it is a regional powerhouse by population and geography, has a sizable military, and is controlled by a theocratic government that is suspicious and hostile to much of the outside world. The more I learned about Iran, the more I was fascinated—especially by its vibrant history and fantastic food. But military personnel could never visit the country as anything other than ordinary tourists until and unless the two countries reestablished relations, which seemed a long way off (and still does).

This left the Farsi team in a confusing no-man's-land. I had a friend who was a Korean linguist who expected to go to Korea. My stepbrother is a Russian linguist who frequently works with the Russian Air Force. This is what normal language specialists do in the US military—use their language skills in countries where they speak the language! So we were eager to figure out how it would work for our jobs—did we secretly have intelligence officials undercover in Iran illegally, or what?

The military intelligence school was in San Angelo, Texas. I was excited to learn from people with actual military or intelligence experience, maybe from someone who had snooped in on conversations between Osama bin Laden and his fellow al-Qaeda masterminds while they strategized to take down the Twin Towers. After all, this was what we would be doing as our profession: not speaking about food and culture in foreign languages but listening to others plot and discuss terroristic activity. I took it seriously: it seemed like vital training, preparation to eavesdrop on sensitive conversations between America's enemies and translate them accurately so that policymakers and intelligence officials could use them to prevent terrorist attacks or bring terrorists to justice. I was ready to be *military*. Plus military intelligence training does sound like it should be exciting. Maybe some James Bond or *Homeland* stuff. Or at worst, learning to decode some local Persian dialects spoken in Afghanistan and Pakistan.

    Nope.

Seven

Generating foreign intelligence insights.
Applying cybersecurity expertise.
Securing the future.

—National Security Agency tagline

The Goodfellow Air Force Base in San Angelo, located 370 miles northwest of my hometown, is a 1,235-acre stretch of flat terrain that exists to serve the air force's mission to "fly, fight and win—airpower anytime, anywhere." There, my professional linguists and I would receive the intelligence training that would be vital in our professional lives. Before we left Monterey, however, the air force finally handed out our assignments, telling us where we would be working after we graduated. Although we were airmen, the Farsi team would be working under the umbrella of the National Security Agency, the agency tasked with monitoring, collecting, and analyzing information for intelligence purposes.

"By 2008, the NSA had become the largest, most costly, and most technically sophisticated spy organization the world has ever known," according to the journalist James Bamford's definitive history *The Shadow Factory*. All branches of the military loan their people to the NSA, but crypto-linguists can serve in only two places in the entire world: Fort Meade, in Maryland; and Fort Eisenhower, in Augusta,

Georgia. Only those two spots handle NSA language-related missions. There would be no awesome top-secret missions in Afghanistan for us, no working with villagers in Pakistan. If I wanted to be in the military as a linguist, I would have to be in Maryland or Georgia. This was knowledge my recruiter either hadn't been privy to, or had decided to withhold from me. Perhaps she rightly knew it would make me rethink my career choices. She had spoken about all the exotic, exciting travels she had done and that I would get to do while I served, as an expert in languages. Nope. It was either Maryland or Georgia for me. For other linguists, this was good news—they wouldn't have to put themselves at risk in some dangerous part of the world. But doing that was exactly what I wanted! That was why I'd joined up. When I said I didn't want to be some person sitting in a dark room with headphones on for the rest of my life, the administrator in San Angelo smirked. "They're spending a fortune teaching you languages. You really think they'll let you out of the country after that?" he said.

The response shocked me. I asked if *any* linguist could be deployed. The administrator said the army sometimes dispatched linguists into the field alongside the rangers in Afghanistan or Iraq. Linguists there could be either interrogators or debriefers. Interrogators question non-English-speaking individuals detained by the US military or its allies. Debriefers question friendly allies who speak foreign languages. The latter seemed better suited to my personality. I was a lover, not a fighter. Although I didn't speak Iraqi Pashto, I figured I could learn it. They told me I would have to finish my enlistment and then switch to the army. So I had to complete my training. But I planned on making a lateral shift once I was done.

Somehow, our instructors in San Angelo were even more jaded than the DLI guys had been. One of our teachers lived in his van down by the river (like Chris Farley's character in the *Saturday Night Live* skit) and looked like Count Chocula. He consistently showed up hungover, with bags under his eyes. And he insisted we watch funny YouTube videos: "It's YouTube Friday!" But as the course progressed, the other days of the week became YouTube Tuesday, YouTube Wednesday, YouTube Thursday, and lastly the holdout: the strong start to every week became YouTube Monday. Every single morning began with a viewing of Rebecca Black's "Friday," or every internet remix and parody, and the corgi version of "Call Me Maybe." One of his favorites was *Guy on a Buffalo*. It's a series of clips about . . . a guy on a buffalo. I highly recommend it, a top-notch musical.

Some of our instructors told us about military contractors like Blackwater and CACI, though I thought they were saying "khaki." They would say candidly, "If I wasn't so comfortable doing my twenty years in the air force"—meaning the length of service required to qualify for retirement benefits—"I would have gone into contracting and made twice as much money for half as much work." This is a big secret to military retention: reenlisting is really comfortable. Yes, you could make twice as much money in contracting, but the military provides a lifelong safety net. You don't have to figure out what health care to get because it's always provided on base. You will never be homeless so long as you wear a uniform. You'll never not have a doctor. Even your taxes are simpler. So many people stay in the military because it answers many big questions in life, from where to live to what kind of work to choose. Your infinite life options are narrowed down to more manageable levels. When my enlistment ended, I was twenty-five years old and had no idea how to adult as a civilian. It was easy to complain at the time, but it was hard to see how well taken care of I'd been until it was all gone. I should have stayed, but I couldn't live the lie anymore.

Our classrooms in intel training resembled hotel rooms from the 1990s, with plain gray thin carpet sliced in tiles. There were four rows of desks, each with six computers. An early version of Windows Media Player on each screen would play a recording of silence interspersed with speech while a graphic of rising and falling lines indicated the volume and the frequency of the speech. Our task was to look at lines on the screen and try to find where the speech was, clicking through ninety minutes of static while our instructor gave us thirty minutes to translate every piece of human speech.

We could speak college-level Farsi by the time we got to San Angelo, but for crypto-linguists, military training consists of listening to voices speaking a series of numbers as static overpowers most of the speakers' audibility. Imagine turning a radio dial to a distant, poorly powered station, where two people talk for hours about their refrigerator serial numbers. All you do is try to discern the precise figures muttered by human voices beneath the sonic boom-ish crackling sounds. You don't need to understand what the numbers mean, or what the speakers are counting or measuring. They're not official communications or anything: they are short snippets of esoteric chatter, not full conversations. Brief. Predictable. Structured. For example, if somebody in the Iranian military is doing a box drill in a plane for thirty minutes, they must report how many kilometers they go turning, turning, turning. And there's a different number code for how they're turning. It's our job to report every turn that pilot makes and when they return to base. The recordings would be of military operations at the lowest level, not of any critical people or decision-making.

It was robotic, mind-numbing work—and yet I found it incredibly difficult. Almost impossible, actually. I flunked every single assignment because I couldn't hear over the static. You either had the ability or you didn't. And no matter how much I worked at it, I didn't have it. Even worse, I couldn't improve. No matter how hard I shut my eyes and pressed the earphones against my auditory canals, I couldn't make out what the Farsi speakers were yapping about. Another student had been a truck driver before joining up. He was a semi-functioning alcoholic, but he had been listening to CB radio for years, making out instructions and conversation beneath the crackles. He would come into class hungover or even after a few drinks and attain perfect scores. Me, I started failing my classes. This was the first time in my life that I devoted myself to something at which I couldn't advance at all. And graduating from military intelligence school—and my career—depended on my improvement.

The prospect of failing terrified me. I would be letting down my entire family and ruining my career before it even began. There was no plan B for me if my military education went south. Turning down that engineering scholarship was starting to seem like a bad decision. Meanwhile, my relationship with Xander was crumbling into mutual verbal abuse, where we both said things to each other that we instantly regretted but could never take back. At the same time, the cramped dorms at intel school were coed, and my roommate brought her boyfriend over every night. It was awkward at best, but also infuriating. I spent long nights across the street at the base fitness center, which only closed between 0100 and 0200. I could nap in the laundry room or the Pilates room and be on a treadmill by 0400. Our squadron had physical training at 0430 two days a week, but I found those to be a massive waste of time, as much of each session was spent getting into and out of formation instead of in pure, grueling exercise. For the first time, I began to excel at running, as I would round out an hour at a time on the treadmill. Every run finished with sprints too. At night, when there were fewer people, I explored weight lifting. At first, I would do everything I could remember from weight room days on my high school tennis team: the same upper-lower body split every Tuesday and Thursday during class, self-paced, with a clipboard and checklist. A friend and I would take these sessions seriously, always trying to bench more than the other. This laid the foundation for a growing passion, and this gym, where I spent hours alone, became my sanctuary.

This was an extremely stressful time in my life, and I was desperately trying to resist the impulse to binge. Nevertheless, I started suffering panic attacks and bingeing and purging almost every day. Ridding myself of my food seemed like the one thing I could control in my environment, my sole reliable anchor. But it was something I hid from everyone. It's a twisted irony that anyone struggling with mental health troubles knows well: connecting with other people is most vital at times of great pain, when it can be a unique balm to soothe the burns of our suffering; yet deep shame, the humiliation of having a malfunctioning brain, prevents us from seeking or accepting that connection precisely when we need it most. The strain of keeping my eating disorder a secret became an added burden, and I was searching for any relief.

My Farsi course friend Sadie had never mentioned running to me as a way to lose weight or cancel out calorie intake—she was smart enough to know that talking to a person with disordered eating about food is never wise. When we were in DLI, she would casually ask if I wanted to join her at the track before eating dinner at one of the places at the post exchange. For years, I'd noticed that if I exercised right before I ate a meal, I wouldn't throw up after and could even control the portion a little better. So now I began running every day for sixty minutes, since that was when the treadmill reset the numbers tracking miles and pace. Because of my OCD, I couldn't go longer than sixty minutes and just add the new stats to the previous ones, nor could I stop any time before the sixty-minute mark; instead, I would calculate in my head to the hundredths place the percentage of distance or time completed and the difference in the mile pace of this run compared to the run from the day before. After class, I would return home, but when the roommate's boyfriend arrived around 1900 each night, I'd head back to the gym, where I had the whole place to myself. With no need to feel self-conscious about trying new stuff and no waiting for machines to free up, I would experiment with different exercises in this playground. My feet have always been injury-prone for some unknown reason, and I developed fractures in each one after running so much. But the injuries were a small price to pay, since exercise was my sole source of sanity and stability at the time. It was in that dark, lonely gym, and only in that gym, that I found some peace of mind. I would work out for a few hours, go home, shower, and then pursue a less healthy activity. I bought a Nintendo 3DS and would carry it upstairs to the laundry room, where I would sit on a washer-dryer and play video games all night, in between gym sessions. My sleep suffered badly without a proper bed to sleep in, and that probably reduced my stress tolerance. I was falling apart. However, I was excelling at *The Legend of Zelda: Ocarina of Time.*

Then came the final exam. Intel training was structured so that the entire class would pass or fail it together. If we failed, graduation would be pushed back two weeks, while we were given another chance to pass. The graduation ceremony is a big deal in the military, requiring practice drills and marching in formation, with exact timing for everyone involved. Training instructors from the other analysis fields and the fire school, who were on the same base, would be in attendance too. But as linguists, we were used to being informal, including when we'd graduated from DLI, where we hadn't even needed to stand at attention, let alone march; there, we'd walked across a stage in what looked like a high school theater from the 1960s and received our certificates from the civilian teaching team leader. So the instructors in the military intelligence class worked hard to get it right. They were annoyed that they had to reteach us things that we had learned at BMT but not practiced since. They only cared that we didn't embarrass them in front of the other sergeants.

By the time exam day came, we had already rehearsed our graduation and were ready for it. And I knew how horribly I was doing with my assignments, screwing up one after another. If I failed the final exam, or couldn't pull my weight in a group setting, I would be dragging down my entire class, making them stay in school an extra fourteen days.

The final exam was set up in a way that simulated a live mission, with the entire class participating as part of the crew, except that the technology was outdated, on the verge of obsolete. Indeed, this had been an overarching theme of the intel training at San Angelo, where the instructors' unspoken message seemed to be: *This is* really *important but also completely unrelated to what you will be doing once you get to your permanent duty station.* Halfway through the exam, which lasted about four hours, I started having extreme abdominal pain. I thought it was anxiety, or perhaps menstrual cramps even though I was on birth control. At one point, during a bathroom break, the pain took me down to my knees in the stall. My anxiety was growing still worse when, with thirty minutes or so left in the exam, our instructor announced that the air force was having a mandatory formation, all-call, in service blues, within the hour, but also that we couldn't leave the class until the exam was over. Not only would we be late, we would also be in the wrong uniform. Between worrying about arriving late to formation, failing the final exam, and these sudden and intense pains, my heart rate was sky-high.

Then the exam was over. Some of the others in the class took off as quickly as possible to arrive, late, to formation. I had had enough. I raced home and changed into civilian attire. I peeked out the window until I saw the crowds of airmen in service blue uniforms begin to thin and I no longer recognized as many of the people filing past. I went to the base exchange and got in line to pick up my dress blue uniform, which was now dry-cleaned and ready for a graduation ceremony I did not yet know if we had qualified for. I fought off another wave of lightning cramps, fearing that I was going to start my period in line.

After receiving my uniform, I took off for my dorm and rushed into the bathroom. But what I found was no simple period mess. It took me a while to figure out what was going on. By throwing up every day, I had probably vomited up my birth control. And my pregnancy had been the cause of my weight loss during those months in San Angelo, where, for the first time that I could remember, I weighed 130 pounds. I didn't even bother telling Xander. We hadn't spoken in a week, and it was clear we wouldn't talk much after we got to our duty station, even though both of us were going to Fort Meade, Maryland. Truthfully, I didn't even feel much. I can't say I was traumatized, or even really bothered, even though I cried for hours from the shock of it after the adrenaline and nerves of the day. Everything else in my life already seemed like a dumpster fire. If some growing creature didn't want to be a part of me, I could understand why. When I eventually told Xander about the miscarriage a few months later, the only thing he could think to say was that I should have told him earlier. Xander was very smart—he reminded me of the character Sheldon from *The Big Bang Theory*. The same rationality and detachment that made him a great linguist also made him emotionally unintelligent and incapable of empathy. Linguists can be like that.

Amazingly, our class passed the exam and was given permission to graduate. It didn't make any sense, because there was no way I did well on the final assignments. Then someone explained it to me: you basically could not fail out of intel training; they needed you that badly at the duty station, qualified or not, as you would be completely retrained once you got there anyway. Only people whose security clearances were denied were kicked out, and even they were given honorable discharges, so long as they didn't have any other ethical infractions. I wasn't too worried about what would happen once I began my actual job, because I was determined to transition from Iranian missions to Afghanistan missions, and I figured the audio quality would be superior once I was tracking conversations in a country we were actually at war with and where the stakes were higher. Somehow, I had faith that I could figure out how to be a good crypto-linguist, even though I had faith in little else about myself.

Mostly, I was just relieved to be leaving behind military training. It had been a slog, but I had made it. The term "winning ugly" is something I heard once, and it describes well my year and a half in military training. I won, but it was very ugly. But I won. But it was ugly. And look: a lot of lawyers hate law school. Medical students hate med school. I didn't have to enjoy military training to enjoy being in the military. I was looking forward to finally working.

Before you arrive at your duty station, the military allows you thirty days' leave, as long as your recruiter agrees. Fortunately, mine did, and I had a blissful month off, at home with my family in South Texas. By the time the next month rolled around, I felt somewhat refreshed and eager to start my career. I was joining the Ninety-Fourth Intelligence Squadron, 707th Intelligence, Surveillance, and Reconnaissance Wing, in Fort Meade, Maryland. However disappointing and taxing BMT, language school, and intel training had been, however much I'd failed at the latter, I knew I could be an asset to the military in the right circumstances. Putting my skills to good use for the country's benefit was deeply exciting. So was the thought of living in Maryland alone, with an apartment and a job, like a Real Adult. At last!

And indeed, the following year, 2013, would turn out to be one of the best of my life.

It was time to start eavesdropping on terrorists. I wanted in.

Eight

> It is time to dismantle government secrecy, this most pervasive of Cold War–era regulations. It is time to begin building the supports for the era of openness that is already upon us.
>
> —US Senator Daniel Patrick Moynihan,
> *Secrecy* (1998)

I am not proud to say that when I received my assignment to Fort Meade, I wasn't exactly sure just where Maryland was within the United States. When you grow up as far south in Texas as I did, every other state is simply "north." I didn't know which side of the Civil War Maryland had fought on, or what the landscape was like, or the food or culture. I was so new to the state that I wasn't sure why there were so many NASCAR-ish flags everywhere until I realized that *is* the state flag. It would be a few years before I could appreciate the enigma of Maryland, how one can find disparate worlds within short driving distances.

Although I was in the air force and still wearing the branch's uniform, I was on a joint mission with the National Security Agency. As I mentioned, it's a monster agency, three times the size of the Central Intelligence Agency, and controls one-third of the entire US intelligence budget. The Fort Meade base itself is mammoth, containing the Defense Information School, the Defense Media Activity, the United States Army Field Band, the headquarters of United States Cyber

Command, the Defense Courier Service, the Defense Information Systems Agency headquarters, and the United States Navy's Cryptologic Warfare Group Six.

Fort Meade's buildings are sterile, gray, and drab, with squat ceilings. Some people find the campus forbidding, the sprawl and size of the place intimidating. But my living quarters were the opposite: my "apartment" was small, nothing more than a dorm room, really, and I shared a bathroom with someone else. I was just happy to have my own space.

My security clearance wouldn't come through for over a month, a problem because I couldn't start working until I got it. Sometimes when people hear the phrase "security clearance," they imagine work that is highly classified, top secret, VIP eyes only. If that was ever true, it's true no longer. More than 4.2 million Americans have security clearances. Fewer than one-third of them can access materials labeled "top secret," but that's still 1.3 million Americans, four times as many people as live in Iceland. When that many pairs of eyes can look at top-secret documents, the information is not very secret.

Here is probably a good time for a brushup on Security Levels 101. (Note from experience: knowing this classification system will not prevent you from leaking classified documents anyway.) The government has three levels of classification:

> **TOP SECRET:** This is the highest level of secrecy. According to a 2009 presidential executive order about the classification system, something is labeled "top secret" when its release would "cause exceptionally grave damage to the national security." Some top-secret materials are given the added designation of "sensitive compartmented information." That's for pieces of information derived from intelligence sources, and fewer people can look at that info. "Top secret SCI" means that something is *extra* top secret, just as KFC's extra tasty crispy chicken is tasty and crispy like regular KFC chicken, only more so. Some of the items the

FBI found at Trump's compound in 2022, after he left office, and in Joe Biden's home and think-tank office, were top-secret SCI documents, for instance.

SECRET: This is the mid-level tier of classification. It's for information that could "cause serious damage" to national security.

CONFIDENTIAL: The lowest rung on the classification ladder. A stamp of "confidential" on a piece of information means that its disclosure would "damage" national security.

Those three categories sound simple enough, but the politics around concealing information are extraordinarily complicated. According to the 2009 executive order, "If there is significant doubt about the appropriate level of classification, it shall be classified at the lower level." In practice, the opposite happens: lots of harmless, useless information is kept secret unnecessarily.

Why? Because anyone deciding upon the appropriate classification level of a given piece of information has every incentive to restrict materials. People don't get fired for overclassifying things. They might potentially get in trouble if their decision somehow inadvertently leads to information falling into the wrong hands, however. Better just not to take chances. In an editorial on the massive overclassification problem in the United States government, the *Washington Post* opined, "While leaks can be damaging, excessive concealment is also corrosive, undermining trust and credibility in the very policies that the government seeks to protect." That's true, but excessive concealment is wrong even if it doesn't undermine trust. It's wrong because the public has a right to know what the government does on its behalf. The bias should be toward making all information available to everyone, not just those in the national security state. That's called democracy.

Few people who work in national security tradecraft doubt that far too many secrets are kept by the government. "It quickly becomes apparent to any person who has considerable experience with classified material that there is massive overclassification and that the principal concern of the classifiers is not with national security, but rather with governmental embarrassment of one sort or another," according to Richard Nixon's solicitor general Erwin Griswold, who argued the government's case against Daniel Ellsberg in court (more on Ellsberg to come) but later had a change of heart. "There may be some basis for short-term classification while plans are being made, or negotiations are going on, but apart from details of weapons systems, there is very rarely any real risk to current national security from the publication of facts relating to transactions in the past, even the fairly recent past."

Nothing is too trivial for the government to hide from the public. In 2010, Thomas Drake, a manager at the NSA, was charged with leaking classified information for taking a document from the NSA's intranet and giving it to a *Baltimore Sun* reporter. "In doing so, the defendant knew that he exceeded his authorized use of NSANet," prosecutors grimly intoned in their statement of facts entered into court. "This is not an issue of benign documents." For his crime, Drake faced thirty-five years in prison under the Espionage Act.

What was this information that the government deemed so delicate and vital? The document was later declassified, so everyone can see it. It is an email about an internal presentation attended by the then-head of the NSA, General Keith Alexander. Subject line: "What a Wonderful Success." The note relayed Alexander's enthusiasm about a new tech program that was being demoed and some of his comments about its applications. Two paragraphs in the email were labeled secret. The first relayed how Alexander testified to the need to process information quicker. The second reported, "He left the conference room, but before he left the building, he greeted the entire test team in the lab (who worked behind the scenes to make the demo successful)." That was the ultra-important information a bureaucrat insisted needed to be kept from public view. And the government was so willing and eager to punish the note's disclosure that they wanted to put Drake on trial, to make an example out of him.

Drake had good reasons for his actions: the tech program Alexander was so enthusiastic about was a disaster: illegal and wasteful. It allowed the NSA to capture and save Americans' emails and phone calls—without having court permission. Another term for this process would be "warrantless domestic spying"; think Fourth Amendment violations times three hundred million. Rightly alarmed at this un-American initiative, Drake took his concerns to his bosses, NSA lawyers, and the Pentagon's inspector general. Only after they all did nothing did he talk to a reporter, taking care to reveal no sensitive information in the process.

J. William Leonard, a Pentagon official who was later the "classification czar" at the federal government's Information Security Oversight Office, signed an affidavit in support of Drake. It declared that the document Drake leaked "contained no information which met the standards of the classification system." Leonard told reporters, "I have seen many equally egregious examples of inappropriate assignment of classification controls to information that does not meet the standards for classification." The entire process of classification was broken, he said. "The system clearly lacks the ability to differentiate between trivial information and that which can truly damage our nation's well-being."

What struck observers was that prosecutors were willing to take a sledgehammer to Drake's entire life because of that one email. The constitutional law professor Stephen Vladeck told the *Washington Post*, "As a tool for prosecuting leakers, the Espionage Act is a broad sword where a scalpel would be far preferable. It criminalizes to the same degree the wrongful retention of information that probably should never have been classified in the first place and the willful sale of state secrets to foreign intelligence agencies."

All this was far from my mind when I arrived at the NSA, though. I just wanted to get to work. Until my security clearance came through, however, I couldn't do any language-related mission. I couldn't even enter the NSA building. The agency sent me to the records department, where I spent days alphabetizing twenty-five thousand files pouring out of filing cabinets—the names of everyone with a security clearance through NSA Maryland for the year. Busywork.

Finally, at the beginning of 2013, my security clearance was approved, to my immense relief. I had worried that the delay somehow meant there was something in my background that was giving the air force pause, something I had forgotten. But I was as clean as a waterfall.

The first day began with "indoc," short for "indoctrination." In a university-style lecture hall with small desks, some other newcomers joined me in watching a video. A man's voice welcomed us to the NSA. With ominous music floating in the background, the narrator gravely explained that "some individuals violate United States national security laws." A PowerPoint commenced, featuring mug shots of the evildoers, with captions explaining their crimes. The offenders included Ana Montes, who spied for the Cuban government for seventeen years while working at the Pentagon's intelligence unit. Others passed secrets to the Soviet Union and China. Some of these people, the voice explained, were charged under the Espionage Act.

A historical primer is in order because the act figures into our story in a big way. As the name suggests, the legislation is designed to root out and punish individuals who spy for foreign adversaries. Although the United States initially stayed out of World War I, President Woodrow Wilson outlined to Congress the need for the act in 1915, saying that it should target those "who have poured the poison of disloyalty into the very arteries of our national life; who have sought to bring the authority and good name of our government into contempt, to destroy our industries wherever they thought it effective for their vindictive purposes to strike at them, and to debase our politics to the uses of foreign intrigue." Wilson explained that native-born Americans were not the problem. Rather, citizens who were "born under other flags but welcomed under our generous naturalization laws" were the traitors. The notoriously racist president was particularly panicking about Americans of German origin, who he assumed would be loyal to Germany in any conflict.

Two months after the US entered the war, in 1917, Congress passed the law. Although it didn't grant Wilson the freedom to censor the press, as he had requested, it was sweeping and draconian legislation that included the death penalty for transgressors. Among other provisions, it prohibited conveying information that interfered with the war effort or armed forces, and outlawed retaining or disclosing any information about national defense if it could potentially injure the United States or aid foreign adversaries. Attorneys general were tasked with implementing the law, and they used it to prosecute socialists, pacifists, anarchists, and others who were against the war. Most infamously, Socialist Party leader Eugene Debs was sentenced to ten years for urging obstruction of the draft (his sentence was commuted after nearly five years). A filmmaker was prosecuted for making a movie about the American Revolution called *The Spirit of '76* because it allegedly undermined Britain, America's ally.

The hysteria spurred by the war and the Russian Revolution in 1917 led Congress to pass an extension to the law, called the Sedition Act. This went even further than its predecessor, barring any dissent at all against the government or war effort. Even after the war ended, the sedition amendments allowed the Justice Department to prosecute and deport all manner of nonviolent dissenters, such as an individual who passed out pamphlets opposing US intervention in Russia following the revolution. Thousands were arrested and kicked out of the country.

The Supreme Court soon ruled the Sedition Act unconstitutional, but it left the Espionage Act in place. The law fell out of use in the 1920s and 1930s, and it was deployed less in the four years the US fought in World War II than it had been in the year and a half the US was in World War I. However, in 1951, Julius and Ethel Rosenberg were convicted under the act of passing secrets to the Soviet Union and were executed two years later, in a case that symbolized the hysteria of the early Cold War. Others were suspected of spying for the Soviet Union throughout the late 1940s and 1950s. And that's who the Espionage Act was meant to target: spies. People actually engaging in espionage, to benefit America's enemies.

But in 1971, the infamously secretive and vindictive Nixon administration charged Daniel Ellsberg with violating the law for leaking national security secrets in the form of the Pentagon Papers, a Defense Department study of US involvement in Vietnam. The Nixon team's decision was monumental: it showed that the government could deploy the country's harshest anti-espionage law against citizens who didn't spy but merely revealed secrets—secrets that perhaps shouldn't have been classified as such in the first place.

Ellsberg was a former Pentagon official then at the RAND Corporation, a quasi-government think tank, who had turned against the war. He knew firsthand that successive presidents and administration officials had lied to the public about the conflict, and the study proved it. After copying the papers and offering them to uninterested senators, he gave them to a reporter at the *New York Times*. The newspaper printed excerpts, enraging Nixon and his team, who obsessed about discovering the source of the leaks.

The US attorney general soon told the *Times* that the documents were protected by the Espionage Act. A court issued a temporary restraining order against the paper, but the *Washington Post*, the *Boston Globe*, and others picked up the slack, printing excerpts. The Supreme

Court soon reversed the restraining order, so the FBI went after Ellsberg. They charged him with violating the Espionage Act, among other crimes, even though he was certainly no spy. If convicted, he faced up to 115 years in prison.

But the legislation, broad and harsh as it is, was never intended to go after whistle-blowers or leakers—because the entire national security state apparatus didn't exist when it was written. When Wilson put his pen to paper to sign the bill, there was no hierarchy of secrets in the Pentagon, the White House, or anywhere else. As the lawyer Jesselyn Radack has written, "The law was written 35 years before the word 'classification' entered the government's lexicon."

The charges against Ellsberg were dismissed because the FBI had been wiretapping his phone without a court order and Nixon had authorized his henchmen to break into Ellsberg's psychiatrist's office in search of information that would discredit him. They, not he, were the criminals. But the administration's illegal, punitive actions foreshadowed the ways in which the government would act against leakers. Nixon had set the precedent: slapping anyone passing on classified information to reporters with the Espionage Act was deemed an appropriate method of punishing them.

"The Espionage Act has repeatedly been deployed in times of war to limit free speech, a free press, and freedom of information in regard to US foreign and military policy," write the scholars Ralph Engelman and Carey Shenkman in their recent study of the law, *A Century of Repression: The Espionage Act and Freedom of the Press*. And yet the law's use was still relatively rare. In 1984, an intelligence analyst at the Naval Intelligence Support Center named Samuel Morison gave three satellite photographs of Soviet aircraft under construction to an obscure publication called *Jane's Defence Weekly*. He said that if Americans and Britons knew how serious Soviet capabilities were, they would support increases in their respective national defense budgets. This militaristic rationale didn't fly with prosecutors, who charged him under the Espionage Act, and he was sentenced to two years in prison. Senator Daniel Patrick Moynihan of New York, deeply concerned about the overuse of government secrecy now that the Cold War was won and there was no longer even a nominal justification for so much overclassification, wrote to President Bill Clinton on Morison's behalf. "We now have in Samuel Loring Morison a man who has been convicted for leaking information, while so many real spies are discovered but never prosecuted," Moynihan wrote. Clinton pardoned Morison on the last day of his presidency.

One more person should be noted here: in 2002, an analyst at the Pentagon, Lawrence Franklin, spoke about classified information regarding Iran policy to two staffers at the American Israel Public Affairs Committee. He, too, was charged under the Espionage Act, and eventually sentenced to ten months' house arrest.

Ellsberg, Morison, and Franklin. That's it. Between the administrations of Woodrow Wilson and George W. Bush, a total of three people who leaked government secrets were subjected to a draconian law designed to root out German spies during wartime. The law was used infrequently not because only three individuals leaked national security information over those ninety-some years. Far from it. As anyone who peruses daily newspaper coverage knows, leaking is more common in Washington than in a badly built bathroom. Rather, those three individuals were deliberately targeted for political reasons, while countless others were overlooked, if not encouraged.

That's one reason organizations promoting freedom hate the law. "The Espionage Act is a fundamentally unfair and unconstitutional law," according to the American Civil Liberties Union. "It allows the government to prosecute leakers and whistleblowers that it dislikes, while leaving untouched the many leakers within the security state who release classified materials to advance those agencies' bureaucratic aims.

Perhaps worse, it doesn't allow leakers to defend their leaks by trying to demonstrate in court that they served the public interest."

The ACLU's conclusions are broadly shared by other civil liberties advocates. A report by PEN America, a nonprofit organization that advocates for the protection of free expression, found that the Espionage Act is "a broad, vague charge not easily defended against" and stifles the free speech of not just government workers and contractors but journalists and publishers. Unlike most laws, the Espionage Act doesn't take intention into account. Even homicide is normally ranked on a hierarchy, which includes first-degree murder, second-degree murder, manslaughter, and so forth; the accused is always offered a chance to explain their reasoning and actions, whatever the crime. That's not the case with the Espionage Act.

PEN has suggested that lawmakers "repeal the overbroad Espionage Act and replace it with narrower laws designed specifically to address leaking to the press and, separately, actual espionage." Alternatively, the group has called for Congress to carve out an exemption for whistleblowers who advance the public interest with their disclosures. It has also recommended that courts allow defendants to submit information about the public interest of their actions in their defense.

This little history lesson is critical to understanding what ensued between the government and me. But I will be honest: none of us paid much attention to the indoc presentation. It felt like death by PowerPoint, another in the endless set of instructions the military delivers to its trainees and rookies. The thought of acting against the country I was serving in uniform was nutty anyway. My main priority once I had this classified access was to wiggle my way into an experimental Pashto crash course that condensed the curriculum from sixty-three weeks to a mere twenty.

Then I began to help the United States to kill people I never met.

Nine

Afghanistan is not only the mirror of the Afghans: it is the mirror of the world. "If you do not like the image in the mirror, do not break the mirror, break your face," says an old Persian proverb.

—Quoted in Ahmed Rashid's book, *Taliban*

While I was sitting in the squadron break room, somebody important, carrying a clipboard, told me about an experimental Pashto program the air force was trying out. He said they didn't have enough Pashto linguists coming in from DLI to fill missions in Afghanistan, so they were offering a crash course in the language. Instead of the class being sixty-three weeks, as it was at DLI, they wanted us to go zero to fluent in Pashto in twenty weeks. I volunteered, and since I'd already spent months studying the language, the course was a breeze. My high test scores were a welcome reassurance that there were some things I could do well, whatever had happened at intelligence school.

I decided to live off base. One place I spotted on Zillow looked nice—anything with well-maintained grass, big trees, and brick buildings looked safe and pleasant to me. The apartment I took was a cheap, nine-hundred-square-foot, one-bedroom nook in a complex right off the highway, in a neighborhood called Berkshire. It had wooden parquet floors, and the living room wall was dark brown. The wall directly by the balcony was painted a sunshine yellow, and then I had a wall in the kitchen painted red. The only cooking I ever did was in a rice steamer, which I used for everything from oatmeal to red peppers. An excellent device.

It turned out that my neighborhood was less than safe and pleasant. Over the subsequent months, I witnessed several knife fights in my parking lot. But the move was worth it. Sure, the heating was so bad that I unwisely used the oven to flood the entire place with warmth. But for the first time, I had a place of my own. It was mine. All mine. I cherished every square inch of it.

I was young, with no family responsibilities, and making more money than most people my age. It began to feel like the unusual career path I'd chosen—hell, my unusual personality—was paying off. I spent most of that cold winter, my first in a northern climate, running an hour a day on a treadmill, then playing in the weight room, at a gym at NSA headquarters. The regulars began to talk to me. Including a fitness instructor named Dan.

Dan saw that my feet were bothering me from running and suggested I get into cycling, which is easier on the feet. "And you should take my class, because the others suck," he offered. He was right. The cycling class he instructed helped repair my feet, and I was able to start running again, eventually getting up to ten miles every day. He knew what he was talking about because his feet had been reconstructed with surgical titanium after his convoy went over an IED in Iraq during the early years of that war.

Being a fitness devotee himself, Dan gave me the courage to try for my first half-marathon, which I signed up for and ran alone, unsure if I would finish. We lifted weights together and laughed all the time. I didn't know that type of thing could happen in a relationship; my previous relationships had only been with either broken people I wanted to fix or cruel individuals I locked horns with, creating some kind of toxic passion. Dan was different. He was kind, cared about me, and adored fitness as much as I did.

But we were both very obsessive, moody people, people whose idea of hell was having their workout routines disrupted. Also, Dan was married. But he said he was leaving his wife, and I stupidly believed him, and we began a romance.

Dan was a functioning alcoholic, which I had never encountered before. He lived to exercise and drink but little else. This was still 2012, the year I turned twenty-one. I had never been much of a drinker before, but Dan invited me on a concert and bar-hopping adventure. He seemed to know every bartender and owner in town, and they offered us samples of craft beers. Instead of drinking to get shit-faced, we drank for the enjoyment of the taste and the sociability. I found that I loved getting buzzed and wandering around. Together, we'd drink during weekend days in Annapolis, about twenty miles from base, and laze around the water. It was heavenly. Every time, we took the tour, visiting the same shops, making the same small talk with the same friendly people. We were invited to tasting dinners and were asked for seasonal menu ideas. I felt like I was living my dream within an episode of *No Reservations*.

Around this time, a doctor told me that I had a lot of scar tissue from my miscarriage and would be unable to have kids. I mostly tuned that information out, waiting in agitation to go to the gym while trying to get a prescription for a birth control pill that would leave me with the fewest possible reminders of being female. I had never wanted to birth children, because the best way to reduce your carbon footprint is not to have any, though I imagined that I might one day open an orphanage in Afghanistan for children whose parents were killed in war. Professionally, I felt competent, smart, at the start of something great. But my mental health fluctuated between stable and disastrous. I didn't have any faith that I could handle all the havoc and upheaval that comes with devoting one's life to raising a single child. But running an orphanage? Somehow, in my mind, that seemed more manageable, and that way I could help two dozen kids instead of one. To be young and ambitious is to dream—and, in my case, to be ignorant of the critique of the white savior complex— and I enjoyed imagining various plans for my life, even if they were hazy and grandiose. I didn't know how I would accomplish all that I wanted to do, but I knew it started with getting to Central Asia via the military. And I was one step closer to achieving that goal in June when we graduated from Pashto school and began training for a mission.

I was put on the night schedule and tasked with shadowing someone for one month for training. I showed up eager to meet my new mentor, only to find I would be shadowing . . . Xander. Xander! Fucking *Xander*. We had not spoken in months and were on bad terms. So the person I had to sit and watch work every night happened to be my ex-boyfriend, whom I now disliked. It was not fun avoiding any small talk and pleasantries for twelve-hour stretches. But we couldn't talk without fighting, so we didn't say anything at all. He was excellent at his job, I had to admit. The idiot savant. But mostly the idiot part. Our team included me, maybe another woman or two, and all of Xander's friends (awkward!).

The setup was strikingly like any modern office: people with dazed facial expressions wearing headphones, sitting at desks, watching multiple computer screens that visualized the audio of conversations being surreptitiously recorded. On one screen was a visual of the frequency of whoever was speaking—you could see when they were talking, because the graph rose. And then you clicked on that spot on the graph, and the audio played the voices. You could adjust the pitch and the volume, and the crypto-linguist's job was to discern what the people were saying.

We were listening in on people living in the mountains in Afghanistan. Some were members of the Taliban. Others were off-brand Taliban, sort of Taliban-adjacent, fighting for scarce resources and carrying out centuries-old ethnic violence. Still other people we tracked were fighting just for the sake of fighting. Some were old-school warlords, defending their territory. And, most amazingly to me, some were people who thought they were still fighting Russians—even though the Soviets had departed Afghanistan in February 1989. Christ, the Soviet Union hasn't even *existed* since 1992. More than twenty years later, the men we eavesdropped on had not learned, or did not believe, that the Russians had abandoned Afghanistan in defeat. They were like Shoichi Yokoi, the famous Japanese soldier discovered in the jungles of Guam in 1972, who thought he was still fighting World War II, having hidden from Americans for nearly thirty years.

The people we were listening in to were *not* like al-Qaeda or other anti-American terrorist groups. They were not savvy professional terrorists speaking in code, which al-Qaeda and related organizations did because they assumed they were being monitored. Before the attacks, al-Qaeda sometimes referred to what they were planning for 9/11 as "the Holy Tuesday operation," since the murders were planned for a Tuesday. At other times they called the attacks "the day of the planes." Al-Qaeda members have code names, and some don't know one another's real names, and they work in compartmentalized cells, which makes it impossible for them to confess anything useful if they're captured and interrogated (one of many reasons torturing them is stupid). That was the sort of nimbleness the amateurs we monitored weren't capable of. Sometimes they used nicknames, but they didn't have code names. We just logged them as "unidentified insurgent male" ("UIM").

Our audio picked up every radio frequency in the area all at once, a process we called "hoovering." Anything could be heard on those frequencies. We picked up Taylor Swift songs sometimes because Afghans were listening to them. We knew which frequencies to avoid because they were used by the US-led coalition forces. We built a database of oft-used frequencies, as in, "Ali and Ahmed usually talk on 157.7," or "163 doesn't work." Most of the time, the speakers talked about everyday topics like weather and food. Not about missiles or guns or anything, although that happened occasionally. Often we listened to two guys trying, for an hour, to find each other's respective frequencies, like some sort of Abbott and Costello routine.

"Hey."

"Hey."

"Heeeeeeyyyyy!"

"Can you hear me?"

"Hey?"

"Can you hear—"

"Hey, I hear you."

"My brother, how are the friends? Are the friends well?"

"Thank God, brother, the friends are well. How is everything? What is the situation there?"

"Here?"

"There."

"Here everything is well. It's cold outside."

"It's very cold here, and we don't have any work to do."

"Work" could mean everything and anything. It could be nefarious, an attack or a reference to gathering ammunition. Or it could be chopping firewood because the weather was cold.

An airplane or drone filmed the individuals as we listened. The camera was, of course, in the air, so the footage was only of tiny figures. They looked like the characters on an old Nintendo Game Boy video game. The only time the camera got a detailed shot was if the drones were flying over the mountains during the day. The whole landscape was visible then. All the other footage was pixelated, and then at night, it was all infrared. And most of the video was shot at night because the American military coordinated its attacks just before dawn.

Fortunately, the audio quality was much better than it had been at DLI, so I was able to do my job. Unfortunately, most of our language teachers had been from east Afghanistan, and one had been from Pakistan, so we had been taught the far eastern Pashto dialect. Our NSA mission—called Cougar Reach—was monitoring communications in Kandahar and Helmand Provinces, in the south. The speakers we overheard sounded like they were speaking an entirely different language. Xander taught me the common phrases. Once you sounded out the most basic conversations and realized there were only about a hundred different phrases these guys ever said, it simply became a matching exercise, winning a game of broken telephone.

But there was no direction or organization to what we were doing; we never had specific goals beyond writing down what was being said. Some linguists tuned in, typed what they heard, and went home, doing only what was required. But I pulled up the video feed onto a screen so I could see the people I was eavesdropping on, even if they were minuscule and pixelated. Just following their body language helped me make sense of their words. As best I could, I wanted to put the conversations into context to understand the intricate players on the ground, to learn the hyperlocal politics and customs. If I was going to live in Afghanistan, I had to know these people, and hearing how they spoke privately to one another was a great way to do that.

If we heard something relevant, like a convoy going through an area and transferring weapons, we typed it into a computer forum, and sometimes someone else far away would act on what we typed and drop a bomb on the people to whom we were listening. Someone had to count the number of enemies we killed in action, especially when it was time to submit awards packages for airmen on the mission. Yes, awards are given for airmen who help kill people—that is a prized accomplishment in the military. It was what I had signed up for, I knew. But it fucking horrified me how many people we were killing.

"Nausea" is the feeling that the French existentialist Jean-Paul Sartre said humans feel when we realize the universe is meaningless. That feeling began to sink into me when I tracked the number of people we killed. The tally went up, inevitably, day by day. Sometimes I felt like I was killing these people directly; half the day I was eavesdropping on conversations to better help others in the military identify people to kill. As I mentioned, the air force eventually gave me an award for "aiding in 650 enemy captures, 600 enemies killed in action and identifying 900 high value targets." Again, think about that: aiding in killing a lot of "enemies" and "high value targets." Being good at identifying large numbers of people to kill didn't make me feel proud.

The real mindfuck was that we were mostly killing people who were *not* enemies or high-value targets. They were just people in the wrong place at the wrong time. Very often, we didn't even know who they were, and the military was not interested in finding out. We were killing so many people that we were making more enemies than we could ever hope to win over as friends. My Afghan instructors had been right, I realized—we were losing the war, and killing scores of innocents in the process. And then seeing on television and reading online that leaders from both political parties, and senior members of the military, were lying to the American people, telling us the war was going well and we were winning . . . it fucked me up.

As linguists, we were permitted to label the individuals we listened to only as "insurgents." We were prohibited from differentiating between al-Qaeda and the Taliban, or anyone else. The only thing we were asked about was how many strikes we called in—how many times we offered actionable information on the people we were observing—not whom we attacked, or why, just how many. The intelligence community, the military, the NSA—they didn't care, because at the end of the day, there was no coherent strategy in Afghanistan. Looking back, I see that it took me an astoundingly long time to realize that. But I never imagined that America was sending thousands of troops and pouring trillions of dollars into a war it had no idea how to fight, let alone win. Douglas Lute, army lieutenant general who served as the White House's Afghanistan "war czar" under Presidents Bush and Obama, summarized this well in an internal interview during the last years of the Obama administration (later obtained by the *Washington Post*): "We were devoid of a fundamental understanding of Afghanistan—we didn't know what we were doing," Lute said. By the time he said those words, the US had been at war in Afghanistan for fourteen years. I had been working on Afghan missions in the military for over two of those years and could see he was correct.

My job didn't demand counting what the military calls "collateral damage"—the civilians we killed during our strikes and missions. It's a revolting euphemism, designed to hide from ourselves and others that war involves killing innocent human beings. And since we didn't count the casualties officially, their deaths never happened, according to the US government. Sometimes I was the only person in the world outside Afghanistan who knew we had killed these people, and my colleagues, my supervisors, and the institutions where I worked—hell, the whole country—not only didn't care but also didn't want to know about it. I did want to know, though. I needed to know. Those deaths began to haunt me, and I was already, shall we say, mentally vulnerable, what with my anxiety and eating disorder.

My fragility was not unique to me. In 2013, the Pentagon released a study showing that drone pilots experienced PTSD at the same rate as regular pilots, despite being continents away from the people they were bombing. The *New York Times* write-up of the data included this perspective from one of the study's coauthors, an epidemiologist: "Remotely piloted aircraft pilots may stare at the same piece of ground for days. They witness the carnage. Manned aircraft pilots don't do that. They get out of there as soon as possible." In addition to PTSD, drone operators were found to have similar rates of anxiety disorder, depressive disorder, substance abuse, and suicidal ideation as compared with traditional pilots.

In 2011, a different Pentagon study found that almost 30 percent of air force drone pilots had burnout, with nearly half having high operation stress. One of the study's coauthors told NPR, "When they have to kill someone, or where they are involved in missions and then they either kill them or watch them killed, it does cause them to rethink aspects of their life." Indeed, it does! Killing people for a living will do that.

But one of the strange things about doing this kind of work is that you're prohibited from talking about it with anyone. My mom, my friends, people I was dating, even a therapist I began seeing—none of them knew what I was doing, because it was classified. Had I told them, I would have been charged with leaking secrets (irony alert). So I kept to myself the violence I was helping inflict, leaving the office after a hard day knowing that I had ended someone's life, someone who might have been entirely innocent.

Although people working in intelligence are banned from discussing work with others, some things were shared. With my security clearance, I could access lots of classified information. I was able to see every mission set, not just my own. Overall, the computer system looked like the internet from the '90s: drab and slow. If you didn't know exactly where your information was, it was easy to get lost in expired links. The system was a labyrinth, but some people, those who had been around long enough, knew how to find the secret meme pages, which featured cartoons and visual jokes.

Whenever a leaker emerges, critics struggle to understand how the military could allow such a suspect individual into its ranks and grant them security privileges. But who else is supposed to fill the millions of military and intelligence roles? The United States has built the biggest military and intelligence bureaucracy in world history. The defense budget is more than $800 billion and will likely reach $1 trillion this decade. We have eight hundred bases, eight uniformed services, the largest air force in the world, and the only active space force. According to the best estimate, by *Washington Post* reporters William M. Arkin and Dana Priest, there are "1,074 federal government organizations and nearly two thousand private companies involved with programs related to counterterrorism, homeland security, and intelligence in at least 17,000 locations across the United States—all of them working at the top secret classification level." They wrote those words in their 2011 book *Top Secret America: The Rise of the New American Security State*, and I don't think the numbers have gotten any smaller.

Well, when you construct a behemoth of a military and intelligence bureaucracy, you staff it with human beings, millions of them. Some of them will have views they keep private because they might be unpopular. Others will develop attitudes at odds with the organizations and institutions where they work. That isn't a screening problem. It's an inevitability. You cannot have a huge national security state with millions of employees and contractors and account for the views of everyone. It isn't possible, any more than it is possible to predict who among the general population might one day commit a criminal act.

I had never committed a crime in my life. But gradually I fell out of love with what I thought was the ethos of the US military. Doing crypto-lingual work on the night shift was difficult. My daily routine involved sleeping as little as possible, exercising as much as possible, and completely falling apart when anything disrupted my schedule, even the most routine or banal distractions. Staying an hour later after a shift for a random drug test, for example. Needing to take my car to the shop and missing an hour at the gym. These everyday annoyances wreaked havoc on my psyche—I once begged an auto shop to drive me to my yoga class so I wouldn't miss it.

Dan and I had a great relationship at first, but it consisted exclusively of lifting and cycling, with an occasional Saturday spent looking for pizza or watching football at Mangia in downtown Annapolis. Our entire relationship was spent at bars and gyms. Great places both, but not always the healthiest ones. Even though we were lifting together for hours every day, it didn't feel like overexercising for us, because we normalized it for each other. Every addict knows that camaraderie, bonding over unsafe or unhealthy practices, can be treacherous. The friendship itself, all the warmth that results when two people connect, becomes dangerous. And even if we want to stop, we don't want to lose the relationship.

It took me a while to realize that my eating disorder was getting dangerously bad. I was still bingeing and purging. I weighed myself each day, frantic to lose weight, but if I lost a pound, I wondered why it wasn't a pound and a half. And if it was a pound and a half, I wondered why it wasn't two. By the end of 2013, my weight had plummeted to 120 pounds. Dan convinced me that my eating disorder was going to destroy me if I didn't get it under control. For the first time, I found a therapist. It seemed to help for a while. I needed to talk to someone about how to cope with having so many things I couldn't discuss because I was prohibited from talking about anything work-related. It's bizarre to spend your day helping to kill people and then withholding that information from your mental health supporter. I ended up speaking with a few different therapists. The longest stretch I had, with a male therapist, was starting to go well. He found ways to encourage me to eat enough of what limited food items I had allowed myself. Finally, during one session, I raised the subject of my father, his dementia, and how stressful his delusions had become. I mentioned the year he left our family. Suddenly, my therapist looked worried.

"This is really bad," he stammered. "We shouldn't have brought this up today. I need to tell you that I'm switching practices and will no longer be here at this clinic."

He was the last good therapist I ever had. But there was now a very serious disconnect between my mental health and my job. When people brought food to share at work, I would compulsively wolf it down and then go throw it up in the NSA's automatically flushing toilets. I hated those fucking toilets; they flushed way too soon.

Helping to kill people for years at a time takes a toll on a person, and I was becoming destabilized. My sister Brittany knew *something* was wrong with me, but I couldn't say what it was. Things with Dan eventually fell apart, the largest obstacle probably being his still-existing marriage. And really, who, having such grave responsibilities and access to top-secret information at their job, would listen to concerned friends and family about a doomed relationship? Nobody could tell me anything, until everything crashed and burned. Not even a black rescue cat with big green eyes named Mina that I got at a shelter around then was able to save me.

Ten

STOICK: They've killed hundreds of us!

HICCUP: And we've killed thousands of them! They defend themselves, that's all! They raid us because they have to! If they don't bring enough food back, they'll be eaten themselves!

—How to Train Your Dragon

In January 2015, ISIS militants threw a Jordanian pilot in a cage, lit him on fire, and burned him to death. I sent an email about it to my friend, who later gave it to the journalist Kerry Howley. I'm quoting from my email because it indicates my mindset at the time. My language hasn't been filtered or changed, so hopefully it gives some insight into what kind of person my younger self was, and how I saw my place in this world:

> Getting out of work, I felt such a rush of emotion that I had been suppressing throughout the shift. I could not escape, or allow myself to put aside thoughts about the Jordanian pilot. . . . I spent hours playing mental chess with the world, who should strike first, hardest, what message should be sent, revenge, etc. . . . So on all fronts I just felt really helpless and overwhelmed. Naturally my thoughts had turned to yoga, because it is the means by which I can really understand and

acknowledge powerful emotions and put them aside to gain more clarity and peace. But I didn't want to just hide in asana and meditation because it made me feel good. In the pain I felt, I did not want the "moral" to be compassion and forgiveness.

I became consumed by despair at what I was doing to people I was watching on screens and knew by their voices. The hopelessness was a kind of cancer that grew in me and began to spread. In the summer of 2015, I finally got to the point where I could not balance going to therapy with working the night shift. I went to the air force administration and told them I was losing it and needed to prioritize therapy. Two weeks later, I got an email saying that I had been selected for an assignment in NSA Georgia. For six months, I lived and worked just outside Augusta with fewer hours and a looser setting. I got to know the area and loved it, which factored into my thinking a year later when I left the military.

While I was living in Georgia, Trump launched his presidential campaign, sliding down an escalator in Trump Tower in front of a small crowd of reporters to blather about the evils of people who came from Mexico. His campaign revolted most of us at the NSA, in both Georgia and Maryland. We wanted to help people, Americans and Afghans, and it was clear he didn't care about the former and despised the latter, and generally hated anyone with too much pigment in their skin. Since I'd spent time in my childhood visiting Mexico and reading about that country's history, I knew his vile words about Mexicans and the border were lies. Over the next year, watching his campaign contributed to my sense that the country was adopting an outlandish anti-immigrant mentality. Xenophobia had returned to America, more powerful than it had been, maybe since World War II, when the government put Japanese Americans in internment camps because they were assumed to be disloyal after the attack on Pearl Harbor.

But at least with our existing president, democracy seemed salvageable. In the spring of 2016, I participated in a protest organized on Facebook against the Obama administration's decision to keep the US mostly out of Syria, even though the country's dictator was using chemical weapons on his own people. In Damascus, Aleppo, and around the country, the Syrian government was, with the help of Russia, Iran, and other unsavory regimes, destroying its country, razing Aleppo to the ground with barrel bombs. "Aleppo is burning," our signs read. The humanitarian crisis was catastrophic, and our government seemed largely indifferent to it. The protesters, the majority of whom were Syrian American, carried candles and posters demanding heavier US involvement. We went from the White House to the hotel where the Correspondents' Dinner was being held, that annual shindig where comedians and politicians flatter one another with easy jokes. I mention this because it illustrates where my head was at, and also because some people tried to paint me as some sort of Democratic Party functionary when I became famous (or infamous). But I spent my free time protesting Democratic presidents, not worshipping them. If Hillary Clinton had won the 2016 presidential election, I don't think she would have been a good president. She was far too enthralled with the goodness of US power, having campaigned for the wars in Afghanistan, Iraq, and Libya. But at least there would have been someone somewhat accountable.

In September 2016, the air force sent me an email offering reenlistment. After two years of school and training, I had remained at the NSA for four years with the air force, even as I became progressively more disillusioned by my work and scarred by its effects on Afghans. Sometimes people ask me why I stuck it out so long. How does a deeply idealistic person, someone who cares passionately about helping people and wants to devote their life to it, end up spending years in the bowels of the NSA helping the US government kill people?

The answer is that I thought I was being strategic. History is my jam; if I had gone to college and been able to study whatever I wanted, it would have been history and anthropology. Instead, I just read furiously on my own time. Not just the history of South Asia and the Middle East but letters and government accounts from ancient Rome, and histories of religion by scholars like Reza Aslan. I devoured so-called pseudo-archaeology by the investigative journalist Graham Hancock, who is adamant that advanced human civilizations extend much further back in time than orthodox archaeologists maintain. Maybe it was my father's influence on me. Maybe it's that I intuitively understood that the present is only the result of a series of historical events culminating in a specific time. And as I read history, I saw that every leader endured jobs where they were unhappy, did work they disliked or objected to, all in the service of eventually obtaining better, higher positions where they could have valuable impact.

The thing is, I wanted to be in the room with the cruel people, where they make the cruel decisions. I wanted a seat at that table. If our country is doing awful things in foreign countries, I want to know about it, to see up close how it works and why. Other, more innocent people look away from the grime, or dissociate. But I always refused to look away. I was willing to do whatever I needed to get into that decision-making room, where I would finally be able to exercise power on behalf of something positive. If people didn't do that, I believed, then change wasn't possible. To get things done, I felt, required playing the game. People with pristine politics don't make it into the Situation Room. You want to do something humanitarian? Hitch a ride with the soldiers. They're the ones with the resources. That was my goal: to ride the military's coattails and take the first opportunity to get to Afghanistan to help the people there.

Look, I learned all the names of the senior commanders in Afghanistan, all the different factions and tribes. I learned how they worked, what their command structure was like, how they operated in the field, how they cried when somebody they knew was killed. You don't get that intimate knowledge in Afghanistan as some random person. You need to be part of an organization with lots of money. And nobody has more money than the US military.

But by the fall of 2016, I knew that Trump might win the White House, and if that happened, any good the US was doing overseas would come to a halt. I had slowly realized that there was no way to advance as a linguist in the military. No matter how much I progressed, even if I made sergeant, I would never be eligible for deployment. The odds were tiny, if not zero.

Good advice came to me in the form of a conversation with my last supervisor, a wise, cynical Turkish linguist who had, in the early 2000s, actually gotten stationed in Istanbul. He'd since been forced to return to Maryland for what was his third stint in that dank, cave-like office. Nearly twenty years after first being there, he was in literally the exact same spot—the only difference was that we were watching suspected militants on flat screens instead of television boxes. When I discussed my plans with him, he asked me, "Are you really going to come back to this shithole squadron and sit in a basement until you retire?" When your own supervisor tells you that there's no future for you at a job, it's smart to listen. I was ready to leave, even without a concrete plan for what to do next. Surely with my multilingual abilities and unique experience tracking militants in the region, people told me, finding a spot at a nongovernmental organization would be within reach.

But when you leave your job doing classified work for the military, they get authority over what information you're allowed to share with potential employers (and they get authority over what I'm allowed to tell *you*!). When I submitted my résumé for approval, the air force sent me back a version of what I could distribute for prospective jobs. They had compressed my six years of experience and training, including awards, to three bullet points—and one of those points was "fitness instructor." My mission, intelligence work, and regional specialization couldn't be mentioned to anyone! And since I'd gone to language school instead of a university, I didn't even have a college degree, except for a vague "Associate of Arts Degree: Persian Farsi." "In the job market, candidates signal their fitness for jobs by pointing to college degrees," writes W. David Marx in *Status and Culture*, the book I happen to be reading at the time I'm writing this. Well, I couldn't signal my fitness for anything but instructing actual fitness. Looking at the job ads on the United Nations' website, and those of other organizations doing good work overseas, I saw that I wasn't competitive. They all required at least a bachelor's degree, often a master's degree (and preferably from an Ivy League university), plus some international experience, internships, and whatever else rich people provide for their kids to ensure that they get good jobs. I realized I was no better off than if I were applying right out of high school. The air force might have told us that we were the elite, and that linguists were the top 1 percent of that elite, but it was clear that in the job market, military experience was devalued. It was deeply disappointing to me, and angering.

But I didn't give up on my dream of doing mission work in Afghanistan; I just felt I had to rethink my strategy and expand my time horizon for making it happen. My impromptu plan was to get a contracting job, do it for a year to burnish my résumé, and then find something overseas. Doing government contracting was the only thing besides teaching yoga and spin classes that I was qualified to do.

How dedicated was I to moving to South Asia? Well, to help my chances, I had my fallopian tubes removed. I was tired of taking birth control pills that could be ineffective during a relapse into bingeing and purging, and I already knew I couldn't have a child anyway. The whole thing was just a hassle. Plus, I thought that not needing birth control pills—medication that can be difficult to access in some developing countries—would make me more competitive over other women for deployments. Does that seem extreme? Well, I am a person who goes to extremes. The whole point of my life was to help humans in Afghanistan, I felt. Taking out my useless reproductive organs seemed a small price to pay.

While still looking for jobs, I packed up my white Nissan Cube I had recently bought and took a brief trip to visit my parents in Texas to surprise my mother on her birthday, December 20. On the way there, I passed the turnoff that would have taken me to where my dad was, in hospice care, with my sister Nikki. It would have been a two-hour detour, and I planned to do it on the way back. According to my GPS, without the detour I would arrive at my parents' house shortly after noon, meaning there would be time to unpack and settle my cat Mina in my bedroom before heading into town to find a gym. The hours on the road felt like poison in my body, and a very pressing anxiety weighed on my mind. I didn't know what version of my dad I would eventually find at my sister's house, and I was terrified.

Early the next morning, I was finishing at the gym when I noticed that I had missed a call from Nikki. Between sets, I called her back. Dad had fallen out of bed, she said, and although my nephew had done CPR until the first responders arrived, he was dead.

I sat on the floor of the gym bathroom and considered my options. My mom and I were going to get Brittany from the airport in an hour, where she was flying in from graduate school in Michigan. But it didn't seem right to tell anyone in my family yet. Besides Nikki and her kids, I was the only one still in touch with my father, and this news would ruin my sister's visit. But whom did I have to confide in? The sad truth is, at the time, I didn't have anyone. A few weeks before, in Maryland, I had started a fling with my CrossFit coach. It wasn't something that would have normally happened, but I was leaving and wouldn't be a client much longer, so I didn't view it as inappropriate. With nobody else in my life, I called *that* guy in the early morning and told him what had happened. I was in shock, and so I sounded stable.

I had long been anticipating this moment, imagining what it would be like to receive the call. And when my dad finally died, I was alone at a gym, talking with a guy I'd slept with twice because . . . I'm not sure what I wanted from him. Comfort? No, but I knew I needed to at least practice saying that Dad had died, even though I would wait hours to tell my mother and sister.

Once I finished at the gym, I met up with Momface in town. We took an unusually quiet trip to the airport to pick up my sister and her first husband, Chris. There was no telling how she would take the news that our father had died. Brittany hadn't spoken to Dad in three years. She arrived; we ate, shopped, and went home. After we put the groceries away, I sat with my mom and sister at the table. Chris was in the bathroom. Mom wanted to go clean something. I knew I had less than a minute before the two of them wandered off, like cats. Without a pause, I told them about the call from Nikki that morning. Seconds later, Chris casually walked into the room and stood by the table, sensing something was wrong.

"What's up?" he asked.

"Dad's dead," Britty replied flatly. Chris nervously drummed on the table with his knuckles a couple of times, then softly said, "Well, damn." This broke the dam of tension and the room flooded with laughter. Ex-wife, estranged daughter, son-in-law who had met the man only once, and me. I don't think any of us knew how to process the news, or even exactly what we were processing. I had lost my father years before, to his dementia and his inability to speak.

Since everyone else there was estranged from Dad, I didn't have anyone to talk with about my pain. So I just ran on those empty country roads, and cried, and ran, and cried.

Eleven

> What truly matters is not which party controls our government, but whether our government is controlled by the people.
>
> —Donald Trump, inaugural address

At the outset of 2017, I was in Georgia, mourning my father and excited about a new career.

The year ended with me in handcuffs and shackles.

That wasn't quite my plan.

Between Christmas and New Year's, on a run just a mile from my parents' home, I received a call from Pluribus International Corporation, a Defense Department contracting company to which I had submitted my résumé. They were offering me a one-year contract. Desperate to fill my days with meaning, I accepted immediately, even when I wasn't sure if the job was back in Maryland or in Augusta, where I had just recently moved all my possessions into a rental home. Luckily it turned out to be in Augusta.

A few weeks later, on February 9, orientation began. Pluribus operated within the John Whitelaw Building, in Fort Gordon. (Fort Gordon was named after a Confederate general, one of many official government properties honoring the traitorous Confederacy. It was renamed Fort Eisenhower in 2023.) With thirty thousand military and civilian workers, it looks like any other military base, but it's all about eavesdropping: it hosts the United States Army Signal Corps, the United States Army Cyber Command, and the Cyber Center of Excellence. The Whitelaw Building hosts NSA Georgia. Unlike NSA Maryland, it's a gorgeous, ultramodern facility. A $300 million one, in fact, reflecting the enormous post-9/11 infusion of cash into cyber-surveillance. But these immaculate, gleaming buildings with high-tech spying equipment are surrounded by horse stables and trails because Fort Eisenhower is an army base that hosts ballistics and infantry training. The entire place feels like a resort in the middle of the brush.

Shortly before I began, Trump was sworn in as president. His press secretary, Sean Spicer, went up in front of the entire world and made the laughable claim that the crowd that attended the inauguration had been the largest at any inauguration ever. The way he could just say it, the way he could lie so brazenly and openly, seemed like the starting whistle in a race to fascism. This was how Trump's whole presidency was going to be, I realized. The contempt he showed for foreigners, especially people of color, refugees, and those from developing countries, made me recoil. Listening to him call Mexican immigrants "rapists" and "murderers" felt intolerable. In Trump's view, people like me, who wanted to help others in faraway lands, were suckers or, worse, "globalists" who disdained America.

A few weeks later, Trump said that the White House didn't get "one call" complaining about his decision to approve the Dakota Access Pipeline, which would run from North Dakota to Illinois, crossing under the Missouri River, where it would threaten the safety of the water supply at the Standing Rock Sioux Reservation. Trump's claim was absurd and insulting in its shamelessness: there were daily protesters putting their lives at risk to stop that cursed climate-killing pipeline. I had been thinking of driving to South Dakota for their "Veterans'

Stand," a strategy to put vets on the front line of the protests to see if the police would shoot us. My surgery prevented me from attending the protest, but I was still haunted by our rapidly burning world. At the time, I wrote on my Facebook wall: "You have got to be shitting me right now. No one has called? The White House shut down their phone lines. There have been protests for months, at both the drilling site and outside the White House. I'm losing my mind. If you voted for this piece of shit, explain this. He's lying. He's blatantly lying and the second largest supply of freshwater in the country is now at risk. #NoDAPL #NeverMyPresident #Resist."

It was difficult to understand how the world's most powerful person could tell lies to people who knew he was lying and suffer no repercussions. I realize how naive this sounds now—I thought that officials were supposed to resign if they lied. I actually expected there to be an uprising against Trump's comments about the pipeline, and when that didn't happen, my belief in the basic sanity of the American system of government began to crumble. Here's how Kerry Howley put it, after speaking with my friends and family:

> To those around her, Reality was a never-ending, frequently exhausting source of information on the world, its problems, and our collective obligation to pay attention. She gave her sister a marked-up copy of the Koran, rife with Post-it notes, and told her to read it. With an organization called Athletes Serving Athletes, she pushed wheelchair-bound kids through half-marathons. ("Athletes Serving Athletes," said her ex-boyfriend. "She'd never shut up about that.") She donated money to the White Helmets, a group of volunteers performing search-and-rescue missions deep in rebel-held Syria. She told those around her to watch *13th*, a documentary about racial injustice in the prison system. . . .

What remained abstract and distant to the news-consuming public was neither abstract nor distant to Reality. "She was really, really passionate about Afghanistan and stopping ISIS," says [a friend]. "We would go to lunch, and that's pretty much all she would talk about. She was despondent that ISIS was the way that it was, that we can't do anything to help the whole situation, that it's so fucked up."

I booked an appointment with a local staff member for Georgia's then-Senator David Perdue and explained the situation—that the White House press secretary was lying, along with the president himself. I showed her photos of the protests and explained the Dakota Access Pipeline's impact, the broken promises that sacred indigenous lands would not be invaded for oil pipelines that leaked before they were even declared operational. I showed her the data that the North Pole would be all but melted by 2025, and how the fossil fuel industry was lying to the American people. Maybe I wasn't heard that day, but that was my first time speaking with someone from an office of an elected official to ask for accountability.

As Kerry Howley mentioned, seeing *13th* had a devastating impact on me. Britty and I watched the documentary film on Netflix and talked often about it. Even though our father had been in prison before we were born, we had no idea how pervasive and brutal America's prison complex was, or how racist. Jails and prisons became my new mania. I read newspaper and magazine articles about the millions of Americans locked up at higher rates than anywhere else in the world, for longer, often in awful conditions. (Later, when I worked in the education department in prison, tutoring women to earn their GEDs while incarcerated, I repeatedly requested and recommended that the film be included in the social studies portion of the curriculum.)

I realize that all this makes me appear insufferable to be around. In my defense, a Fox News examination of my Facebook page included this line: "As for non-political interests, her social accounts also suggest she's a workout buff and donates to veterans' and children's charities." See: I'm into normal things like exercise and charity too. It wasn't all doom and gloom.

During my thirty-minute commute from home to my new job, I started listening to podcasts on Spotify. The second season of the hit true-crime series *Serial* told the story of Bowe Bergdahl, an army soldier who deserted in Afghanistan and was then kidnapped by the Taliban before returning to the US as part of a prisoner exchange. Although his ordeal was splashed widely across the media, Bergdahl's tale was news to me.

That's because people who work in intelligence are prohibited from reading or watching any news stories or shows that include information derived from classified information that was leaked. In fact, I was paranoid about ever reading the *New York Times* or the *Washington Post* or any other news source on my computers and telephones because if they contained anything that came from government sources disclosing unauthorized information, I could be charged with possessing those secrets! In other words, people working in intelligence are sometimes *less* knowledgeable about national security than the average newspaper reader because they fear what might happen if they consult the news. No prosecutor will charge Joe Six-Pack or Sally Housecoat with reading in the newspaper about some classified Pentagon program. But intelligence officials could be charged. Although I knew their names, I had no idea what information Edward Snowden and Chelsea Manning had leaked specifically, for instance, because I was too afraid to look it up. If that sounds absurd, that's because it is. But those are the rules.

But some intelligence officials are seemingly exempt from these rules. If you read newspapers or watch the news regularly, you'll notice that the stories often include anonymous or background quotations from high-level officials in the United States government, who are revealing information they are not supposed to give to journalists, who are not supposed to have it. You might remember an anonymous White House official who in 2018 wrote an entire op-ed for the *Times* concerning the danger of Donald Trump! President Obama, who went after leakers and whistle-blowers with astonishing vindictiveness, said that he went after only "a really small sample" of the many people leaking information. There were so many leakers during his presidency that his administration began strapping officials to lie detectors. Trump raged against leakers, tweeting once that "leakers are traitors and cowards, and we will find out who they are!" A conservative writer named Gabriel Schoenfeld complained to reporters, "The system is plagued by leaks."

How plagued? "As a matter of reality there are leaks every day on all sorts of subjects. Some come from the top. They are part of the way the government functions," University of North Carolina law professor Mary-Rose Papandrea told the *Christian Science Monitor*. But while leaking is common, it is acceptable only when done by some people. "High government officials feel no compunction about leaking, and the rare times anyone is prosecuted, it's usually someone at a low level," CNN legal analyst Jeffrey Toobin said during the Obama years. Steven Aftergood, head of the Project on Government Secrecy for the Washington-based Federation of American Scientists, asked, "Is it only the army privates and the mid-level bureaucrats who are leaking? Is it never White House officials or senior agency officials? Judging by the government's prosecution record, you'd think that senior officials never leak, because they're never being prosecuted, and we know that's not true." He added, "What appears to be a pattern of selective prosecution is another aspect of the unfairness of the way these statutes are being enforced."

At orientation at Pluribus, we went through the routine security covering the dangers of spilling secrets and distributing information. It was the typical boring shtick, and I blamed Edward Snowden and Chelsea Manning for it. For those of us who worked on national security issues, Snowden and Manning were nuisances. Practically speaking, their actions had led to increased security measures for anyone dealing in (or adjacent to) intelligence. They had also led to measures that were meant to look like they increased security and to reassure people but were actually useless, just causing hassles and inconvenience ("security theater" is the term coined for this sort of thing). Turnstiles, cameras, searches when entering and leaving the building, signs on the wall reminding us of the secret nature of our work—it all increased after Snowden and Manning.

Without thinking twice about it, I signed the usual training documents, security agreements, and nondisclosure acknowledgments regarding insider threats, handling sensitive information, and distinguishing between different levels of classified documents. On a sheet of paper, I confirmed that "I make this agreement without any mental reservation or purpose of evasion." Texting with my sister after enduring another round of these presentations, I joked, "I have to take a polygraph test where they're going to ask if I plotted against the government. #gonnafail."

"Lol! Just convince yourself you are writing a novel," she responded.

"Look I only say I hate America three times a day. I'm no radical. It's mostly just about Americans' obsession with air conditioning."

These comments proved to be deeply damaging to me in court, when prosecutors presented them not as harmless jokes between siblings but as declarations of a lethal hatred. They did not quote other parts of the conversation, the context that would have shed light on the unserious nature of my exchanges with Brittany.

Pluribus seemed a ramshackle operation, devoid of designated rooms or even a desk for me. My supervisor wasn't an analyst, and the person who was supposed to show me my assignments didn't even work for Pluribus. The agency was internally going from one dumpster fire incident to the next, so it was burdensome to have to train, orient, or even acknowledge a private contractor. As part of orientation, various offices gave me some papers, one of which included my email address and a temporary password, which I logged in with and dutifully changed to something I would easily remember. A few hours later, I went downstairs to get an iced Americano from Starbucks in the cafeteria. "Security" was a guy in a suit sitting on a metal chair at a small table—he could have been an extra from the *Men in Black* films. There were metal detectors farther down the hall by the turnstiles, but he didn't make anyone walk through them.

"Where are you going?" he asked.

"Starbucks," I said.

He looked through a folder I was carrying. "Okay, see you in five."

I went past him to the cafeteria, still within the turnstiles, bought an iced Americano, and returned.

"Did you get anything else besides the coffee?" the guy asked me.

"Nope, didn't even get a receipt."

This time, the guy looked more carefully through the folder I was carrying and saw that it contained my email password, which I had already changed.

"This was a security infraction. This was classified information you took to Starbucks."

Christ. You didn't say that when you looked through it the first time. Nobody told me I couldn't take this to the internal coffee shop. Hell, all the paper says is "Confidential: For Official Use Only."

I kept my irritation to myself. "Okay. What do I do?"

"It's not a big deal, but I have to write it up. And Human Resources will let you know when to see them," he said. "I have to go upstairs and report it to my supervisor."

"It's just a piece of paper with a password on it that doesn't work anymore," I protested. It was my first day and I was already getting in trouble.

"Well, why didn't you leave it here?" he asked.

The Human Resources officers said that I had committed a serious offense, even though one of them was quick to wave it off as something that always happened. The paper I had taken outside was "confidential," the lowest secrecy level. But I feared losing my job before it even began, so I kept quiet about the security-ish guard failing to search my papers properly on the way out and the fact that nobody had told me that the cafeteria downstairs didn't count as being within the building, although it was within the building. (Although I was outspoken on social media, I have trouble advocating for myself in person sometimes and am nonconfrontational.) The Human Resources people told me that usually when someone committed an infraction like the one that I did, they must take a course on security. Instead, they instructed me to peruse a PowerPoint and take a ten-point quiz, which I did. But now I had a record.

This, too, came back to bite me in the ass when prosecutors made it seem like my Starbucks run had been part of a grand conspiracy to begin funneling documents to America's enemies. In retrospect, I should have told HR that they, not I, had screwed up by being lax about security and failing to tell me which papers needed to remain in the building, and what constituted the building. But I tried to be cooperative, and it backfired. Not for the last time.

Eventually, Pluribus placed me on the second floor, in a room with a lovely patterned carpet and floor-to-ceiling windows. The space was round and flowy and open, with people working in clusters of three around the room. There were barriers between the three desks, so you weren't staring at someone all day, but another person was always there, just to your left or right. Each person had at least two desktop computer screens in front of them, and some had four. The whole place looked more like a cutting-edge tech company than any government building I had ever seen. Even the kitchen was nice, with two sinks and two microwaves. The "burn bag," which was where we put any classified documents we printed out, was also in the kitchen, on top of the fridge. The office made it easy to be sociable, too: if you needed to talk to your colleague, you just stood up and talked to them. Once, during a thunderstorm, people stood shoulder to shoulder at the colossal windows, watching the drama of the Georgia lightning.

My job, such as it was, consisted of translating documents from Farsi to English. This was around the time that Trump was threatening to pull the US out of the nuclear deal with Iran, so Pluribus felt those efforts were more important than anything happening in Afghanistan. But there wasn't much work to do. My supervisor didn't speak Farsi and wasn't even cleared to be on my floor, so I couldn't talk to my boss about my work. Nobody else seemed to know or care what I should do. That wasn't unusual, I learned. My coworkers all seemed to have extra time on their hands. One older woman who shared my group of desks commonly brought huge bags of Tootsie Rolls to her desk and fashioned the candy pieces into sculptures resembling the famed poop emoji. She distributed her unique folk art to people's desks. In honor of Harambe, a gorilla who had been shot after a child fell into his enclosure at the Cincinnati Zoo, one guy built a small shrine at his desk to the slain animal (who he mistakenly thought was an orangutan), consisting of a glass jar containing a tangerine from the day of his death. *TangHarambe* never grew mold, a testament to his everlasting memory. My contribution to the silliness was placing my prized fake-signed Anderson Cooper portrait on my desk alongside my two screens.

In our oodles of downtime, another thing Pluribus employees did—as virtually all NSA personnel did at one time or another—was read NSANet. It's the agency's home page on its internal computer system, containing information about upcoming speakers, news articles, reports of interest to the intelligence community, fun daily puzzles, human resources stuff, and other miscellanea. The website consists of news-style summaries of intelligence reports. Anyone working for the NSA goes through a process of receiving permissions to access various sites and programs and then, if their position and assignment mission warrant it, they can file requests to see reports and analyses concerning their immediate missions. But that rule doesn't apply to anything that just comes our way by being posted on what's called NSA Pulse, an offshoot of NSANet. Scouring NSA Pulse was better than reading the news because it was raw and exclusive, and we couldn't get in trouble for it. The materials there are available to anyone with a high enough security clearance.

Humans are curious by nature, but that feeling of exclusivity shouldn't be underestimated. It infects people with security clearances, the sense of being part of a special club that is entitled to be trusted with the nation's most precious confidences. In his excellent memoir *Secrets*, Daniel Ellsberg describes the effects of having access to government secrets as a process. "First," he says, "you'll be exhilarated by some of this new information, and by having it all—so much! incredible!—suddenly available to you." Second, he goes on, you'll feel foolish for having opined on these topics without having known all this information existed. Third, you'll start to see people who voice opinions without being able to reach this information as foolish, just as you once were. Which includes most of the public, of course. "You'll eventually become aware of the limitations of this information," Ellsberg continues. "There is a great deal that it doesn't tell you, it's often inaccurate, and it can lead you astray."

Indeed. After *Serial* ended, Spotify recommended that I listen on my commute to a different podcast about national security, one hosted by Jeremy Scahill, a journalist at a publication called the *Intercept*. The program, called *Intercepted*, was at once revelatory and familiar to me. Scahill and other journalists specializing in foreign affairs, like Glenn Greenwald and Naomi Klein, would discuss what the United States was up to in Afghanistan and elsewhere in minute detail, including information, perspectives, and voices that I had never heard. Literally, the first time I heard the specifics of what Snowden had leaked about national security secrets, I was in my Nissan Cube listening to that podcast.

But the *way* that the *Intercepted* crew spoke—the jargon they used, the issues and people that commanded their concern—was the same as mine and the people I knew and worked with. This podcasting crew sounded like others in the national security world: ex-military, CIA, and NSA. Even the pace at which they spoke was like a briefing. Listening to the podcast on the way to Pluribus, I felt like I was at work except that I was learning more and different things from these experts than I was at my actual job. They were coming to conclusions I was already living through, completely immersed, in real time, and yet they spoke from a point of authority, one that was extremely skeptical about the national security state and informed by American history.

It was profoundly cathartic to listen to debates about the NSA's work while driving to and from work, where I was seeing the agency's dysfunction from the inside once again. Scahill, Greenwald, Klein, and others were reinforcing, with impressive erudition, what our Afghan instructors had told us about the war's failures and damage. From my own work, with my own worn-down eyes, I saw how cavalier the military was about so-called collateral damage. *Intercepted* corroborated what I knew to be true from my own experience, with the same passion I had and the factual basis I desired. They added context I hadn't known about. The podcast had an enormous, immediate impact on me. Maybe I should have paid closer attention sooner in life to what my country was doing around the world. But we were a pro-military family, from a pro-military part of the country, and we had been sheltered growing up.

During the summer before, to augment my work, at home I had watched Afghan news and followed the Taliban's social media profiles. Like the rest of the world, the Taliban used Twitter, YouTube, and Facebook. Since I could speak Dari and Pashto, I tuned in. The feeds live streamed their firefights, and when I watched them, I realized that the NSA had been predicting their movements and decisions incorrectly. That in turn helped me realize that when we were calling in strikes on militants, we were not striking them at their most potent. We were too late—the Taliban fighters had already spread out, making it impossible to find them together in the same place at the same time. Instead, we killed them on their way to and from the conflict zones, often with their families. Even worse, I saw that the Taliban were sometimes fighting ISIS, who were committing the most heinous crimes imaginable worldwide and were our top enemy. And while ISIS was battling the Taliban, we were weakening the Taliban. We would call in a strike after the Taliban defeated ISIS in a battle, kill some Taliban members, and then ISIS would return stronger in that region, wreaking even more havoc and killing more Afghan National Army and Police forces than the Taliban would have killed.

Even worse, the Trump administration seemed to have contempt for the idea of helping Afghanistan at all, and for the entire intelligence community. In mid-April, someone at work said something shocking. Toward the end of the day, my colleague stood up in the room and announced, "Hey, I think Trump is gonna be dropping the

Mother, in Afghanistan." The Mother of All Bombs was the nickname for the GBU-43/B Massive Ordnance Air Blast. It was the largest nonatomic bomb in existence, a 21,600-pound, $16 million weapon that had cost $300 million to develop and contained ten tons of high explosives. "It's so large that no U.S. warplane is big enough to drop it: it has to be offloaded from the rear of a cargo plane, with the help of a parachute," as the *New Yorker* described the weapon. It had never been used.

I was puzzled and horrified by the prospect of dropping the Mother. It didn't make sense—we were spending trillions of dollars trying to build a functioning state in Afghanistan, not to destroy it. American troops had died for that goal, and many others were wounded. Successive presidential administrations had committed to that project. On top of that, countless civilians would be killed if we dropped the Mother on them. What could possibly justify doing it? Remember, this was a country I had come to know well, albeit from a distance, through years of schooling with native speakers who'd fled Afghanistan and pledged to help the United States. Afghanistan was not Iraq, where ISIS had gained control in key cities a few years earlier. It was not even pre-9/11 Afghanistan, where al-Qaeda had planned major operations from the unstable and obscure southern and eastern provinces with relative security. Even with some ISIS members running around, there was nothing in the country that posed the kind of threat that would require dropping the Mother of All Bombs, which would spread untold devastation.

Someone had to bear witness, so I found a feed where I could watch it happen live. People gathered around my desk to watch in real time as the Mother was ejected from the back of an airplane, pulled by a parachute out of the cargo bay. It plummeted to the earth, guided by a GPS system, and exploded six feet above the ground, creating a giant cloud of smoke and fire designed to obliterate everything within a thousand-yard radius. Of course, we couldn't see any of that, just the cloud of smoke that rose from the ground.

Watching the bomb, I felt so goddamned guilty and angry. Why did we drop the bomb *there*? How had I not known about it? I couldn't figure out why that location had been chosen, which I thought meant that I was not keeping up with the area as I should have been. Even though I had moved on from Afghanistan work to Farsi stuff, I was still tracking my old missions. I reached out to my old colleagues, but they told me that nobody in intelligence had called for that strike. No targets were named to higher-ups as spots that should be hit, let alone hit by the Mother. We looked at everything leading up to it, trying to determine why they had chosen that spot, on that day, at that time, on those individuals. Nobody at the NSA had identified it as a place that should be hit. We all felt that we had just thrown $16 million down the drain.

The Mother's deployment went against all the intelligence provided to the administration. It was a direct contradiction of every policy that had been pursued during the Bush and Obama administrations. The same thing was happening with Syria, where Trump was doing the exact opposite of what the intelligence community was recommending. It felt like all our work was for nothing. Worse, it gave cover to the administration, which falsely claimed its actions were based on intelligence. I knew that a new president would bring a shift in policy, but I had not anticipated that he would make a 180-degree turn and do the opposite of what we at the NSA had been told was vital for us to do for the previous sixteen years.

By the next morning, the media had gotten hold of an unclassified version of the video of the bomb's descent and were showing it on a loop. "We targeted a system of tunnels and caves that ISIS fighters used to move around freely, making it easier for them to target US military advisers and Afghan forces in the area," Sean Spicer said. "The United

States took all precautions necessary to prevent civilian casualties and collateral damage as a result of the operation." Trump said he was "very proud" of the operation, which he called "very, very successful."

But I knew how these strikes took place, I knew the area, and I knew the players. Those tunnels had been there for two thousand years, and they were not occupied much by ISIS members. And despite what the military and administration said, to this day nobody but the people on the ground collecting bodies knows how many civilians we killed. There are parts of the area that have not yet been excavated. (We, of course, never excavate the areas where we've killed people.) Nevertheless, the *Guardian* reported a local eyewitness as saying, "There is no way that civilians were still living there." Even though the law mandates that the military be nonpartisan, all the televisions on the walls at NSA Georgia were tuned to Fox News, and of course, their talking heads were all praising the bravery of the commander in chief who had the guts to drop the Mother. All I could think about was how the United States had just launched the biggest recruitment video for ISIS, and how many innocent people we'd killed. I kept imagining what it looks like when you pull somebody out of rubble after a bombing, their charred and broken remains. But by the next week, the media had moved on to something else and totally lost interest in the most devastating bomb dropped since 1945. Our nation's superficial, erratic, and destructive approach to countering terrorism was reinforced to me when, a few weeks later, a man pledging loyalty to ISIS bombed people at an Ariana Grande concert in England, killing twenty-two people and wounding five hundred. Destroying chunks of Afghanistan had done nothing to prevent that. Meanwhile, the United Nations had declared the world at risk of the largest famine since World War II, with twenty million people in Yemen, Somalia, South Sudan, and Nigeria facing a hunger crisis. We weren't doing anything to prevent that either.

The truth seemed to be degrading around me. In May, it was revealed that Trump had disclosed "highly classified information" to Russia's foreign minister about a planned ISIS operation, information provided to him by Israel. "The information the president relayed had been provided by a U.S. partner through an intelligence-sharing arrangement considered so sensitive that details have been withheld from allies and tightly restricted even within the U.S. government," the *Washington Post* reported. The president was not authorized to share the details, which concerned the inner workings of ISIS, since they jeopardized a vital source of intelligence by citing the city in Syria where the source picked up the intel. That could help adversaries (like, say, Russia) identify the Israeli source and how they got the information.

Of course, the president was not disciplined for his illegal sharing of highly classified intelligence with Russia. That was an important lesson to me in how unequally the government treated leakers. The collapse of American democracy was inescapable. At work, having to watch Fox News all the time—the bigotry, the xenophobia, the contempt for democracy on the network—was nauseating. My extended family had been ruptured by some of my relatives' support for Trump, and I wasn't going to put up with that at work. I filed a formal complaint with the NSA's HR department, since having the partisan network on all the televisions violated policy. It made no difference, of course.

Intercepted became a lifeline of sanity for me. They had a terrific episode about climate change, and I emailed the podcast requesting a transcript of the show. The email exchange was about three sentences long: I asked why the transcript, usually available by Thursday, wasn't posted yet; they assured me it was in progress and would be up by Friday at the latest. That brief, innocuous email exchange would prove to be fateful for me. In the meantime, I contacted Georgia Senator David Perdue's office again, by which time the transcript had dropped.

I spent the last two hours of my workday citing their evidence on climate for Senator Perdue's staffer, the woman I had visited back in February. I don't know how well that was received, but at least I was doing something.

And then on June 1, Trump announced that the US would unilaterally withdraw from the Paris Climate Accords, destroying the planet's best hope of averting disaster from climate change. God, I was angry about it. How could anyone take our country seriously if every four years, a new president came into office and reneged on our global commitments? Trump had done the same with the Iran nuclear deal, unilaterally renouncing something that was not only good for both the US and the world but necessary for our well-being. But severing a pact with Iran was at least reversible. Climate change was an impending catastrophe, and we needed to devote our best resources and efforts toward averting it. Our actions couldn't be undone. The awful irony was that the Paris Agreement was extremely weak, simply establishing a consensus on the *goal* of reducing global temperatures. There was nothing binding about it; each country was allowed to chart its own path toward lowering its emissions. No penalties were levied on countries that failed to meet targets, and there were no international inspections or anything like that. But our country could not even commit to doing that, so selfish and shortsighted were our leaders. I felt nearly hopeless.

I needed to do more. That was a common feeling for me, but the Trump era made it an urgent priority. It was dawning on me that my career plans were mistaken; I would not, in fact, be able to use service in the United States military to help people in Central Asia. The little work Pluribus had for me consisted of translating arcane documents about Iranian aerospace programs. Trump had no interest in helping people in Afghanistan, or anywhere else. "We are building roads and schools for people that hate us," he once tweeted about Afghanistan. Indeed, his administration seemed intent on bragging about being cruel and disdainful toward others. Refugees, peace, aid, climate relief—all the things I cared about were under attack by my own government.

As bad as all this was, my distress was amplified by the tone in the media. It's easy to forget now, but the atmosphere then was one of impending authoritarianism. In February, the *Washington Post* had adopted a new slogan: "Democracy Dies in Darkness." This was the newspaper that had exposed the Watergate scandal during the Nixon administration—surely they knew what they were talking about. Respected political scientists, historians, and pundits were publishing books with titles like *How Fascism Works*, *On Tyranny*, *Twilight of Democracy*, *How Democracies Die*, *How Democracy Ends*, *Fascism: A Warning*, and *The Road to Unfreedom*. "Trump Is Following the Authoritarianism Playbook" was the headline of an op-ed on CNN .com written by a specialist in Italian fascism. The media had a vested interest in fostering hysteria, and I admit that I fell prey to it.

Amid the plethora of crises, a classified intelligence report appeared on NSA Pulse, the NSA's clearinghouse. The stuff posted there is usually boring and dumb. Not this. For anyone able to decipher the bureaucratic language, the report's contents were riveting. On the issue of Russia's interference in our elections, the hottest, most disputed topic of the day, the document in front of me had exclusive, critical details.

This report seemed like a bombshell. But one thing confounded me. *Why is this secret? Why isn't this getting out there? Why can't this be public?* It was labeled top secret, but that didn't mean it *should* be top secret. For one thing, everyone who had access to NSA Pulse could read it. One helpful feature of NSA Pulse is that, like Twitter, it shows which articles are trending. That narrows down the content and directs readers to what others are finding most interesting. The piece began to trend on the site, eventually becoming the most read article, which meant that it was being read by countless intelligence agents around the world. This is the national security state version of going viral.

I read the report over again, and then again. Once more again. People in the office were talking about it. Someone asked, "Dude, did you see that?" "Yeah," someone responded, "I wonder when someone's going to leak that to the press." Surely the information would make its way to the media, I figured. It was only a matter of time. But I kept watching the news, and it didn't happen. The whole country knew that Trump had volunteered classified intelligence information to fucking Russia, but *this* was somehow being kept under wraps?

Still, I didn't plan on doing anything drastic. But as it turned out, that's just what I did.

Twelve

I'm all for leaking when it's organized.
—William Daley, President Obama's chief of staff

Daniel Ellsberg described feeling exhilarated the first time he engaged in an act of civil disobedience. It "had freed me from a nearly universal fear whose inhibiting force, I think, is very widely underestimated," he wrote in *Secrets*. "I had become free of the fear of appearing absurd, of looking foolish, for stepping out of line."

That wasn't my experience. After I mailed the report to the *Intercept*, I felt relieved, but not free. The report was out of my possession, the NSA had not caught me with it, and it could not be traced to me, or so I thought. If the NSA somehow got wind that someone had leaked the report, they would surely be looking for a tech-savvy perpetrator; all leakers in the modern era, from Edward Snowden to Chelsea Manning to Thomas Drake, sent their stuff digitally. And anyway, I had not written or used my address or name anywhere. I didn't want credit or fame or notoriety. The information needed to get out to the public, and since nobody else was circulating it, I had to do it. But now it was in the hands of expert journalists who would understand its value and share it with the country. And so I was done.

I waited to watch the drama unfold. I kept looking at the *Intercept*'s site for any mention of what I had sent them. And waited. And waited some more. What I didn't realize, what I had never considered, was that once you send out information, you lose control over what happens to it, and to your own narrative in the world. I had imagined that the *Intercept* would treat what I had sent them as sensitively as it had treated Snowden's revelations. Experienced journalists that they were, they would surely understand the value and delicacy of the top-secret document in their possession and act accordingly, factoring into their calculations the dangers the leaker had voluntarily brought on themselves to get them the materials. I chose to send the report to the *Intercept* because I figured that they alone were principled and smart enough to understand what was in their hands, and to report it in proper context. In his memoir, Ellsberg wrote about handing over the Pentagon Papers to a *New York Times* reporter: "We didn't talk about protecting me as the source. I took it for granted that it would do that, to a point." I believed the same thing.

I was wrong. Days went by, and nothing happened. I was mystified. I felt stupid, risking my career over nothing. I didn't tell anyone because it would be like bragging about failing at something. I had no plans to send the report elsewhere, or to leak anything else. Normal life resumed for a few days, with me cycling between my routine at the gym, boredom at work, and a bad date. I was considering my next career move because it was clear that working at the NSA was leading nowhere, but without a university degree, I wasn't competitive elsewhere.

I decided to go to Belize for the long Memorial Day weekend. It was time; I had expected my life after the air force to be travel-packed. Months before leaving the military, I'd planned an extensive trip to

Mexico City. I knew which hostel I would stay in, one block away from a CrossFit gym. Both were within walking distance of a bus terminal that had shuttles to various historical sites and art districts. In my mind, the perfect vacation started every morning with a 5:00 a.m. CrossFit class, followed by a day of hiking to ancient pyramids, pacing around art museums, or simply exploring a city on foot. But since I'd retained my security clearance, my first trip back to Mexico since childhood would have to wait—US government employees are prevented from traveling to the country except for a few designated resorts in Cancún. And there was no way I was going to some all-inclusive place that looked like Florida. Instead, I began to dream of Peru and Bolivia. My sister and I were supposed to see Machu Picchu in the fall of 2017. I couldn't wait for the fall, though.

Coincidentally, I received an email about a small airline offering direct flights to Tel Aviv for eighty-nine dollars. Of course, I wanted to visit Israel for historical and religious reasons, but also, I enjoyed the street artist Banksy, and a new project of his had opened its doors in Bethlehem that March. It was a parody hotel, called the Walled Off Hotel, boasting floor-to-ceiling views of graffiti-covered concrete walls, plus, according to their website, "the best hummus in the region." Not only were original Banksys featured in the hotel rooms, but local artists displayed their works in the hotel gallery. Adjacent to the hotel was the "Wall-Mart," where guests could rent their own equipment and add to the graffiti. Graffiti is one of my favorite art forms; I have a tattoo inspired by the graffiti artist A1one, or Tanha, as he goes by in Persian. I clicked the link and wondered what a trip to Israel and Palestine would look like. (This would also come back to bite me. During my first detention hearing, the court mentioned that I had been looking at flights to Israel. I immediately scribbled a question mark to my attorney, who whispered something about extradition. The government repeatedly suggested that there was something nefarious about my dreams of global travel.) But the Middle East seemed impractical, while Belize was closer to home.

I had reason to want to go there. The sudden disappearance of the ancient Mayans in Belize was among my father's favorite topics for speculation, about which he would speak at length during the drives to and from his house. It haunted him that a civilization with a calendar and clock more accurate than the ones used in his own lifetime had declined so rapidly, without a clear cause or catastrophe. He even claimed to have Mayan earrings, carved from solid pieces of jade, stolen from a graveyard. His obsession had become my own, and I found a small, family-owned resort called the Howler Monkey Resort, aptly named for the howlers who frequented the trees around the cabins.

I intended the trip to be a quasi memorial to my father. There had been no funeral when he died the previous December. I had paid for his cremation, but since his final arrangements were carried out by Nikki, I didn't have even a portion of his ashes. When we were younger, Dad talked about driving up to Indiana to spread our grandparents' ashes (where they had retired to), a plan he might have carried out. Spreading ashes at a place where one belongs was always important to him. Sadly, when he passed away in my sister's home, no one found a will, where he might have expressed his wishes. Apparently, he didn't have one. Part of me wanted to leave his ashes at the top of a Mayan pyramid. They were an enigma, and so was he. However, I didn't know if it was legal to mail human remains, and considering how I would get through TSA and US Customs into Belize with his ashes kept me up at night. I had pretty much consigned to oblivion the fact that I had just committed a major felony with my leaking; the thought of breaking any law terrified me. I scrapped the plan for the ashes but booked the flight.

What I didn't know was that the *Intercept* had indeed received the envelope I sent them. It had landed in their mailbox and was casually given to two senior editors. "If you get a document that purports to be from the NSA, it should be a five-alarm fire," one of the publication's security experts later said. "Go to a secure room, with an editor, freeze where you are. You are not aware who you are exposing or putting at risk." The *Intercept* had an experienced, brilliant security team who knew how to deal with secret national security documents. The Snowden files were kept in Fort Knox–like conditions, in a locked room with a camera, for instance. No individual was allowed to be in the room without another person.

Conversely, the report I sent bypassed the veteran security team and was instead handed over to two new reporters who came from television news, Matthew Cole and Richard Esposito. They had little expertise with digital secrecy or classified NSA documents, but they were hired by the website because the editors felt the *Intercept* needed more insiders with connections to the national security state and federal government to do things like, you know, verify classified documents they received in the mail from anonymous sources.

And that's just what they did. In the exact wrong way. The new guys were unsure whether the document was a hoax. So Cole put it in his bag and took a train from DC to New York City, putting the document at risk of being lost, destroyed, or, yes, intercepted. "I thought at the time there would be an audit if they printed on a government printer," Cole later said. "I forgot about that thought." Whoopsie-daisy!

Cole, or someone else at the *Intercept*, texted someone in Tampa regarding the leak and described what they'd gotten. "Was mailed May 10 from Augusta, Georgia," the *Intercept* reporter texted this source. This source showed the text message to the FBI. And that's when my life began to unravel, unbeknownst to me.

I had flown to Belize while the *Intercept* was helping the FBI realize I had leaked something. I arrived on May 27. The lack of heavy Spanish accents amazed me, and I realized I would be just fine speaking

English. I admit I never knew that Belize was part of the British Commonwealth until recently. I traveled with only a camouflage rucksack filled with shorts and summer dresses. After I checked in at the main cabin and was shown the filtered water dispenser, which I immediately knew I wasn't going to use, I was led along a wooden walkway to my cabin. Behind the cabin was a gentle slope down to the river, and there were large metal signs with silhouettes of alligators. My cabin had a bed, a nightstand, a table with two chairs, a sink, and a shower and toilet in a water closet. It was perfect. I changed into a sundress and wandered around a little outside my cabin while I waited for my first tour of the pyramid at Altun Ha. The monkeys weren't there that afternoon, but they would be the next morning, or so I was promised. On the half-hour drive to the historical site, I stopped at a shack for food and enjoyed the best beans and rice topped with fried fish that I'd ever had. Everything came with a side of caramelized plantains. I tried not to scarf it down, but I did.

A guide and I were the only ones at Altun Ha that afternoon. He took pictures of me looking pensive, sitting between two carved rocks overlooking a courtyard below the pyramid—it was Instagram-worthy, so I posted it, captioned with a few sentences about how much I missed my father. Just outside the ruins were a few stalls. I hated being "that tourist," but I also wanted to leave some money for the locals, since there were no other tourists that day. I bought a few bracelets and a wooden cross (allegedly) hand-carved by the guide who'd given me a personal tour of the site. I say allegedly because every tourist shop had those same crosses, but that transaction also allowed me to tip him generously for the tour without feeling awkward.

Back at the resort, watching the river behind my cabin, I hoped to see a massive alligator (Crocodile? Sometimes I don't know the difference) floating down the river. I was nervous about dinner. On the drive out to the ruins, as we pulled out from the resort driveway, my driver had pointed to a flock of chickens.

"That's dinner tonight," he'd said. "My brother is killing one this afternoon and cleaning it for the guests."

I had been a vegetarian heading toward veganism for more than two years. There was never one stand-alone reason for my diet, but I was gradually realizing that staying as close to vegan as I could would be the most ethical lifestyle possible. I've never thought that humans eating meat per se was wrong; it was mostly the gross negligence and abandonment of dignity and compassion found in factory farms that bothered me. The carbon footprint and water waste kept me from eating beef, though I suppose I also have an emotional affinity for cows (they're cute!). I simply avoided dairy, meat, and anything else from the industrialized and subsidized commercial farms that put profit over ethics. It was just another one of those things that probably made me unbearable to be around. I was twenty-four and lived as if all my actions made a difference to the world. It was something I could explain to the imaginary Tony Bourdain who kept me company.

The howler monkeys arrived before dinner. They were little, but I knew they could be fierce if startled. I lay beneath them on the grass as they spread out on tree branches, hanging by their tails to leisurely pluck leaves to eat. Seeing these pitch-black fur balls with long tails made me think of my cat, Mina. The monkeys were a reminder of home, a dozen Minas hanging from the tree.

I decided I would eat the chicken, part of a simple meal: a small portion of chicken breast, potatoes, and greens. Dessert was a cocktail glass of oven-warmed banana slices with a little syrup and cinnamon. All this food navigation surely sounds complicated and exhausting, but that was my life then. There was no vacation from being myself.

My final day, I had a late breakfast of cornmeal pancakes and hung around the resort, walking around the property and taking a stroll by the river. At 10:00 a.m., I headed to the airport in Belize City and made a huge rookie mistake. While waiting to go through security, I bought some fifty dollars' worth of hot sauces, anything to spice up my meals of lentils and kale. Not one of those bottles made it through security, though, being over the security size limit. I was mortified, realizing that the shop deliberately sold merchandise it could immediately reclaim from the gate. Once I made it past the gate, there was an identical shop, and I dropped more money buying the same sauces. One more plate of fried fish, beans, and rice, and what the federal government later called my "suspicious" trip to Belize was over.

There was no secret meeting in Belize, and at no point was I unaccounted for. I never left the resort without being accompanied by someone who worked there. I didn't eat or go anywhere without posting the pictures to Instagram, which I could do only when I returned to the resort's common room and had Wi-Fi, since I didn't know how to make my phone function outside the US. But my harmless trip would be a major point of contention in court.

On May 30, the day after I returned, Cole actually phoned the NSA itself and told the head of public affairs about the leak. When the spokesman asked to see the report, Cole snapped photographs on his phone of all five pages and sent them over to verify their authenticity. He didn't read from the document to the NSA spokesperson, describe its contents, or send him a retyped copy—all standard Reporting 101 protocols for journalists who need to confirm the authenticity of leaked documents. Hell, he could have looked for ways to verify the report without contacting NSA officials, like finding other sources or even checking online to see if anything would corroborate the leaked report. All that would have protected the leak's source, who might be risking their career (and much else) by sending the *Intercept* information the government had deemed top secret. Nope. Cole sent the NSA actual shots of the document.

Most modern printers use a machine identification code. That means that whenever any document is printed, it contains unique printer markings indicating the type of printer used as well as the date and time of printing. The markings are invisible to the naked eye but detectable with special equipment like image-processing software and ultraviolet lights (though sometimes a magnifying glass will suffice). Again, these are things professional national security journalists know and factor into their decision-making. But when Cole gave the NSA photos of the exact document I sent them, he inadvertently included those distinctive printer markings, the fold in the center of the pages (which suggested it had been printed and hand-smuggled out of an NSA facility), and other things that provided the NSA with vital clues as to the source of the leak.

Cole called a source he had in the intelligence community and relayed how the report made its way to the *Intercept*. He said it came via snail mail, postmarked from Fort Gordon, Georgia. "There's a logic to that," the intelligence source responded to Cole, who didn't realize he had just casually revealed important information about my whereabouts. And so the NSA, armed with indispensable evidence from Cole, went furiously searching for the source of the report's leak. This being the nation's leading spying agency, they swiftly determined that six people had printed out the document, including me. Of those six people, only one was found to have emailed the *Intercept* from their work computer (damn my stupid question to them about their climate podcast transcript!). On June 1, two days after Cole called them, the NSA contacted the FBI. They told the bureau everything from start to finish: the *Intercept* had given them what it believed was a classified, top-secret NSA document that had been folded in half, "suggesting it had been printed and hand-carried out of a secure space," according to the FBI affidavit for my arrest warrant.

Why did Cole have carte blanche? Why was the report not given to more senior, experienced people, or even run by the *Intercept*'s multi-person security team? There has never been a good answer to this question. Glenn Greenwald, one of the *Intercept*'s founders and the person who had handled Edward Snowden's leak as a reporter at the *Guardian*, was in Brazil then and was not interested in reading what I'd sent. He considered the link between Russia and Trump during the 2016 elections a "hoax" and was contemptuous of anyone—or any documents—that suggested otherwise. Otherwise, I have no idea why the publication acted as it did. But the *Intercept* made disastrous choices, with grave consequences for me.

Look, this isn't just Reality Winner saying the *Intercept* screwed up. The documentary film director and producer Laura Poitras, who, as one of the founders of the *Intercept*, helped report the Snowden documents, said the organization had failed badly in its handling of the NSA report. After she went public with her complaints, Poitras was fired by the outlet. "I haven't seen a mistake this consequential before," veteran *Washington Post* national security reporter Barton Gellman later said about their handling of my document. The *Intercept* "knows a lot about this stuff—they have arguably the best operational security experts in journalism over there," he added. "So it's baffling that they didn't make use of them." Columbia School of Journalism professor Bill Grueskin, who had long been a newspaper reporter, said, "We had rules around this kind of thing: You would never just turn over the original or a copy of the document [to the government]." Stephen Engelberg, editor in chief of *ProPublica*, the top investigative news site in the country, said, "We shouldn't assume that if something comes in a plain brown envelope, that we don't have a very high level of duty to protect the identity of a person, even anonymous to us." Alas.

Cole himself later acknowledged that not speaking with the *Intercept*'s top-notch security team was a "face plant." Betsy Reed, the

Intercept's editor in chief, later admitted that "at several points in the editorial process, our practices fell short of the standards to which we hold ourselves for minimizing the risks of source exposure when handling anonymously provided materials." She added, "We should have taken greater precautions to protect the identity of a source who was anonymous even to us."

But they didn't. And so, five days after I returned from Belize, some nice-looking gentlemen I didn't know showed up in my driveway to ask me some questions.

Thirteen

I was eager to find leakers and would like to nail one to the door as a message.

—FBI Director James Comey (2017)

Saturday mornings are my favorite part of each week. At 6:30 a.m., when most reasonable people are catching up on their sleep, I get to be one of the first people at the gym and enjoy having the spin studio to myself. My usual routine is to start with cardio conditioning and then proceed to strength training. June 3, 2017, started like a typical day for me. But it ended with my imprisonment in the county jail (not typical for me).

At the gym, I was finishing my last exercises—deficit Romanian dead lifts—when a guy I was interested in, an army intelligence officer, showed up for his CrossFit workout. We completed his regimen together, ending the session with partner box step-ups while each carrying fifty pounds on our shoulders. My body was jelly by this point. After showering, I put on tiny cutoff jean shorts and a three-quarter-sleeve button-up top that was off-white but almost transparent. And because the shirt was so tight, probably only half the buttons were done up. This ho-ass outfit choice proved to be problematic later. But in the meantime, the army guy and I went for a sushi lunch, and he asked me to hang out that evening. I said that sounded cool. After a grocery shop run for kale, ice cream, and beer—the essentials—I headed home.

It was a perfect, sunny day, which made the events that followed seem even more unreal. When I arrived at my rental house around 2:00 p.m., I parked the car in the driveway. After I stepped out of my vehicle onto the pavement, a black sedan and a black SUV pulled up behind me. Two middle-aged white men in pastel-colored collared golf shirts emerged from the cars. Well-dressed men driving nice cars rarely appeared in my neighborhood. *Real estate agents*, I thought. Or maybe they were in town for the Masters Tournament, the golf championship that had recently been held in Augusta, and had gotten lost?

The men approached me. Figuring they needed directions or information about the neighborhood, I smiled at them.

But they did not smile back.

They flashed their badges and introduced themselves as FBI Special Agents Wally Taylor and Justin Garrick. Garrick looked the part: he was tall and had an army-style haircut, one you set your watch to, although his hair was gray. Taylor also had short hair, but he had buck teeth and was shorter and heavier. He spoke with a strong Southern accent, the kind even us Texas natives make fun of.

Garrick explained in a friendly tone that they had a warrant to search my house.

"Do you know what this might be about?" he said.[*]

"I have no idea," I answered.

It was an honest response. The day before, I had submitted my security packet to renew my security clearance, so when they said they were from the FBI, I figured they'd come to clear up some mistake I had made with the paperwork. But sending two agents to visit my home in person on a weekend seemed excessive. Hours later, after we

---

[*] All the dialogue between the FBI agents and me here is taken verbatim from the FBI transcript.

were almost done talking, Garrick said I hadn't looked surprised to see them, as if I had been expecting some G-men to turn up on my rented property one day. But I'm just a friendly person. Sometimes that gets me in trouble. This would come to be a pattern—the FBI continually interpreted my words and body language in the most nefarious possible light.

"This is about possible mishandling of classified information," Garrick said.

"Oh my goodness," I said.

They know. Oh my God, they know. Panic set in. I figured I was done for, that somehow they knew I was the person who'd leaked the document to the *Intercept*. In seconds, my mind searched for ways they might have discovered my identity. And then I realized that their method didn't really matter—what mattered was that I come clean. Maybe if they heard my rationale, they would be understanding, even forgiving.

But then another thought came to me. Perhaps they didn't know *everything*. Garrick said they were there to search my house for classified stuff. But I didn't have any classified information in my possession, in my house, my car, or anywhere else. It wasn't as though I had stolen a stash of top-secret documents and squirreled them away somewhere. Nothing classified had been illegally taken and kept for nefarious purposes or, for that matter, for my personal amusement or ego gratification (as Trump would do when he left the White House). I hadn't brought papers to read at home and left them at the house. Or mistakenly slipped even a single cover sheet or memo into my backpack or pocket. If they scoured through every piece of paper in my home, they wouldn't find anything classified. So as my brain scanned possibilities for my next move, I figured there was a chance these guys might take a quick look around my place, see that there weren't any secret governmental materials, and peace out. That would buy me some time to figure out how to salvage the situation. I knew I wouldn't be in the clear in the grand scheme of things, but maybe I could talk to an attorney and figure out how to survive professionally.

Garrick said that he wanted to sit down and discuss the warrant. "Kind of go over what's going on. Talk to you, kind of get your side of it," he said. "And of course, [it's] completely voluntary to talk to me. We can talk here. Our office is about five minutes away. If you want to—if you'd rather talk there, then we can do either one. It makes no difference to me."

Okay, so this is not *a friendly visit,* I thought. *They might take me somewhere I don't want to go.* I glanced around and noticed that my street, usually bustling with activity, was empty. It was a lovely weekend afternoon. Why was nobody around? It seemed like maybe the road had been deliberately cleared or closed off. And I observed for the first time that these middle-aged men in clean, calm clothes had guns attached to their hips and poking through their thin polo shirts. It was just me and them, and they had power, the state's authority, and deadly weapons. In that moment, I began to fear not just for my security clearance or even my job but for my life.

You see, I'd never thought of the FBI as a national law enforcement agency, or as any kind of law enforcement agency, actually. I was badly wrong. But I had not watched those popular cop shows like *Law and Order* or *CSI*, programs that portray the FBI as a helpful institution devoted to catching crooks. I had not even watched any of the countless movies in which an FBI profiler gets inside the mind of a serial killer. My world was the military. Having spent years in the service and in intelligence, I saw the FBI as just another in a long list of agencies and departments known by their initials devoted to protecting the United States from foreign threats: the NSA, CIA, DOD, DHS, DCHC, and so forth. The roster is extensive, and the FBI is a major player in that world. We worked with them all the time on counterterrorism stuff. So I thought these men were representing something like a branch of the military. In their looks and demeanor, they seemed similar to the army guys I hung around with.

That's exactly why I was terrified.

Chelsea Manning flashed through my mind for the next few hours. I knew that Chelsea Manning had been court-martialed from a deployed position in the army, in Iraq. After holding her in a military camp in Kuwait, they took her to solitary confinement in Quantico, the hidden Virginia town that consists of a military base and the headquarters and training academies of the Drug Enforcement Administration, the FBI, and the marine corps. Quantico is basically one giant military place where ordinary American freedoms are absent.

Manning suffered abuses at Quantico. Because it was a military situation, she wasn't considered a civilian, so she had few rights. And the clearly armed FBI agents at my house suddenly confronted me with the same fate. Simply put, I feared I would be disappeared. There were no potential witnesses around. Even the old man across the way, who was usually sitting in his rocker on the front porch, was nowhere to be found. I had the terrible sinking feeling that a black cloth was about to be thrown over my head and I would be whisked away somewhere. If that sounds paranoid, well, you don't know how the United States military treats those it deems dangerous.

As I desperately searched for an off-ramp from the situation, the FBI men asked if I had pets. That question sent a wave of terror through me. Mina was fussy and could hiss at people she didn't like. Before I adopted her, would-be owners had twice returned her to the shelter; she's so afraid of humans that when first brought into a home, she acts feral, even though she is domesticated. The shelter said that someone had separated her from her kittens, and she therefore hated all humans. They told me that if I could tolerate her for one week, they would waive the adoption fee because nobody had kept her that long. Challenge accepted! Three years later, we were enjoying our lives together. But Mina didn't like men, which could be a problem at this moment. A big problem.

And then there was my dog. Mickey was a funny-looking beagle mix I was fostering from a rescue shelter. She was delightful—except when there were men around. She could chew her way through a door in a blind rage if men were afoot. Just a few weeks earlier, a guy I'd briefly dated had told me to get rid of Mickey because she'd growled at him a few times. But I didn't get rid of Mickey; I got rid of the guy. These FBI fellows would not be turned away so easily, however.

Worse, they might be trigger-happy. Despite my comfort with guns, I was in a situation where guns seemed terrifying. If these two military men (I thought) were inside my house and felt threatened by Mickey or Mina, they could simply, quickly, and legally kill the animals. In the days and weeks before Taylor and Garrick showed up at my driveway, I'd watched countless videos online of police officers with deadly weapons, agents of the state, gunning down Black men in the streets. I had watched *13th*, the documentary about racism and mass incarceration. I had lived about five miles outside Baltimore in 2015 when Freddie Gray was killed in police custody and had been deeply affected by his death. It was easy to imagine the men in front of me offing a dog or cat—or me—just as ruthlessly and instinctively. It happens all the time. My panic intensified, and I felt like I was beginning to drown.

Thinking as fast as I could, I informed Taylor and Garrick about my pets and asked to put my groceries away. My ice cream was melting. My impromptu plan was to get inside my home, scramble to put my dog and cat in a safe place, and then let the FBI do their search.

But Taylor said, "What we're going to have to do is we're going to have to go into the house first and make sure it's—it's safe. We have a—"

"Absolutely," I interjected.

"—search warrant and so we're going to—"

"Absolutely," I repeated, sounding like a stuttering parrot.

"Okay. And what we'll do is we'll keep you out here until we do that."

There went my first plan. They wouldn't let me go inside my house alone to secure my pets. Before I could form plan B, they asked about Mickey. I immediately told them that she disliked men. I wanted to minimize the chances of any deadly encounter between my dog and these guys; at least if they knew she might be hostile to them, they would be unsurprised. They couldn't say I hadn't informed them.

Taylor again mentioned that my discussions with them would be "completely voluntary." But then he added, "Maybe it'd be worth your time to listen at least for a little bit." I couldn't tell if that was genuine advice for my well-being or a veiled threat. In any case, I was having trouble focusing on anything besides my pets. *Please don't shoot Mickey. Please. What if they kill her? I would freak out, which could endanger my life. God, I hope she doesn't act up.*

"I can move her straight to the backyard," I offered. I was practically begging. They said they would permit me to put a leash around her and bring her into the yard. But Taylor gruffly warned me, "You're not to touch anything else, you're not to do anything else but get the dog and bring it out here." That clarified just how free to act I was in this situation: not very. They were manipulating the situation and making it seem as if I could do certain things, but also making me feel extremely cautious about doing so. It began to feel like I was caged, a prisoner on my own property, unfree to leave or even to move around. But I still had to go in, lest Mickey lash out at one of them. I could practically hear my mom's voice yelling that I was risking my life for a foster dog who hated all men, including the ones with guns on standby to use against her owner. But when you take a rescue dog into your home, you assume some responsibilities, and protecting her from death at the hands of FBI agents tops the list.

Taylor asked if I had weapons, and I told them about my AR-15, Glock 9, and 15-gauge. They warned me not to make any moves for the guns. I wasn't planning on it! But the warning confirmed the danger I was in: if I made one move these guys didn't like, they could shoot me. And if this were Texas, they wouldn't think twice about doing that.

Taylor told me they had another FBI guy in the car, and that more people would be joining them. That made me even more nervous: How many people did they need for this? I wasn't El Chapo. They asked if I had other pets besides Mickey, and I again mentioned Mina, the other man-hating animal in my care. "Starting to see a trend here," I joked, nervously. They didn't laugh.

And that's how it began, the interrogation that would ruin my world. The next three hours determined much of my life's fate, and I regret everything I said to those two nice men in bland golf shirts. I should never have said so much as "hello" to them before demanding to speak to a lawyer. In the days, months, and years since I talked to the FBI, I've often been asked why I didn't immediately clam up and demand to speak with an attorney, and God knows I've berated myself for not doing just that. But the truth is, doing those things seemed like a death sentence at the time. I wasn't under arrest or charged with a crime, yet somehow I was still wholly controlled. Garrick and Taylor kept the reason for the visit vague, along the lines of, "Oh, well, we're just doing an investigation. We're just doing a search. We don't really know anything." I was unaware that my words could and would be used against me in a court of law, deliberately twisted to imply or convey meanings that were the opposite of what I had intended. The two men in front of me were not friendly or even neutral; they considered me their enemy and would act accordingly.

But of course, I knew none of that. All I knew was what they told me: my best chance of getting out of this was to answer their questions and play along. I told myself: *Do whatever these guys instruct, and don't ask for anything until you're about to pee yourself. Because if you so much as ask the wrong question, they could take whatever extreme, violent response they want. And then you'll be dead and your animals will be alone.* That self-guidance proved to be unwise.

We stepped inside my home slowly, them alert and suspicious, me terrified and baffled. The house itself was a brick one-story, two-bedroom 836-square-footer, built in 1954. Whatever they expected inside, I doubt it was what they got: my home looked like a messy, overachieving hippie had decorated it. Which was true! I have furniture commitment issues, so there wasn't much there. Virtually no furniture, in fact. My dining room doubled as my yoga room, filled with rugs and an altar for incense. There was a meditation cushion, where I ate my meals. Books were strewn around. I had some journals in which I was sketching out ideas to do with Jesus and early Christianity, what Salman Rushdie did in *The Satanic Verses* with early Islam: fictionalized and played around with myths.

I'll admit it: my decor was best described as "boho poor"; that is, bohemian, implemented by someone who cannot afford to be boho chic. There were no ceiling lights, so I had purchased a lamp from Target after agonizing over the purchase for three weeks. My barbells sat comfortably on my floor beside my acoustic guitar, in front of my television. Framed pictures of Garth Brooks, Billy Joel, and the Beatles hung on the wall. My pencil drawings of Martin Luther King Jr. and Mahatma Gandhi were on the wall too. Post-it notes littered the rooms, with my written exercise instructions and thoughts ("further research: deserts versus rainforest"). All my five rugs were authentic Persian and Afghan antiques; a friend had sold me two of them, and then I accidentally bid on three rugs on eBay simultaneously and forgot about them until they started showing up on my porch.

After successfully putting Mickey into the front yard, coaxing Mina into a separate room, and closing the door, I felt some relief. At least if I were shot, my pets probably would be unharmed. Taylor asked again if another person was inside, or if anything else would appear to surprise them. He seemed concerned that I had someone stashed in there, ready to shoot him. I assured them again that I was alone, and then Taylor and a third FBI guy who showed up but didn't introduce himself began walking through my home. Taylor eventually came back to the room where Garrick and I were standing. I thought we would get down to business, but Garrick wanted to talk about Mickey first.

"How long have you had your dog?" he asked.

"She's actually a foster. I'm rehabilitating her so hopefully she can get adopted later on. She's a rescue. I think I got her in March."

Garrick told me about his own rescue dog, whom he had nurtured back to good emotional health. Discussing dogs with the FBI made me feel like they might see my pets as individual living creatures and perhaps see me as one too. With Garrick's permission, I placed my Popsicles, beer, and other groceries on the kitchen counter, slowly, carefully, deliberately, like I was defusing a bomb. Turning my back to him while I completed this most routine and domestic of tasks made my stomach turn. I had left my car keys and wallet on the table, so they knew I wasn't going anywhere. But there was nobody around to act as a witness if they decided, for whatever reason, that I was a threat to their safety. I just kept praying my animals didn't freak out suddenly. What if my cat got out? Or Mickey started barking up a storm? All hell could break loose, and someone would die.

But the animals kept quiet for now, and I was able to put my groceries where they belonged. Meanwhile, some FBI man took my Pokémon blanket from my bed as part of his search. Garrick asked again if I preferred to talk in my home, or at "the office." That option sounded potentially ominous to me, so I stuck with my decision to talk in my home. Our "conversation" could now begin. Except there was nowhere obvious to sit down. No kitchen table and chairs or living room chairs. Just one frumpy couch and some floor rugs. Garrick offered to sit on the floor to talk, but I suggested instead my back room, the second bedroom. It was a bit isolated from the rest of the home, so would offer us some solace from the troop of other FBI people now arriving to stomp through my home. I could hear my front door open and close; people were walking throughout my house while talking to one another. These people were clearly in charge. Each time someone new came in, I wondered if they knew about Mina's confinement, and what would happen if she went after one of them.

The back room was about ten by twelve feet, with the closet taking up a big chunk of the space; in most homes, it would be a laundry room. Two folded dog crates were leaning against the wall, but Garrick and Taylor took them out into the hall. The door in the back room was on one side of the closet, and Garrick and Taylor closed it behind them. Not all the way, I would come to find out—they had left it a crack open—but from my vantage point on the other side of the closet, it seemed completely shut. With no seats of any kind, we had to stand up. "Very hard without a table and chairs," Garrick complained. I apologized, but I hadn't anticipated my spare space doubling as an FBI interrogation room. There was no ceiling fan, no lights; sun poked through the blinds, which were crooked because I had broken them the night I moved in, when I trapped a wandering stray cat in the room. I leaned against a wall and kept reminding myself to keep my hands by my sides lest I make Garrick or Taylor feel threatened. Taylor stood closer to me, with Garrick hanging back. Now that we were packed together in this small room, I suddenly became conscious that I was still dressed for a date. My outfit, revealing and nightclub-appropriate, made me feel even more ridiculous and vulnerable in front of these two military-like men who controlled my fate. But it also seemed clear in my mind that they couldn't perceive me as some huge national security threat—what kind of terrorist wears Converse shoes and cutoff jean shorts?

Garrick began by asking how long I'd lived in Augusta, and we discussed my linguistic training. But then Mickey started barking. My stomach dropped. Mercifully, instead of rushing outside with a gun to shoot her, one of the agents asked if she was okay or needed anything. "If you can tell, we're all dog people," Garrick said. "One of mine, she's fine, you can leave her out all day long, all she does is sleep and snore. Shakes the whole house."

I gave my best forced laugh. "Yeah," I said.

"My rescue, we left him out for probably the first two weeks. He destroyed the couch. Clean through, chewed it. And, uh, three Apple power cords. The computer power cords. Ninety bucks a pop."

"Yep," I said.

"Yeah. I was thrilled."

I tried to fake-laugh again. This was starting to feel slightly less menacing. Maybe these nice FBI men would understand me and where I was coming from. They asked about my military career and workouts and told me about theirs. As Garrick kept talking about his dog and exercise regimen in self-deprecating terms, he seemed like a familiar type: a gruff, good-hearted military guy. *I know this guy*, I thought. *I work with this guy.* I asked permission to put Mina on a leash and tie her to the bed so she didn't go after one of the other people searching the house. They allowed me to do so. They offered me a glass of water and told me I could use the bathroom. But all this generosity had the unintended effect of making me feel *more* like a captive whose every move was controlled than like someone with freedom. Needing permission for the most basic of tasks, getting them granted sometimes and rejected at others, reinforced the fact of my detainment.

I'm not attempting here to criticize how the FBI did their job that day. The agents were told I was some major threat, and they acted professionally. But I am trying to convey my honest thoughts and feelings at the time. I didn't even realize our interaction was an interrogation, because I was not read my rights or told I could contact an attorney. They just told me that they had a warrant to search my house, that it would be in my interest to cooperate with them, and that they could always take me to their "office," which for all I knew was some lawless place like Guantánamo Bay. It seemed better to talk with them than to keep my mouth shut, which would only make me appear guilty—I didn't know they already *knew* I had sent documents to the *Intercept*. Believing in the value of speaking with agents of the state might seem naive. But, well, I am a naive person at times. In the *New York Times* review of *Is This a Room*, a 2019 Broadway play based verbatim on the official transcript of these exchanges I had with the FBI, the critic observed of the actress playing me, "She seems like a teenager." The truth was not far off. Before these guys showed up at my door with their clean-cut haircuts and guns, my only experiences with police were reprimands for my terrible driving.

"All this stems from a report that we received that you had mishandled classified information, okay?" Garrick said. "So, that's the broad scope of it. My question is, does that ring any bells to you whatsoever?"

"It does now," I said. My new plan was to offer them a tidbit of harmless information that would satisfy them, without revealing anything serious. Sometimes when I'm anxious, I close my hands and dig my fingernails into my palms—this time I was doing it so hard I could feel the skin start to peel.

On one occasion at my current job, I explained, I had a piece of paper with my temporary email password on it, and I didn't have a desk at the time, so I took it with me to a Starbucks that was in the office building. When I returned with a cold brew in hand, security looked through my stuff, saw the email password, and filed a report for that, I said.

But Taylor and Garrick seemed unconcerned by my disclosure. I told them that I sometimes printed stuff out at work because it was easier to translate by hand than on the screen.

"So you said you printed out stuff?" Garrick said. "Why did that come to mind as far as security?"

"I guess it always—I just think about having actual papers," I said, which was true. "I can't imagine any other way to get things out of the building, I guess. I'm old-fashioned, so I'm just thinking about that." The air seemed uncomfortably warm and stale without a fan in the room. There was no breeze.

"You didn't carry anything out of the building?" Taylor asked.

"No, I definitely let everything get searched all the time," I said. "So, I haven't had any other accidents."

They seemed satisfied with my assurances, and we moved on to the subjects I studied at work, which then concerned Farsi translations.

"Have you ever inadvertently, either by accident or intentionally or whatever, gone outside your access, or outside your need-to-know on items?" Taylor asked. He wasn't as friendly as his partner, and he seemed to be getting less friendly the more we talked.

"Outside of my need-to-know on items. Um, I do, from time to time, look at a website called MyOnline, and it is the drone feeds," I said. "I used to work on a drone mission, so sometimes I'll be in chat with my air force friends up in Maryland and I'll be watching the mission that they're executing." I also sometimes read news articles on NSANet, I added.

"Have you ever gone searching for stuff that's not related to your work role?"

"Not unless I have somebody in Maryland ask me a question," I said.

Garrick asked me again if I'd taken something out of the building, and again I told them I hadn't.

"Have you ever downloaded anything? Emailed anything out?"

"No."

"No? Okay. Hmm."

It didn't sound like they knew much. The thought crossed my mind: *Maybe I'll get out of this alive after all.* They asked if I'd discussed anything classified with anyone, and I said I hadn't. They asked about my neighborhood, and I said it wasn't very good but that I was well armed. When I was in Belize, someone had taken it upon themselves to mow my lawn in my absence. That person would surely show up soon asking to be compensated, I predicted. They returned the conversation to my printing things outside of my work role. They wouldn't let it go, so it seemed wise to reveal a little more. I admitted that I printed out reference materials from NSA Pulse, the offshoot site of NSANet.

"So that's probably fraud, waste, and abuse right there," I said, laughing nervously. I kept bringing up these little inconsequential infractions and then tried to explain them away. In the stress of the moment, my mind sought any safe harbors where I might be able to exercise control—taking care of my cat, laughing at my own behavior.

"We're not worried about fraud, waste, and abuse," Taylor said curtly.

Well, what *were* they worried about? They finally got down to it.

"Reality, what if I said that I have the information to suggest that you did print out stuff that was outside of that scope?" Garrick asked.

"Okay, I would have to try to remember," I said.

Taylor was clearly getting tired of my act. He raised his arms in exasperation. "Reality, we obviously know a lot more than what we're telling you at this point," he said. "And I think you know a lot more than what you're telling us at this point. I don't want you to go down the wrong road. I think you need to stop and think about what you're saying and what you're doing. I think it's an opportunity to maybe tell the truth. Because telling a lie to an FBI agent is not going to be the right thing."

Still I wasn't sure what they wanted to hear, or what they knew. Their knowing more didn't mean they knew everything. So I told them about the report that I had printed out. I explained that it was easier to read in hard copy, and it sat on my desk for a few days. It didn't require digging to find; NSA Pulse had lots of news articles and reports.

"I don't know if you saw the one about the miniature ponies, but that one was number one for like a year," I said, hoping to both endear myself to my interlocutors and suggest the casual nature of my action. I told Taylor and Garrick that I went to NSA Pulse to see gems like the pony article, and the Russia report was right there. After reading just half the report and leaving it on my desk for three days, I said, I'd put the document in the company's "burn bag," the little white box with a slit in the middle, for the disposal of sensitive documents.

Garrick asked if I was sure I put the document in the burn bag. He asked again. He asked if I took it out of the building. He asked again. He asked if I sent it to anyone. He asked again.

"Reality," he asked, sounding like a father disappointed in his misbehaving child, "can you guess how many people might have printed out that document?"

"No," I said. Uh-oh.

"It's not many. That document has made it outside. Okay? Obviously, because we're here."

"Obviously, yeah. Crap."

"The most likely candidate, by far and away, is you," Garrick said. He sighed again, like he was saddened by my behavior. "I don't think you are a big bad master spy, okay? I don't. I don't think that. I've looked at the evidence and it's compelling. Now, I'm not sure why you did it, and I'm curious as to that, but I think you might've been angry over everything that's going on, politics-wise. Because you can't turn on the TV without getting pissed off. Or at least I can't. And I think you might've made a mistake. Now, why I'm here, and why I want to talk to you, is to figure out the why behind this, okay? So, I ask you again—did you take it out and send it?"

"I didn't. I put it in the burn bag." It didn't sound like they *knew* it was me, just that I was "the most likely candidate." If they couldn't prove anything, maybe I would be able to get these guys out of my home and regroup.

"I mean, I'm trying to deploy," I said. That was true. "I'm not trying to be a whistle-blower." That was less true. "That's crazy." Arguably true.

"So how would you think that a document would end up getting out?" Garrick asked.

"I mean, let's be straight, there's little to no security on documents," I said. "Nobody pats you down." Staff members would talk about it all the time, how we had to show security our food but not the papers we carried, which was the stuff that could be classified, I said. I could feel myself starting to babble anxiously. "But no, I mean, that's the last thing I would've wanted to do with that. Especially with, you know, right now, trying to get somewhere else, trying to increase my clearance." And I explained again that after printing the report out, I slid it into the burn bag. "Folded in half. I mean, I remember it."

Garrick sighed again. He seemed deeply disappointed in me. The act worked: I felt horrible for lying. Not just lying, but lying to this man who clearly had my best interests at heart.

"What if I tell you that that document, folded in half, made its way outside of NSA?" he said.

They know. They know it's me. Oh Jesus. There was a pause. It seemed to last for an hour. If they knew about the document's fold, they had clearly traced it directly to me. Of course they had. How could I have thought otherwise? A team of FBI guys were rummaging through my house in their muddy shoes. I felt stupid and ashamed.

My stunned look must have told him everything. "I don't—I don't know that," I sputtered.

Garrick continued. "It made its way out in an envelope, postmarked Augusta, Georgia. See, things are starting to get a little specific."

Yes, they were.

"Okay," was all I could manage to squeak.

"It made its way to an online news source that you subscribe to. Getting really specific. So, I'm going to ask you again."

Again there was a pause. I couldn't speak; I was paralyzed with fear.

Garrick could speak, though. "What is very, very, very compelling. I'd like to know the reason, because I don't think you make habit out of this at all. At all. I really do. I think you just messed up. Now, I'm not quite sure why you did it, and I'd like to hear from you on that, but the what and the how is, would you agree, looks awfully bad?"

"It looks really bad," I said.

Another pause. "If you're angry about what's going on," Garrick continued, "if there's something that . . . Look, you've had a good career. You have. If there's something that just pushed you over the edge on this, now is the perfect time. This is a podium." He just wanted to know the truth, it seemed.

Taylor chimed in to reassure me. "You know, like he said, I don't think we're coming in here to say you're some big bad mastermind prolific spy kind of thing. I think what we both think is that maybe you made a mistake. Maybe you weren't thinking for a minute. Maybe you got angry, like he said. I mean, that's what I'm hoping. If that's the case, then that makes us feel a little better, knowing that we don't have a real serious problem here. You know, that's something that concerns us, too, this isn't an ongoing problem. But we need to figure it out. And if it was a mistake, let's deal with it."

They wanted to help! When it became apparent just how much they knew, I didn't try to talk my way out of it. I confessed. They were right: I'm not some kind of criminal mastermind. I was just someone who thought the world needed to know what Russia was doing in our national elections, and I'd fucked up royally.

"So how did you get it out of the office?" Garrick asked, staring into my eyes.

"Folded in half in my pantyhose," I said. When I was indicted, the media seized on that pantyhose detail. On *Full Frontal with Samantha Bee*, someone asked the rhetorical question: "Who even wears pantyhose anymore?" A Fox News headline read, "Reality Winner Transcript Reveals Pantyhose Caper." The pantyhose made me sound ridiculous, like the "Underwear Bomber," the Nigerian-born jihadist who tried to detonate a bomb hidden in his underwear on a flight from Amsterdam to Detroit in 2009. But hurting anyone was the opposite of what I'd intended.

I spilled everything out, admitting that I'd sent the report to the *Intercept*.

"Had you communicated with Glenn Greenwald prior to you doing that?" Taylor asked.

"No. I wasn't trying to be a Snowden or anything," I said.

"I don't think you were, either. I really don't. But, I think you made a mistake. But I don't think either one of us think you're trying to be Snowden."

Those words were important to me. They made me feel that the FBI understood what I had been after with my actions. I wasn't an activist determined to bring down the national security state. My complicated feelings about Snowden aside, his motivations and actions were radically different from mine. Once the FBI agents saw that I had been driven to leak a single harmless document for pretty benign reasons, I thought they would have no use for me. The case would be cracked, and we could each go on our way, with me maybe losing my job, at worst.

And so I told them everything. I started with the complaint that I'd filed at work about Fox News blasting on televisions endlessly. "For God's sake, put Al Jazeera on, or a slideshow with people's pets," I said, describing my grievance. "I've tried everything to get that changed."

In detail, I walked them through the leak. How I'd sent the document from a mailbox at the mall because it was near my yoga studio the night I taught there. How I'd wanted the *Intercept* to publish the report and hadn't sent it anywhere else. How it was the only thing I'd ever leaked. Using a screenshot on my cell phone, I showed them the address I had put on the envelope. We talked about where I had purchased the envelope and even the stamps.

They let me drink a glass of water, after which I told them about the Tor browser. My possession of Tor might seem suspicious, so I preemptively came clean about it and explained that I'd used the underground browser once, when I was curious to learn more about WikiLeaks, and never looked at it again. For those not in the know, Tor is an internet browser, just like Google Chrome, Mozilla Firefox, and Internet Explorer (RIP). Except that Tor allows users to remain anonymous and undetectable. Hackers, internet service providers, corporations, governments—they cannot trace users who scour the web with Tor browsers. There are many reasons to use Tor, such as maintaining privacy and evading giant tech companies' surveillance. But accessing what's called the "dark web"—where you can purchase every illegal thing imaginable—is among them.

After I gave them the passwords to my computer—I had nothing to hide—we went through my motivations for leaking the article.

"Like you said, I just, I saw the article and was like, 'I don't understand why this isn't a thing.' And it—I just—"

"It made you mad," Taylor interjected.

"It made me very mad, and it's right there. I guess I didn't care about myself at that point, and just . . . Yeah, I screwed up royally."

Garrick sighed again. I felt like I was letting down my own father. "Well, I believe you when you say that you didn't take anything else. I do. I think you made a mistake."

A mistake! That's what it was. That didn't sound bad. Everyone makes mistakes, right? But then Garrick suggested otherwise.

"In regards to the document that you did put out, when did you realize the technical capabilities in that article?"

That sounded evil. "Technical capabilities" made the document seem like it contained blueprints to a nuclear weapon or something.

"Sources and methods," I said. That's a buzz term intelligence types frequently throw around that refers to anything that would indicate how intelligence was obtained.

"Sources and methods are valuable to adversaries," he said. This was something we heard often at work—if targets know how they are being surveilled or recorded, they can change up their patterns to escape detection. But since the report I had sent was obsolete, it wouldn't reveal a thing. It felt like making that distinction to Garrick would only have been making excuses for what I'd done, though.

"Yeah."

"Did you know that before you printed it off, as you were taking it out?"

"Yes."

"Okay. Did you know that if that got out, that those sources and methods could be compromised?"

"If they haven't been already, then yes."

"Okay. With that in mind, why did you make the decision to send it anyway?"

I answered that since the election was over, I figured that it no longer mattered. "Honestly, I just figured that whatever we were using had already been compromised, and that this report was just going to be like one drop in the bucket." This was the most honest and complete explanation of my motivations and thinking that I had given throughout our entire interrogation. I only wish the FBI had cared about it. Instead, they were concerned with portraying my actions in the worst possible light.

Garrick asked me if I knew for a fact that the intelligence in that report had already been compromised.

"No, I wasn't smart enough to check that out," I said.

"Okay." He sighed again. I felt ashamed, as if I had just flunked my SAT. He asked me if I was aware the *Intercept* didn't have authorized access to classified information.

"I am aware of that," I said.

"And you were aware of that at the time that you sent it?"

"I was aware."

"Okay," Garrick said.

READING THIS EXCHANGE NOW, I can see clearly that the FBI was not interested in what drove me to leak the document, or in my state of mind. They were more concerned with building a robust criminal case against me. But I didn't get that at the time. I really thought they just wanted to understand where I was coming from, and to confirm that my efforts had not been extensive or designed to hurt the United States. Like I said, I can be naive.

"You don't seem the type to do this," Garrick went on. "I believe it. I want to believe it." He really had the disappointed-dad shtick down. He knew what would most resonate with me emotionally and get me to confide in him. I hate letting people down, especially those concerned with my well-being.

"I'm not," I protested. "You know, I want to go out with our special forces. That's why I got out of the air force. I mean, that's why I'm here in Augusta. I wanted my clearance back so I could get a deployment, and it was just at a time when I wasn't applying for deployments. I had, you know, seven, eight months left of a job that didn't mean anything to me because it's Iran, and I'm a Pashto linguist. Like, what am I doing translating Farsi? I felt really hopeless, and seeing that information that had been contested back and forth, back and forth in the public domain for so long, trying to figure out, like, with everything else that keeps getting released and keeps getting leaked—why isn't this getting—why isn't this out there?"

And that was that. Garrick and Taylor seemed satisfied that I had leaked a document only the one time. That I had felt compelled just to inform the public about something it should have been informed about. And that I hadn't wanted to wound the United States or aid our enemies.

"Do you have any questions for me?" Garrick asked.

"This sounds really bad. Am I going to jail tonight?" I asked.

"I don't know the answer to that yet," he said.

The thing was, I actually wanted to hear that I was going to jail. *Not* going to jail was terrifying to me—I had just confessed to a crime. There is a procedure when someone does that. If these armed FBI men weren't going to read me my rights and put me in jail, what *were* they going to do? In jail, at least, I would retain my constitutional rights. American jails and prisons are brutal places, as I would soon discover firsthand. But they are not like the military base where Guantánamo Bay is located or the CIA's black sites. I recalled again how the United States Army's Criminal Investigation Command had arrested Chelsea Manning and taken her to a military camp in Kuwait before even charging her with a crime. They kept her in a steel cage, where her only human contact was with the guards who brought her meals. She attempted suicide within weeks. That was just the first of five different facilities where Manning was held, in conditions a United Nations expert later called "inhumane" and "cruel." I was thinking of her heinous treatment when I asked about jail.

If I was going to be taken away, I had to take care of some things. I mentioned a woman named Kathy from the local animal shelter who could come and pick up the dog if I wasn't going to be home that night.

"Let's don't get the cart before the horse right now," Taylor said.

"That is my only concern, is getting her . . . and then maybe one more phone call to get the cat covered," I said.

"We'll figure that out," Taylor said.

Agents were still prowling around my home, looking for anything incriminating.

Garrick asked me, "Is there anything at your desk at work that I should be worried about?"

Desperate to ensure that the FBI did not see me as a serious security threat, I did my best to lighten the situation. I said, "I have an Anderson Cooper photo that is signed. It's not legit." But they were asking about classified documents, and those I did not have.

Garrick asked if I had any other questions for him. I said, "I feel like if I ask you what's going to happen to me, you're going to say that you don't know at this point, so that's kind of my only concern. And my ability to keep these two animals alive."

Finally Taylor assured me that, whatever happened, they wouldn't leave my animals alone. He seemed sick of my asking about them.

I felt comfortable enough to ask to use the bathroom. They agreed and asked if there were any weapons there. "There's a nail clipper in the orange bag," I offered. That was not a joke—these guys might use nail clippers, or a razor, or any excuse at all, to say I was holding a weapon and declare me dangerous.

But they turned off the audio recorder, and I went and returned from the bathroom without incident. And that was it, for the FBI and, ultimately, for me. It shocked me when filmmaker and playwright Tina Satter thought the verbatim interview transcript compelling enough to serve as the script of a play—a Broadway play, no less. "Every word, cough, and breath you hear on stage is taken straight from their actual conversation," the promotional material for *Is This a Room* declared. The *New York Times* called it "one of the thrillingest thrillers ever to hit Broadway."

Interview transcripts are not normally the stuff of drama ("There's a first time for everything in the theater," one critic joked about the play, while noting that the transcript itself was "choppy, repetitive, and dull"). But the genius of Satter and her colleagues was to recognize that the raw text alone captured only so much. The power dynamics, gender subtleties, and emotional manipulation are absent from a conversation recounted on a page. But the brilliant theater production enabled this context to come alive, since it could reveal what mere written words alone could not. As a result, audiences got to understand some of the broader forces at work in my interactions with the FBI. I only wish the whole country could have the same understanding. Not that theatergoers all had the same reaction to or interpretations of my actions. A reviewer for *New York* magazine wrote, "More than any other play I have loved in the last few years, *Is This a Room* has surprised me in how differently audiences see it. To me it contains a frightening portrait of male menace; to others it's a picture of men being kind while doing their job. To me Reality seems too good for this world; others watch the same production and see her as a liar and a fool." Some of those things are true simultaneously: I did feel menaced by the armed FBI men in my home who controlled my every move. I also did initially lie. And I was most definitely a fool.

By seeing the play—and later a movie called *Reality*, starring Sydney Sweeney—audience members were able to discern my thought process during the interrogation. "What ultimately drives Winner to the brink isn't being found out," *Variety*'s critic observed. "It's the thought of not being able to keep alive her two pets, whose fragile animality animates the stakes from the outset."

My terrifying conversation with these two men lasted over three hours while I waited for my home to be searched. But even then, it wasn't clear whether I was under arrest. They said they needed to call their bosses to figure out if they would take me in. They gave me a glass of water and let me out into the front yard. I felt like I was just like Mickey, on a leash, but with the tension taut. Mickey was mercifully calm and unbothered. My existential fears were still overwhelming: *If Mina sprints through a crack in the door*, I thought, *if the dog attacks someone, if I do anything other than stand like a statue, that will be grounds to be shot.* Still my street was eerily devoid of other human activity.

About twenty minutes later, Garrick and Taylor approached me again. "We're going to have to take you in," Garrick said. Those were his exact words—nothing about an arrest, just taking me in. He never Mirandized me. He said, "Would you like to call your family? It's gonna be a bit of a drive. I apologize for that. But your hands will be handcuffed in front, and I'll be sitting next to you in the SUV."

That's it, I thought. *I'm going to Quantico like Manning. No rights, no attorney, no official acknowledgment of my detainment. Just a squad of unmarked, blacked-out vehicles, ready to transport me to an undisclosed location that's "a bit of a drive."*

Garrick handed me my phone and told me I could notify a family member. I called Gary, my stepfather, who is famously level-headed and calm in stressful situations. He picked up after a few rings. He was coming in from doing some yard work.

"I'm in some trouble, Dad."

"What is it, sweetie?" he said. He knew something was wrong because whenever something went wrong, Brittany and I phoned him out of the blue.

"The FBI is here. They're saying I have to go with them."

"Why? What happened?"

"I don't really know." Immediately I realized that I didn't know what I was permitted to reveal to him. I couldn't inform him whether I was under arrest because I didn't know if that was the case. If I told him about the intelligence report, would that somehow reveal classified information? Plus, of course, I didn't know where I was going, or when I would be back. The last thing I wanted was to get myself in more shit by saying the wrong thing.

But the FBI agents seemed to interpret my reticence as a sign that I was hiding some horrible deeds I'd committed.

Garrick instantly dropped his nice-guy act and began taunting me. "Why did you say you don't know where you're going? Why did you say you don't know when you'll be able to see or talk to him again? What gives you the impression that it's gonna be a long time?" Well, they hadn't told me otherwise! They hadn't told me anything, including what I could say to my stepfather. Suddenly, Garrick had morphed from my concerned friend into my bully. His new guise would become much more familiar to me soon. In the meantime, he saw that I was tongue-tied, trying to explain my Kafkaesque situation to my father without being explicit.

Finally Garrick got frustrated and said, "Let me just explain it to him." He took the phone from me and walked out of my earshot. Only much later would my father tell me about the conversation. Garrick told Gary that I was "under arrest," using the term he and Taylor had distinctly avoided with me. He said I had violated "section 793 of the Espionage Act of 1917." My dad had no idea precisely what that meant, of course, but it sounded terrible and grandiose. Garrick further said I would be indicted at the federal courthouse the following Monday at 9:00 a.m. This was far more information than anything conveyed to me in three hours of interrogation and confinement, and knowing those facts would have significantly influenced my decisions. Espionage, indictment, criminal counts—the FBI deliberately erased these words from their vocabulary when talking to me. Garrick gave my father his cell phone number and said he could call if he had any questions about when and where I would appear in court. Gary had once considered a career in law enforcement and knew that the FBI wasn't going to release many details to him, so he didn't ask a lot of questions. Momface was in the next room but didn't know that Gary was having a critical conversation with someone.

Garrick returned with my phone and said I could call Kathy, the woman at the animal shelter. I asked Kathy if she could come get the dog. "I think I'm going to jail," I told her. "Can you just come get Mickey? And my family will be here to take the cat." She didn't even ask questions before agreeing—decency and generosity are how people working at animal shelters roll. She said she would check on Mina too.

When my call ended, Garrick came over to me with an annoyed expression. He had just gotten off his own cell phone and said, "I just spoke to my boss, and for the warrant for your person, a female needs to come do it, so we have another person coming now." They knew better than to have a man search me, which is surprising because they sure didn't mind having two men interview me alone in a confined space for hours. Soon after, the first police car showed up, from the Richmond County Sheriff's Office. It was the eighth vehicle parked in my driveway—FBI agents were still scouring my eight-hundred-square-foot home, though none besides Garrick and Taylor had introduced themselves. Seeing the word "Sheriff" on a car reduced my ballooning panic—it was the first marked car there, and at least, I thought, there would be a law enforcement agency that might be semi-accountable if anything happened to me. The woman searched my person, but it was a quick job because I wasn't wearing much clothing. She just patted the pockets of my jean shorts, looked at the bottoms of my feet, and announced, "Yep, she doesn't have anything." Another female officer, younger than the first, arrived on the scene. Despite what Garrick had said about handcuffing in front, she told me to put my hands behind my back, placed handcuffs on me, and said that I was going to jail. Because I am a powerlifter, it hurt to have my arms folded behind my back. That was something I had not anticipated, never having been arrested before. She escorted me to her car.

In the back of the police car, with my hands cuffed behind my back and no way to exit from the inside, I was panicked and claustrophobic, and I finally understood why people sometimes freak out in the back seats of cop cars—it's scary in there! I just prayed the entire way. And yet, compared with the last four hours of visualizing all the different ways that I could set these men off, imagining what catastrophe would befall me if I acted out of turn, being fortified in a cop car with just another woman felt weirdly safe. For nearly four hours, it had been just me surrounded by eleven men with guns, worrying about my cat and my dog and my life. It was all so nerve-racking that it was comforting to have someone show up in a uniform, in a marked car, and say the word "jail." It was concrete, recognizable, professional, straightforward. I would be accounted for. I felt as if the Richmond County Sheriff's Office had rescued me from the FBI.

But I would soon realize that the FBI was not done with me. Far from it. I still had much to fear from them.

Fourteen

> Judgment does not come suddenly; the proceedings gradually merge into the judgment.
>
> —Franz Kafka, *The Trial*

If you have never been arrested by the FBI and thrown in jail on an espionage charge at the age of twenty-five, I advise against it. Zero out of ten would not recommend. Consider this a zero-star review.

The drive from my home to the county jail took us out of the city. The landscape became more rural as we went. I watched the farmland and trees and cows, silver bracelets painfully constraining my wrists behind my back. After ten minutes of silence, the cop driving asked if she could smoke a cigarette. I agreed. After thirty minutes, she said, "I hate driving out here. It's such a long, boring drive." I was trying to breathe deeply to prevent an impending panic attack as my body exhaled from the FBI interrogation. *Well, this trip to jail is actually my first, lady! Whatever else it is, boring isn't on the list!*

After forty long minutes, I arrived at the Lincoln County Detention Center, a medium-security jail. The cop took me out of the back seat and walked me through the back entrance, by the drunk tank. FYI: a drunk tank is a cell common to many jails, where people who arrive drunk or high are placed until they sober up and can be either charged or released. At Lincoln, the drunk tank had an imposing cement bench and cinder blocks scattered around for seats. It was empty and everything was quiet, eerily so. They removed my cuffs and took me to the booking room, a small space containing a telephone they said I could use, and a computer. Nobody else was in there, not even a staff member, and they left me alone and shut the door behind me. Clearly, they didn't know I was supposed to be some master cybercriminal! I phoned Brittany and my parents, but nobody picked up. I guess they weren't waiting around, expecting their family member to be calling randomly from a jail.

A guard came in and instructed me to remove my clothing. I handed over everything but my bra and underwear. I had to give her my prized mustard-yellow low-top Converse; those beauties hadn't been on the market in years. She gave me shower shoes and a filthy plastic mat with filling pouring out of it, for a mattress, along with an orange jumpsuit with the ominous, stigmatizing word "INMATE" on the front in yellow, and handed me a peanut-butter-and-jelly sandwich, which I looked at horrified because I was three weeks away from a powerlifting meet and that white sandwich bread would constipate me and move me out of my weight class. The FBI had made it seem that they were arresting me reluctantly, and I still figured I would get out of jail shortly. Once I had a chance to explain myself to someone in a position of authority, surely we could all then just move on.

Another guard arrived and took my mug shots and let me see them on his digital camera. They weren't me at my best, as you might expect from someone who'd been sweating with fear for four hours. I asked him deadpan, "Can you put an Instagram filter on it?" He laughed but declined. I said that nobody had answered my calls, and he told me that I could try again from inside the jail cell but that I would need a PIN to make a phone call there—and then he added that they weren't giving out new PINs until Tuesday, three days away. I figured I would be out long before then anyway.

As he walked me toward the women's cellblock, he looked over his shoulder and asked, "What did you do?"

By now, I knew not to confess a second time, so I gave him a wise-ass response. "I was serving my country," I quipped. (I think he was confused. So was I.)

The women's cellblock consisted of a single room, probably twenty by thirty feet, with a small phone booth at the cell door with plexiglass windows. There were ten beds, some of which were three-tier bunk beds. A rusted picnic table sat in the middle of the room, behind which were a toilet and sink. About ten women were there, sitting on beds, watching the television mounted on the wall. Two were wearing orange like me, but the rest were in teal-green jumpsuits, which meant they were in on state charges, I later found out.

I had seen *Orange Is the New Black*, the show about an upper-middle-class white woman who spends a year in a federal women's prison. Even though it was a fictional television show, it was based on a real-life account and gave me some context for what to expect. When I entered the cell, I could sense the inmates sizing me up. But one woman approached me and helpfully pointed me to a bunk I could take. I headed over to it and put my mattress-like thing on top of it. Someone asked me what I was in for.

"I worked for the government and looked at something that I should not have."

There was a pause, and the women looked at one another. "What do you mean? Like, *really bad stuff*?" someone asked. It became crystal clear what they were insinuating, but only after a moment.

"No, no, God, no." I didn't know then why that was their first concern. "Not that type of illegal. I just saw some information that I should not have, and gave it to someone that I shouldn't have." It would be a few years before I learned to ask new inmates the same type of questions with the intent to suss out the predators.

"So what are you being charged with?"

"I don't know," I said honestly. "They never told me. The FBI just showed up at my house. They're still at my house." I said that I was worried about my cat, but that nobody in my family had answered when I phoned them.

"Oh, sweetheart, you can use my phone PIN," someone offered. This was the first of many kindnesses my cellmates would provide to me. Again, I wasn't completely surprised, because I had watched *OITNB*. The protagonist, Piper Chapman, might have been richer than me, but we were both misfits with bizarre names and all our teeth, who surely looked like extraterrestrials to the other women already in jail. But it took me a while to remember that I was in jail, which is a state or local facility, and not prison, which is part of the federal system and where the show took place. The distinction matters: everything from the quality of the conditions to the type of people surrounding you is radically different. Jails usually have less funding than prisons, so the conditions are even more decrepit, for instance. There is less room both inside cells and outside for exercise and sunlight, worse food and less access to water, and less accountability for abuses of power.

At 7:25 p.m., I finally got through to my mother. It was the worst phone call of my life.

"Do you know what you're getting charged with?" she asked me.

"Yeah," I said. I didn't know which law I had broken, but I knew my leak was the problem.

"What is it?"

"Mom, those documents. I screwed up."

"Oh." That two-letter word said so much coming from Momface. Disappointment from a parent is far worse than anger, as any child knows.

"I don't know if they give bail for that," I said. "I don't even know which law I broke. They never told me." Hearing myself say it out loud still didn't make me realize that I had not been arrested properly. Those kind FBI gentlemen hadn't followed proper procedure. If I had been told that my words *after* my arrest on a jail phone could be used against me in a court of law, I wouldn't have told my mother repeatedly on that phone line that I had sent classified "documents"—plural. In fact, I had sent only one five-page report, but the government later seized on my use of the plural word to suggest that my crime merited my being locked up before trial.

But in that conversation, based on her experience of courtrooms and legal proceedings from her own work, my mother assumed that I would get out immediately, since I obviously was not a flight risk. My friends were few and far between, I had no money, and my life consisted of nothing besides work and exercise. Plus, most importantly, I had not done anything violent and had no criminal history. Whom was I a risk to?

I said to her, "There's a woman who is going to pick up Mina and Mickey. Can you find her on Facebook? Her name is Kathy Ellis."

I returned to my bunk, which was over a bed occupied by a large Black woman named Tay who had only one front tooth. Tay was in for fraud, but it was clear she had more life issues, including addiction, that had led to the charge. She was going to the federal prison in Tallahassee. To our right was a Black woman named Baby D. She never wore her orange federal uniform but rather made day dresses and wraparounds with the state-issued sheets in a way that made her look different from us, like she was here of her own accord, and not state property; I think it was her way of maintaining her identity in a system designed to convince you that you are less than a person. Once we got to talking, I asked Baby D what she was locked up for.

"I shot a nigga's dick off," she said, matter-of-factly. While I picked my jaw up off the floor, she told me her story. Her ex-boyfriend had tried to rape her, and as she ran away from him, he grabbed her. She reached for the shotgun behind a door and shot his groin, point-blank. The man ended up in a wheelchair with a fractured pelvis and will shit in a colostomy bag forever. She was charged with aggravated assault; in practice, self-defense laws don't protect women. I would learn this later, one case at a time. It was a helpful introduction to how America's justice system really works, and whom it protects.

"So, like I said, I shot a nigga's dick off," Baby D said again, but she was smiling this time, and I laughed for the first time since the FBI arrived at my house. Baby D then offered me a pack of Jolly Ranchers and told me to pick any flavor I wanted, but only because her baby mama had already picked out her favorite flavors. "I'm not telling you you're cute or nothin'," she clarified. Rejection stings.

This was something else that I recognized from *OITNB* and was amazed to discover was true: the inmates in women's jails and prisons, despite in most cases growing up in horrible circumstances, being abused by men, and living in poverty, were often warm, funny, generous, caring people. Few needed to be incarcerated, certainly not for the draconian, lengthy stays they were given. They helped me with everything. Instead of hazing a shy newbie, a dorky white girl who had never even seen a jail and who loved books and languages, they showed her the ropes. Baby D had endured awful sexual and physical abuse, was unjustly incarcerated for defending herself, and somehow had a sense of humor about the whole thing. It was sad, horrible, hilarious, and moving all at once. Most of the women were like that. They walked me through the basics of jail.

"How are you going to pay for your attorneys?" one asked me. I hadn't thought of that.

"Um, my mom and I have a shared joint bank account, and there is some money in that."

"Well, if you have money, they're going to take it. They'll seize it and freeze your account."

I hadn't thought of that either.

That night, the NBA playoffs were on, and we were glued to the TV. At home, I had a television with one or two streaming possibilities, mostly YouTube, so watching the game was a novelty, though a few weeks before, I had gone to a sports bar alone to watch them play. There wasn't even enough space between the three-tiered bunks to fully sit up, so I lay on my bed, staring at the screen. I was dazed, running the day's surreal events through my mind, thinking of how I had survived an encounter with armed FBI men who were intent on putting me behind bars for placing a five-page document in the mail. It had been only ten or twelve hours since I'd met them, but so much had transpired. I'd gone from groceries to jail, from liberty to incarceration.

And then, right then, I remembered the date I was supposed to be on. In my haste and panic following the FBI's appearance at my home, I had forgotten the plans I had made. I had called to get my pets taken care of, and I'd called my parents, but there was no "I have a date tonight" option with the FBI. I didn't know the guy's number—it was in my phone, which had been taken from me. But even if I could have reached him, there was no way I could have explained to him that I had been interrogated by the FBI, arrested, and put in jail on unknown charges. *Where would I be if I weren't on this jail bed?* I thought. I assumed I'd be out on Monday and reunited with Mickey and Mina, but the situation with the guy probably couldn't be fixed. For some reason, maybe because I finally had time to process what I was living, the loss of that insignificant date brought home to me the reality of where I was, of what had happened to me, of my loss of freedom and dignity and opportunities. It was the first real and tangible loss, and for the first time that entire day, I cried. If you're reading this: I'm sorry, Dennis. I really wanted to meet you that night.

Looking around, I saw mostly Black women, mostly there for nonviolent drug offenses, forced to exist in a crowded, filthy room. The walls were painted with layers of gray over what had been an even more nauseating shade of bright, light pink. I would one day carve mandalas through the gray to expose the pink in small, bearable segments. Someone had taken what few crayons they were gifted to draw childlike flowers all over the walls, and, in the shower, an outside scene, complete with a yellow sun. On the walls by the phone were numbers written and scratched out again—that was where people kept their phone lists, the names of their boyfriends, bondsmen, and attorneys. One of my favorite pieces of graffiti in the world might still be in that cell, just to the left of the toilet, about knee level. The artist aggressively wrote "I LOVE IT HERE" in all caps, in serial killer–style handwriting. The effect on its captive audience, every time they used the toilet, was to make them subconsciously whisper to themselves, "I love it here." What a visionary.

Only a bedsheet separated the toilet from the table where we were given our meals. The laundry line and shower curtain were also fashioned from old bedsheets. Mold and rust slimed down the walls, bubbling out under the paint layers used to cover up the mildew, and there was a single watercooler in the room. The allotment of water did not change whether there were four or thirteen women in that cell, or if someone had diarrhea or irritable bowel syndrome. Same thing with the two rolls of toilet paper given to us each day. Outside jail, even a homeless person could use their two feet to find better living conditions, but the women surrounding me didn't have that option. When the toilet overflowed and shit and piss covered the ground, they had to live with it, live in it, live of it. Their food was brought to them to eat inside that awful cell. *This looks like a refugee camp in Afghanistan,* I thought. *Aren't we Americans?*

The day had sped by before I could catch my breath, but the night crawled forward at a horribly slow pace. I didn't sleep much. I cried but forced myself to do it silently so nobody would hear. No clocks were on the walls, so I had no idea what time it was. The thought of missing a training day on a Sunday frightened me, since I was three weeks away from a powerlifting meet, the first I was ever competing in. Sunday workouts were reserved for bodybuilding, hypertrophy, and steady-state cardio, but were also another chance to bench press. The idea of missing training *and* yoga class was unimaginable. So when I thought it was morning, I began exercising while everyone else was still sleeping. I did hundreds of squats and push-ups in the phone booth, back and forth all morning. A white woman with thick brown hair, thick eyelashes, and black teeth from a terrible meth addiction joined me in my exercises when she woke up—I think she hurt herself trying to keep up!

One thing about having an eating disorder is that introducing a new food into your diet is excruciatingly painful. Breakfast that morning was eggs, grits, and biscuits, none of which I could eat. So I went hungry until lunch, when I got two scoops of beans by trading away my fried chicken. Dinner was sandwiches again, with that white bread I feared more than any other food besides meat. I was desperate for Monday to arrive so I could get out and be in the world, where I could survive with my ultra-restrictive diet. It became clear that in jail I would just starve. If the slimy walls didn't suffocate me, my bulimia and orthorexia (an obsession with eating healthy food) would, crushing the air out of my lungs and preventing me from having any rational thoughts about my legal charges.

Because my phone account still wasn't working, a kind inmate offered to call my mother for me. That was how jail worked, I was learning: when a newbie came into the cell, the others took a minute to ensure they weren't violent. Then the other women warmed up and made sure they had food, clothing, and a chance to phone home. Part of this was self-interest: people who made phone calls could figure out ways to leave jail, which made the cell less crowded. But part of it was just sheer decency. I didn't want to get in trouble by speaking on her line—I didn't know if that violated some rule—so she passed messages for me to my mother.

Older and with gentle eyes, Angie was a grandmotherly figure with thick white plastic glasses, short bangs, and a strong Southern accent. She looked like anyone you might find walking around a Walmart in Georgia or Alabama, except she lacked front teeth. She called my mother while I stood beside her. My mom answered the phone.

"Hey, this is her roommate, Angie, but she can hear you, okay?"[*] ("Roommate," this sweet woman said! Like we were two young innocent kids in a college dorm!)

"Oh well, thank you, um. Thank you for being so sweet to my Reality," my mother said. "Everybody has been so nice."

Angie said, "She said will you please log into her bank—"

"Okay."

"And transfer from her savings account—"

"Okay," my mother said.

"In your account."

"Into my account?"

"Yes, ma'am."

"Why?"

"Into your account—"

"Why? Why?"

"Under 'Momface,'" Angie said, the funny name we had for the account.

"'Momface,' okay, but why?"

Angie turned to me and said, "She says, 'Why?'"

"Uh, because they might freeze it," I said.

"They might freeze it," Angie told my mom. "Oh, they said they will freeze it."

---

[*] This conversation is taken verbatim from a government recording of this call that was released in court.

"Yeah," I said.

"Oh shit!" my mom said.

"Yeah, as soon as this conversation's over," I yelled into the phone.

"Yeah, she says like right, like right now, like an hour ago," Angie told my mother.

"Yeah," I said.

"Okay," Mom said. "Okay. Wow, all right, we'll do that. We'll do that immediately, so, good. Okay."

"She said something else," Angie told my mother. "What? Twen—thirty grand."

"Okay."

"She said thirty. Okay."

"All right, okay, we'll do that."

Through Angie's generosity, we talked more in the coming days. I told Momface, who had driven to Georgia with Gary to house-sit for me, to eat the tasty foods I'd brought back from Belize. She told me that someone had established a GoFundMe account for me, that people were supporting me. I told her she had to set up a GoFundMe for herself because she was allotting all the savings she currently had for my case. The house was a mess, she said: the FBI agents had strewn things across the floors and tracked dirt everywhere. But nothing seemed destroyed in the home. We talked about my pets, and she reassured me they were fine.

My mom expressed her gratitude to Angie for treating me so well.

Angie responded, "I know, I'm a mama of two, a daughter and a son, I know exactly, I know it's important, I know. Your baby's okay." Mothers of two who are kind to strangers: that's who America locks up in its decrepit jails.

My mother thanked her again profusely. Knowing her daughter had, if nothing else, some decent human beings looking after her—the inmates cared, if the guards didn't—was enormously reassuring to her.

"Aw, I'm rubbing her back for you," Angie told my mother.

My mom talked to Brittany before I did, so when I finally got hold of my sister after thirteen attempts (she had been at a movie theater), I didn't have to break the news that her baby sister was in jail.

"Oh, Britty," I said. "I screwed up."*

"Well, it's gonna be okay."

"I don't know if I'm getting out of this one."

"You don't know if what?"

"I don't think I'm getting out of this," I said.

"Well, Mom told me that your hearing is tomorrow?"

"Umm, they're just going to decide if I can go out on bail—"

"Oh, okay," Brittany said.

I told her that I didn't even know what was facing me and didn't see how I could survive.

"You survived basic training," she said.

"Basic training is like college. You're getting ready for something. This, I mean, and the food, I don't, I can't even get over the little things, like I was supposed to teach yoga today, I was supposed to be on a date last night. I have a powerlifting competition at the end of the month. I know it's stupid, but that's my whole life, that's all I had."

"It's not stupid," said Brittany, always amazingly generous to me. She was three months out from defending her dissertation, and my predicament was a worry she didn't need in her life. That's what happens when an individual gets ensnared in the justice system: their whole family suffers. All of a sudden, Brittany didn't just have to worry about her deeply stressful exam; she had to worry about her baby sister indefinitely locked in a disgusting jail on mysterious charges!

---

* This conversation is taken verbatim from a government recording of this call that was released in court.

She said her husband was worried about my eating habits. In jail, there aren't a lot of options. "Chris was like, 'What's she gonna eat?' I was like, 'The only thing she eats is kale, so . . .'"

"I know, I feel absolutely terrible, there's so much white bread here, I . . ."

Brittany couldn't help but chuckle at my quirks. "I'm sorry I'm laughing at you." My obsessions were ridiculous, I have to admit, and I almost laughed too.

"I was wondering if you could do me a favor," I said.

I asked her to find someone to teach my cycling class on Wednesday, just in case I still wasn't released or couldn't show for it, and then we talked about Kathy, the woman looking after my pets.

"I just don't want to spend years in prison," I said. "I just—"

"Nobody does."

"I don't care, if I get bail tomorrow, I don't care what the price is, um, I'm gonna find a way to make bail happen. Even if it gets me two weeks of freedom. I just wish it would be something simple, like ten years of probation, or go back to live with your parents. Like, I wish there were a reset button."

We talked about how much I regretted my actions. "It was just a stupid decision," I said. But Brittany could tell that I was already falling into despair, understanding me in a way only a sister can.

"This sounds really dumb, but I don't know what I'm getting through this for," I said.

"What do you mean?" my sister asked.

"What's going to be on the other side?"

"The rest of your life?"

"Yeah, I just don't see it that way. Like I don't want a rest of my life if it's not what I have. I feel like I'm being a diva, like, there are freaking Syrian refugees that have nothing but still go from one day to the next."

Britty did her best to find a silver lining. "Depending on what happens, it could be a pretty big change, but there is hope on the other side. You get through it. It changes you as a person, but I don't know, I'm really naive and I don't really know anything about anything, but, um, I still think it's going to be okay."

"I didn't think," I said. "I did not think of the consequences for even a second."

"You're going to get through this."

"I keep telling myself to act more like I did something wrong," I said, laughing.

"What?"

"That was the thing when the FBI was interrogating me, they were like, 'Look, we just want to know why.' You know what I mean? They were straight-up curious to know why."

"Well, maybe you're right," Brittany said. "I don't mean to discount the effect of being pretty and white and blond. I'm kidding."

When the transcript of this conversation was presented in court, those last two words were completely disregarded by the government and, for a brief while, the world. After watching *13th* and talking about it so much, we were hyperaware of just who had privilege in the American criminal justice system and who didn't. But being privately cynical and sarcastic wouldn't help us in the courtroom, we would soon discover.

"No, I'm definitely playing that card. I'm going to braid my hair, I'm going to look cute, like I'm going to have a small voice, I'm going to, you know—"

My sister laughed. "Cry a lot," she joked.

"Obviously there's no possibility of a repeat," I said. I thought that since I wasn't about to leak any more documents and had already apologized, I would have no trouble making bail.

An automated voice broke through to tell us that one minute was remaining on our call. I told Britty how much I loved her and how sorry I was for what I was putting her through. We made a funny reference to the movie *Step Brothers* and said goodbye.

It didn't occur to me that people might be listening in on our call, that they might want to use my words against me, and that they might be intent on building the worst possible case against me.

The comedian John Mulaney has a bit in one of his stand-up specials about the dangers of emailing. He says, "I like to throw in 'I'm kidding' at the ends of jokes now, in case the jokes are ever played in court. You ever heard a joke played in court? Never goes well." Mulaney imagines his jokes being picked apart by a lawyer: "They're like, 'And that's why you shouldn't give to charity.' Is that something you find *funny*, Mr. Mulaney?"

Mulaney discovered that jokes don't survive well in the courtroom when his college friends were sued for property damage. His friends were guilty, but the lawsuit dragged on for years, and one day, when Mulaney was twenty-eight years old, he got a call out of the blue. His college friend told him that the lawsuit was still ongoing and that the neighbor had just subpoenaed all his emails from college that mentioned the neighbor or the lawsuit. Mulaney expressed sympathy but asked why his friend was calling him. "Because you should be concerned," the friend said. The friend explained that in junior year, he had sent an email saying that he would have to miss practice to meet with the neighbor to discuss the lawsuit. Mulaney delivers the punch line as his friend explains why the comedian should worry:

"And you replied, 'Hey, do you want me to *kill* that guy for you? Because it sounds like he sucks, and I will totally *kill* that guy for you. Okay, see you at improv practice!'"

The crowd delights at this joke.

I don't laugh at it so much anymore.

· · ·

On Monday morning, a guard came to the cell and told me to get ready to go up front. At the drunk tank of the jail, just inside the sally port, another officer put me in handcuffs and shackled my feet. Two cops drove me the forty-minute trip to the courtroom, where I was placed in a holding cell. In walked Titus Nichols, a clean-cut fellow who introduced himself, from behind the glass separating us, as my attorney.

"When do I make bail?" I asked him immediately. Even if I was unsure of that process, I knew enough to do everything possible never to return to those decrepit conditions.

"I don't know," he said. He had just gotten the case minutes earlier and was blindsided. My indictment had been sealed, but why such secrecy for someone leaking an obsolete five-page document? Titus had never handled a national security case before, but he took on public defense assignments sometimes. They'd tossed him my case at the last minute, as he was not only an officer in the military (called a "judge advocate general") but literally the only public defender in all of Georgia who already held the necessary security clearance to even review my case. The government's insistence on total secrecy seemed bizarrely melodramatic to him. We had five minutes to talk before my arraignment began.

My parents were seated in the courtroom, while I was on the other side in shackles, with two burly United States marshals guarding me. Kerry Howley of *New York* magazine was the lone reporter present, somehow tipped off to the proceedings because she's a journalistic badass. Magistrate Judge Brian K. Epps said that I was charged under the Espionage Act, but that didn't register with me, despite my intel training. All I kept thinking was, *When do I get to speak and tell my story?* Had I processed the judge's words, I would have realized their implications for my life. "The playbook of Espionage Act prosecutions is tainted with the settling of political scores, character assassination, illegal break-ins, extrajudicial death threats, and prosecutorial misconduct," Ralph Engelman and Carey Shenkman write in *A Century of Repression*. Even the name of the law is misleading and dangerous because it covers much more than spying—I was accused of leaking, not espionage—but the name automatically taints anyone charged with it as a *traitor*. The government was calling me, someone who had worked all their professional life on behalf of the United States and was willing to die for it, a turncoat. Engelman and Shenkman write of their survey of the Espionage Act's targets: "All defendants paid a high price for their ordeals in their personal and professional lives." *All* defendants. I would not be exempt. My case would set the new price for whistle-blowers and leakers.

The judge asked me if I had ever been diagnosed with a psychiatric disorder, presumably trying to ascertain if I was competent to take part in the proceedings. "Bulimia," I admitted. My therapist while I was at the NSA had walked it through with me. My mother didn't know this; I had always shielded her from it, out of shame and concern for her. This was the worst possible way for her to find out. She cried.

Things got worse. The judge read from a transcript of the jail conversations I had had with my mother about the shared bank account. He said it showed that I had money to hire a high-priced attorney. As a result, he said, "In regards to this account, she may retain her public defender if she chooses. But she will not be provided a public defender by the court." He was wrong—my family didn't have the money to afford some high-priced attorney! How was I going to find someone to represent me if I couldn't afford it but also was prevented from getting a public defender?

The prosecutor said I should be kept in detention. Titus was shocked—I hadn't hurt anyone! Even alleged murderers sometimes get out on bond. He objected, and the judge said we would have another hearing in three days to determine whether I would be released. Which meant three more days in jail at least.

The proceedings ended there. It took only twelve minutes to seal my fate. I never got to speak. I never got to talk to my family, who'd thought I would be going home with them then and there. Aside from being prompted to state my name and identify my eating disorder, I was silenced. It dawned on me that I was no different from the forgotten mothers and castaways who were sharing my cell—I was part of the American criminal justice system, which is to say that I was a nonperson, less than a human being. I always would be in the eyes of the law.

That status, of course, is not unique to me. An astonishing 1.9 million people are incarcerated in more than six thousand correctional facilities operated by thousands of government agencies. Nearly half a million people are locked up just awaiting trial, mostly because they cannot afford the bail amount the court demands to secure their release. I knew all this before, from watching *13th* and doing some reading. But now I was one of those people I'd read about.

That was when I began freaking out. My knees buckled. *I'm not getting out of this. I'm not going home.*

As my parents were leaving the courtroom, Special Agent Taylor approached them. "You should probably expect some phone calls from the press," he said. Momface and Gary were staggered. The press? What? Why? "Well, there's a press release going out from Washington, DC, right now," Taylor said.

Stalwart professional that she is, Momface knew some things. "Will this be local or national press?" she asked.

"Ma'am, this will be national," Taylor said.

THE ATTORNEY GENERAL OF THE UNITED STATES issued a press release announcing the arrest of a traitorous human being named

Reality Winner. "Exceptional law enforcement efforts allowed us quickly to identify and arrest the defendant," Deputy Attorney General Rod Rosenstein said in the release. (It really didn't take exceptional efforts to find me—the *Intercept* basically told them where I was, and then I confessed to the FBI and submitted to arrest easily.) "Releasing classified material without authorization threatens our nation's security and undermines public faith in government," Rosenstein continued in the release.

When I read this line, it struck me as maybe being occasionally true but largely untrue and specifically false in my situation. What I released didn't threaten anybody; and, in fact, I was trying to expose things that were undermining public faith in government. "Suspicion that a secretive 'deep state' is unaccountable even to presidential power fuels conspiracy theories that are sapping the strength of our democracy," writes scholar Matthew Connelly in his recent book *The Declassification Engine*. My disclosure was designed to counter those theories by illustrating that some people working in intelligence want Americans to be as informed as possible, and would go to great lengths to ensure that happened.

I would like to ask people like Rosenstein: Does the release of *all* pieces of classified information threaten American security? What if something shouldn't be classified in the first place? These questions need to be asked, not just for me (my destiny was already determined, like the case against me) but for the country's well-being. "A whole series of government committees and commissions have identified the same fundamental problem: officials have not clearly and consistently specified what information actually requires safekeeping, making it impossible to prioritize what is truly sensitive," writes Connelly, a political scientist at Columbia University. "The government can no longer even estimate how many secrets it creates each year, or how much it is spending to try to protect them all." Connelly founded a team called

History Lab to compile and study all the records the government had unsealed, creating the biggest database for declassified documents in the world. As a result, government lawyers told him *he* might be charged with violating the Espionage Act, even though everything he and his team were compiling was *de*classified, so broad is the law.

Some high-level elected officials pointed to the importance of what I had disclosed. Connie Lawson, Indiana's secretary of state from 2012 to 2021, told the US Senate, "We've learned from a top-secret NSA report that the identity of a company providing voter registration support services in several states was compromised. Of course, it's gravely concerning that election officials have only recently learned about the threats outlined in the leaked NSA report, especially given the fact that the former DHS secretary, Jeh Johnson, repeatedly told my colleagues and I that no specific or credible threats existed in the fall of '16. It is unclear why our intelligence agencies would withhold timely and specific threat information from election officials."

Lawson's comment pointed to the exact reason I had put that document in the mail—so that concerned citizens could discuss the information contained in the five-page report. Claire McCaskill, then a Missouri senator and Homeland Security and Governmental Affairs Committee ranking member, said during a committee hearing, "While I condemn the leak and the person who leaked it . . . I am anxious to get more information about what we know about these attempts. Whether or not they accessed the tabulation, it's clear they [the Russians] were trying to get into voter files. And I don't think they were going there to try to just hang out. Imagine the disruption. We spend a lot of time in this country talking about voter ID. Imagine the disruption if thousands of people showed up to vote and their names were no longer on the voter files. What would we do?"

These statements were notable, and they revealed how much critical research and intelligence were being hidden from the public that should rightfully be shared with them. This is hardly a new crisis. The problem began with the construction of the national security state during the Cold War. As early as 1965, a Pentagon report concluded that "overclassification has reached serious proportions." "For decades, blue-ribbon panels and incoming presidents have observed with surprising unanimity that overclassification has grown out of control—and vowed to fix it," writes journalist Patrick Radden Keefe in *Foreign Affairs*. In 2017, reports Keefe, the federal government spent more than $18 billion to maintain this classification system. Maybe there are too many secrets?

Rosenstein wasn't interested in those sorts of questions, but I was. And I still am, even after the government tried to destroy me. The Justice Department released my arrest warrant. It was written by Garrick, the FBI guy who interrogated me and pretended he was my friend. Reading it was a surreal experience. One line he wrote is particularly bizarre. "WINNER further acknowledged that she was aware of the contents of the intelligence reporting and that she knew the contents of the reporting could be used to the injury of the United States and to the advantage of a foreign nation," Garrick wrote. This was *bullshit*. I would never have leaked something that could help a foreign country harm the US, and I never said that. You can read the transcript of our conversation above (or see the play or movie that uses it verbatim) and see that it was bullshit. What I said to him was that I knew that the document I sent the *Intercept* contained "sources and methods," intelligence jargon denoting a category of things that could, in theory, be helpful to adversaries. But I then said that I believed the document I had sent *wouldn't* be helpful to anyone because it was obsolete and insignificant. He excluded that part from the warrant.

Of course, it didn't matter. They had already arrested me and locked me up. But Garrick's lie was an early sign that the government was determined to portray me as an enemy, no matter what I actually believed and did. Indeed, in the affidavit and press release, the FBI and Justice Department deliberately avoided specifying which publication I had leaked the report to. They called it "the News Outlet" instead of the *Intercept*. There was no reason to withhold the publication's name, but to me it seemed more nefarious and perhaps anti-American or foreign if the outlet was unnamed instead of listed as what it was: a reputable, prize-winning, US-based publication devoted to exposing government secrets. People could have gone to the *Intercept*'s website and seen for themselves that what I had leaked was harmless. But the government wanted to portray me as someone eager to destroy American national security.

The *New York Times* published a story about my arrest that was more accurate than what the government released. "Intelligence Contractor Is Charged in First Leak Case Under Trump" ran the headline. The publication's choice to foreground the political nature of my prosecution was incisive and showed they were savvier than I was about why I was targeted. "The case showed the department's willingness to crack down on leaks, as Mr. Trump has called for in complaining that they are undermining his administration," the article read. "His grievances have contributed to a sometimes tense relationship with the intelligence agencies he now oversees."

So the government wanted to make an example out of me. Journalists from around the country deluged Titus and my parents with phone calls before they even got home. My mom at first told the callers she didn't know anything. And then, when they didn't stop, she stopped answering the calls. And when they still didn't stop, she was overwhelmed and finally picked up. CNN was on the line and asked her for a comment.

"Wait, wait, wait, can you tell me what's going on?" she asked the reporter. "What do you know?" And he was the one who told her about the contents of the press release and sent links so she could read for herself what the government was saying about her daughter.

Of course, the media bombardment didn't end there. Rosie O'Donnell phoned my mom to offer support and asked if she could help. Reporters huddled outside my home, where my parents were frantically trying to put my place, and our lives, back together. I was infamous, and that has unfortunately never changed. I preferred it when nobody knew my name.

About one hour before I was indicted, the *Intercept* published a story about the report I sent them. For reasons known only to them, they decided to publish with their story a PDF copy of the report itself, along with photographs of the report, complete with printer markings, the fold in the center, and the printer serial number. Now the whole world could figure out who leaked the document, not just the NSA.

They published all that evidence even after an NSA source earlier told their reporter that the NSA was actively hunting for the leak's source, and after the agency itself had held several meetings with the *Intercept*. During all those meetings, the NSA never mentioned to their friendly media helpers at the *Intercept* that they had identified me as the likely source of the leak or that they were working with the FBI to find and arrest me. By the time the *Intercept* published the story that I sent them, the NSA had already successfully swindled them: they and the FBI had gotten me behind jail bars, with the *Intercept*'s indispensable help.

Fifteen

> The truth is sometimes a poor competitor in the market place of ideas—complicated, unsatisfying, full of dilemmas, always vulnerable to misinterpretation and abuse.
>
> —George F. Kennan, *American Diplomacy*

Warning: things get dark here. After the court hearing, I was on the verge of a mental breakdown. My anxiety was off the charts, and I was disoriented, walking wobbly. I didn't want to appear weak in front of inmates I didn't know, so I kept to myself. But when the local news came on the television in the early evening, my face was plastered all over it. All the other women with me had been arrested, many more than once. Some had been taken in for big drug deals or violent crimes. But nobody had been arrested like *that*, they said. Nobody had been on the news.

"What the fuck did you do?" they asked me, almost in unison. I struggled to explain, but then the tabloid show *Inside Edition* came on the television following the news. Remember that show? Apparently, it still exists. "Reality Winner—yep, that really is her name—is behind bars and facing a possible ten years in federal prison," the narrator said, speaking over clips of me exercising, taken from my social media accounts. The show interviewed people at my gym, who described me as "quiet," and quoted tweets I had written about Trump being a fascist. They pulled excerpts from a video I'd made for a friend who challenged me to do a twenty-four-minute plank on my twenty-fourth birthday. By the final two minutes in the video, I was howling with pain and said, "I HATE EVERYTHING." With all seriousness, *Inside Edition* suggested that the phrase was related to my mindset when I committed a felony an entire year and a half after the planking session. More excellent journalism from the toilet of TV news. "Winner is being charged under the Espionage Act; her attorney says she is not a traitor," the anchor said.

Traitor?! That was the first time I had heard my name associated with that dirty word out loud. It stung me deeply, but it also made no sense. I had served six years in the military and wanted to help the United States. I had won an award from the air force for my service. Betraying my country was unimaginable. *Where the fuck did that "traitor" shit come from?*

I should have known the answer: social media. "She is a traitor to this country and must be treated as such," some random guy tweeted after my arrest was public. Once Trump's notoriously violent hardcore supporters found my Twitter feeds blasting the president, they swiftly and loudly called me anti-American. And cable news took it from there, always eager to stoke whatever controversial fires would boost their ratings. A CNN voice-over previewed an interview with Titus: "Leaker accused of leaking classified information facing charges tonight. Reality Winner, that is her name, is she a traitor?" Well, no. But just asking the question suggested that it was a possibility.

And that was just the mainstream media. The right-wing media ecosystem is massive, and from Fox News to talk radio, they did not take kindly to me. They rifled through my social media and twisted everything around. Every joke I told, every sarcastic comment, every dissent from the government's policies—they were depicted literally and in the harshest possible light. Fox News host Sean Hannity declared, "She also allegedly vowed to stand with the Iranians" because I declared solidarity with them for being victims of Trump's cruelty. His colleague Tucker Carlson said that "the point of the leak" was "to add the perception that Trump somehow is a foreign agent." He questioned how someone like me could ever be granted a security clearance; clearly the intelligence community was filled with traitors. A headline in the *Washington Times*: "Reality Winner Hates Trump, Hates Whites—Loves Iran?"

This outrage was as phony as a three-dollar bill. Thomas Drake, the former NSA executive who became a whistle-blower, had leaked classified but harmless information, like me, but because the Obama administration prosecuted him, the right-wing press didn't vilify him. Hell, he himself told me that "they didn't really pick up on it because it was under Obama." Attacking Drake would have meant defending something Obama had done, and conservatives never had a problem with whistle-blowing and leaking if it was done under a Democratic president.

Important defenses of me also appeared online, however, a sign of things to come. "A 25 year-old woman has more courage and patriotism than every old white guy in the Republican Party combined," tweeted Charlotte Clymer, a prominent liberal activist. Shaun King, another high-profile activist, said, "I stand w/ this courageous young woman, Reality Winner, who leaked NSA docs. She's a brilliant Air Force veteran disturbed by what she saw." And most importantly, WikiLeaks founder Julian Assange came to my defense. "Alleged NSA whistleblower Reality Leigh Winner must be supported," he tweeted, alongside a picture of me. "She is a young woman accused of courage in trying to help us know." When I learned Assange had done that, I felt my first glimmer of hope that somehow, someway, I could find a way out of my catastrophe.

Later, when it became clear just how viciously and arbitrarily the US government came down on me, these expressions of support would grow louder, more numerous, and better organized. They are a lifeline, and I treasure every single person who has my back. But because I was in jail and did not have access to the internet then, I couldn't see or know about this support. Had I been aware of it, this solidarity would have given me a boost at a dark time. I felt totally alone, despised by the world, including by the leaders of my country that I loved so much. I began having suicidal thoughts for the first time in my life. *Maybe it would have been better if I hadn't survived my arrest. At least I wouldn't have to be watching this shit and become globally infamous, considered a traitor. This is how my family will be branded forever. I should have just written a manifesto and ended it.*

My parents had been instructed by lawyers not to say anything to the media. But the narrative of the government and the conservative media that I was a despicable information-terrorist was coursing through the press and social media without much pushback. The *Intercept*, known for its outspoken journalists who relentlessly accuse the rest of the media of being cowardly and deferential to politicians, was so embarrassed by its huge fuckup that it kept silent while my name was being destroyed. Its reporters were prohibited by its editors from talking about it in public. And for many reporters, the *Intercept*'s inner turmoil resulting from its screwup of my leaked document and identity became much more important than the information I had disclosed.

The first impression most people would get of me was what they saw or read in those initial few days. Every company knows the value of branding, and I was getting branded as something unspeakably bad. If my parents didn't offer a different narrative, nobody would. "A lie gets halfway around the world before truth puts on its boots," Winston Churchill supposedly said. Well, the truth about me was still bootless.

So my mother and Gary decided to speak to the masses of reporters huddled around my home, where they were staying. "It was a swarm with microphones, like you see in the movies" is how Momface describes the gaggle hounding her. One journalist asked my mother what she was most concerned about, regarding me. "Her safety," my mother said. She knew that alleged traitors don't fare well in jail, or anywhere else. My stepdad said that I should pay for whatever I did wrong, but that I didn't deserve anything worse than fairness. My parents went on CNN and were interviewed by Anderson Cooper, a surreal moment considering that his photograph with the fake signature was still on my desk somewhere at the NSA. "She served her country, she is a veteran," my stepfather told Cooper. "She's a patriot, and to see her maligned and slandered in the media is very disheartening." My mom was astute about my state of mind. "I don't think she's seeing a light at the end of the tunnel," she said.

On the night before my bond hearing, Titus visited me. Even though he could have left my side after Judge Epps denied me the right to counsel, Titus said he would have my back pro bono, to his immense credit and to my tremendous good fortune. He told me he was going to partner with a lawyer named John Bell.

The jail did not even have a room for lawyers and inmates to confer, so when Titus visited me, we sat in the booking room. Titus reassured me that, historically speaking, almost everyone charged under the Espionage Act made bail, since it was considered a nonviolent, white-collar crime. Legal precedent suggested I would be getting out the next day. "And you went to Belize and came back, so you have already demonstrated that you aren't moving to another country," he pointed out. Edward Snowden, conversely, had left the US before the authorities could get their hands on him, and the FBI themselves had established during my interrogation that I "was no Snowden." I had no more than $30,000 to my name, and I was willing to put it all down on bond. There was no way I could leave the country even if I wanted to.

One version of me that was mostly accurate was in the *New York Times*. According to their report, "A broader portrait that emerged from interviews and her active social media presence suggests a fun-loving, talented young woman, a workout enthusiast and a wide reader, fond of kale, dedicated to her cats and dog and her work." They said I was an unlikely whistle-blower. "She had no apparent history of leaking or any disciplinary proceedings during her military service." But the government had a different version of me. The next day, back in the courtroom, with two marshals by my side again, I listened as they began to present it in my arraignment and detention hearing. Judge Epps told me something I had not heard from the FBI: "I need to remind you of your right to remain silent. You have the absolute constitutional right to remain silent."* Neither the government nor law enforcement could compel me to make a statement about the actions I was being charged for, or anything else. And if I *did* make a statement, I could stop doing so at any time. "Any statement made by you or the answers you give to any questions asked can be used as evidence not only in connection with this case that we're here for today but also any other cases currently pending against you or that may be brought against you in the future," he said.

How I wished the FBI had said those words to me at my home. I might have known better than to talk to them.

The lead prosecutor, Jennifer "Jenna" Solari, an assistant US attorney in the Southern District of Georgia, looked straight out of an *NCIS* set: designer suits with perfectly tailored pencil skirts, a pixie haircut, and chunky nautical-themed jewelry. My case was unusual, she told the court, because of all the classified information. It needed to be reviewed to determine its classification level, and my defense attorneys needed to obtain security clearances. "We're not sure at this point how long that process will take," she admitted. "We're not at liberty

---

* All quotations in court are taken verbatim from transcripts.

to produce anything more than what's been filed in the public record at this point because, again, it has to undergo a classification review." The government had taken from my home my computers, cell phones, and a tablet. All that material needed to be forensically examined and reviewed for anything classified, she said. "We will give whatever we are able to defense counsel. We're not looking to go out of our way to withhold anything." But she was under strict orders on what she could say and how she could say it, lest she reveal anything classified. This type of concealment is typical for these cases; the government uses the veil of secrecy to make everything sound more complicated and ominous than it actually is. They usually know all the facts by the time they step into the courtroom, but you will never hear a prosecutor admit that to a magistrate.

In practice, all this secrecy meant that my defense lawyers could not examine the evidence against me! That examination, of course, is supposed to be a basic right in any American courtroom. But not for someone charged under the Espionage Act—such a person has few rights. The government's statement that they didn't know how long it would take to determine what information was classified was a sign that this trial would be some scene out of Kafka. We didn't know what evidence the government had, yet we were expected to mount a defense against it to demonstrate why I should be released! It was absurd. But that's how the national security laws are written. And truth be told, much of the country's legal system falls along similar lines.

Solari made the case for why I should continue to be held until my trial. I will say this for her: she came prepared. She had a narrative of who I was, what I had done, why I had done it, and she acted determined to get the court to accept her story. She brilliantly used what the government *didn't* know about me to make me seem more nefarious. "The defendant inserted a removable thumb drive into a top-secret computer," she told the judge. "Unfortunately, we don't know yet what she did with that thumb drive while it was inserted, but we do know she inserted the thumb drive just days before she was read out of classified compartmented programs and her access terminated as she left the air force." Sounds bad, right? Of course, if they'd asked me, I would have told them that the thumb drive had nothing on it—I'd told them everything else voluntarily. Their lack of knowledge about what I had done with the thumb drive somehow became a presumption of my *guilt*, not my innocence. What she didn't say was that authorities had already taken apart the computer the flash was inserted into, and they knew for a fact that no files had been placed on the thumb drive. In the post-Snowden era, software exists on government computers that prevents any files from being burned onto CDs or flash drives. They knew that. Any court experienced in national security knew that. But Georgia and that little court didn't.

She said that any other classified intelligence I had potentially hidden—which the government admitted it was unsure existed—could "put our country in grave danger." Moreover, she was "concerned the defendant may have taken additional documents from her most recent employer and from the physical facility." There was more of this ominous speculation about what I *might* have done. Solari reported to the court that, when speaking with my mother, I had used the word "documents," plural, which suggested I had taken a bunch. "We don't know how much more she knows and how much more she remembers, but we know she is extremely intelligent," she said. Now being smart was somehow indicative that I was dangerous. (Months later, the government would clarify that, in fact, I had indeed leaked only the five-page document that I told them about. There was nothing on the flash drive, or anywhere else in my possession. But by then, the damage was done.)

The FBI had taken photos of pages from my notebooks from my home and was poring through their banal contents. I hold on to these notebooks to this very day, despite how lethal the government said my anatomical and yoga sequencing materials could be. They were also worried because I had written down instructions for how to install Tor. Although Solari conceded that the dark web had "some legitimate uses," it was most widely known as a haven for criminal activity, she said. What concerned her was that if I were released from jail and went on the run, I could somehow scour the dark web while hiding my identity and location. Historically, defendants in Espionage Act cases have been barred from using electronic devices, so that would have been a possible compromise. But I would not even be given that opportunity.

My private journals were where I confessed my feelings and fears and secrets, and Solari seemed deliberately to read them out of context. Solari said, "Amongst the notes about the defendant's new employment with Pluribus International Corporation where she scribbled notes about dental and health insurance, she also wrote, quote, 'I want to burn the White House down.'" As though expressing anger in a private journal were evidence of arson. I had written "ha ha" after it, but she left that part unmentioned.

Solari continued: "Other notes: 'Find somewhere in Kurdistan to live or Nepal. Ha, ha. Maybe Mexico in the spring. Afghanistan in the summer. Asia and Jordan in between.' It seems she wants to be anywhere but the United States." My face grew hot, and I wanted to scream that none of that desire to travel was illegal. But when she read those words, her context became the new truth. I sat there, in chains, and tried to recognize this person they were describing.

Amazingly, it got still worse. Solari said that there were names of Taliban leaders in my journals—which was true. I was thinking of writing a historical novel about the transformation of the mujahedin who once fought the USSR as they morphed into radical extremists and terrorists. Hell, I'd worked on an Afghanistan intelligence mission for years! The first lines of the journal page asked rhetorical questions:

"If Christ were to be on planet earth today, where would he be? Who would he be? What would he say or do? Would people like him? When would he reveal himself?"

The page continued: "Mullah Omar and Akhtar Mansour were the only leaders of the Taliban who were leading with the single cause of an Afghan Nation under a Taliban gov't. That is all. They both understood the need for peace yet were pushed too far by western demand for unconditional surrender. The worse things get, the more desperate means will become. I do not want ISIS mentalities spreading to the Taliban. I must find Yaqub, Omar's son."

As you might expect from an Afghanistan intelligence analyst with the US military, these lines were attempts to understand the movement's appeal among Afghans and think of ways to dampen the spread of global jihadism. But Solari implied that they were evidence of my potential to *join* the Taliban and kill American soldiers.

The rest of the page read: "If there were another Christ, he'd be a zealot. He'd have a Judas-like figure bring him down, too. Perhaps Bin Laden was the Judas to Omar's Christ-like vision of a fundamentalist Islamic nation. Yaqub would know. Where is Yaqub? Pakistan. I can go there. Urdu. Goddamit." I was expressing my frustration with having to learn yet another language in my mission to end international terrorism. Whatever you might say about these half-baked ramblings of someone who had never set foot outside the Americas, the notion that they express a concrete plan to join America's enemies in trying to destroy the country is ridiculous. But the government submitted a copy of this journal page as evidence for why I was too dangerous to be released.

Special Agent Garrick was on the stand presenting the journal entry. At first, he read only the sentence starting with "Perhaps Bin Laden . . ." I sat forward in my chair and frantically scribbled a note to my attorney: "WHERE IS THE REST OF THE PAGE?! MAKE

THEM READ FROM THE TOP OF THE PAGE." He made Garrick return to the top and read the part about Christ. But in that courtroom of people who hadn't heard of a contemporary scholar like Reza Aslan, let alone read the iconic works of fiction by Salman Rushdie or Nikos Kazantzakis, the entire point was lost. They thought I *actually believed the Taliban was a Christlike vision of a fundamentalist Islamic state.* That sentence, to me, when I wrote it, was a premise for an imagined novel. At the age of twenty-five, I was trying to write the next *Satanic Verses.* I wanted to write a blistering parallel between the rise of Christianity and the Taliban, mostly because I didn't fully understand the dangers of receiving a real fatwa. I wanted to follow my hero Rushdie's trajectory into history. What I wasn't expecting was the actual life-destroying consequences that these worlds held for my case, not from some foreign authority but from the United States government. I didn't even have to write the novel for my life to be threatened by it. You never get the fatwa you want.

In Solari's telling, simply writing down those names on paper was indicative of my guilt. Just *mentioning* them. It didn't matter that I had compared bin Laden to Judas (never a flattering comparison, since Judas betrayed Jesus) and expressed a desire to stop his style of anti-American terrorism from triumphing in Afghanistan. Nor that I was an Afghanistan analyst trained to study the region by the US military. Once the government decided my loyalties were suspect, they could find potential for disloyalty anywhere. Solari admitted, "She's very interested in humanitarian work and all those sorts of things, and I don't take any of that away from her." But she did take that away from me.

Solari said that I had visited Mexico many times in the past, forgetting to mention that I was a kid when I had done so. I'd never lived there, or indeed anywhere outside America for more than one week at a time. She kept repeating that agents took "four cell phones, two laptops, and one tablet" from my house. Which was true: I kept my broken cell phones because they had lithium batteries and I had not gotten around to discarding them in an environmentally sound manner. I had broken many of them after phone calls with my father. Hearing him unable to speak, or calling when he wasn't lucid, hurt so badly that I'd thrown my phones and shattered them. Other phones had stopped working in the gym, usually because of sweat. The internal chips worked, but those early touch screens couldn't take the moisture. The government could have looked at the data on those phones and seen that they contained nothing harmful before implying that they were part of some global criminal scheme.

It was bizarre—this government lawyer was suggesting that things like instructions on how to change SIM cards meant that I might be trying to hide my identity. My trip to Belize? "It seems odd to spend the kind of money necessary for a trip all the way to Central America, to go alone, and then to come right back after such a short period of time with very little idea of what she did there," Solari said. Suddenly my trip to Belize, where I didn't do anything but look at pyramids and eat new foods—proud evidence of which was on my Instagram and which I had volunteered to show the FBI—became evidence that I had clearly been doing something nefarious. She filled in all the blanks of my professional life—which were secret because I wasn't allowed to tell anyone about my work life—with innuendos and worst-case assumptions. As an exhibit, prosecutors submitted my internet history. They included as evidence of dangerousness: my Google searches for flights to Iraq and Jordan (both American allies, in fact), visits to the Taliban's news site and Afghan newspapers (which I did as part of my *job*), and views of job advertisements across the Middle East for linguists. My career itself, for which I had been commended by the air force, was now turned against me as a sign of disloyalty. Suddenly my social media declarations that I despised Trump were viewed as having sinister implications.

After this onslaught that made bile rise to the back of my throat, the defense got a chance to present our case. My parents spoke as character witnesses. My mom said all the right things: I had never been in trouble during my time in the military, I always stayed in touch with my family, and I had no criminal record. She said I'd never gotten in trouble in school, except once in eighth grade, before graduation. "They had the biggest, bestest food fight that the school has ever imagined, and she was not allowed to walk the stage," my mom said. That was the sum total of her daughter's misbehavior in life. My mother said that she and my stepfather would be bondholders for my release.

"Is it fair to say that, well, ever since she joined the military, she's been trying to deploy to Afghanistan?" Solari asked my mother.

"I don't know if you would say she's been trying to. I mean, in the military, it wasn't an option for her."

"Well, that's what I mean. So was she frustrated that her position in the air force was not going to give her an opportunity to go to Afghanistan?" the lawyer asked.

"I think, in the beginning, that's one of her—that she had wanted to. But, I mean, very quickly on, she learned that she wasn't going."

"Isn't that, in fact, why she left the air force, because they wouldn't offer her any ability to go to Afghanistan; those abilities were being given to special forces–type persons?" She was implying that I wanted to deploy to Afghanistan with the air force to join the opposing side!

"I don't know if that was the reason. That might have been one of many reasons."

"Did she ever tell you why she took up an interest at the age of seventeen in learning Arabic or Farsi or Dari or any of those?" Solari was implying that I began studying Middle Eastern languages—as a teenager—because I was sympathetic to terrorists and extremists. After which I joined the US military for six years so I could have access to top-secret materials! It was fucking absurd.

"She loves that language," my mother said, meaning Arabic.

"Has she ever discussed with you a desire to go to Pakistan to meet with—I know it's going to sound like a silly question. Has she ever discussed with you a desire to go to Pakistan to meet with leaders of the Taliban government?"

Indeed, it did sound like a silly question. My mother was aghast. "No," was all she could say.

My stepfather was up next. He said I wasn't a troublesome child (bless him) and got good grades but that I was "strong-willed." He mentioned my food fight again (it's now a source of pride). Gary explained that I had so many SIM cards because my phones broke, not because I was a mastermind criminal. "She was just trying to make her cell phone work," he said. He said I hadn't gone to Mexico since I was a kid, and I had gone then because I needed my teeth fixed. It broke my heart, and melted it, to hear him say he would offer the twenty acres of land he owned, and the house that sat on it, as bond so I could have pretrial release.

But Solari told the judge that if I were released, I would try to burn down the White House, move to Afghanistan, and join the Taliban. She seriously said that. I mean, I had taken up Judaism in high school and tried to keep kosher—I would be gang-raped and set on fire if I met with the Taliban! But once the government said it, people believed it. A headline in the local news after that hearing was "Prosecutors: Contractor wanted to 'burn the White House down.'"

"The defendant certainly appears to come from some very nice parents who had little if any idea specifically what she did for a living, how she felt about it, or why she would steal and disclose classified information," Solari said. Now the fact that I *hadn't* broken laws to reveal information about my job to my family became a sign of my commitment to lawbreaking. But what the FBI took from my house was "downright frightening," she said.

And then there were my jailhouse conversations with family members. My joke with my sister about how I would try to gain sympathy in court? Solari suggested this was proof of my deceitfulness. "She said she didn't want to spend the rest of her life in jail and that she was, quote, gonna play that card being pretty, white, and cute; braid my hair and all, gonna cry. *That* is the defendant's character." No chance to explain the sarcasm and bitterness in our voices as we were criticizing the systems in the country.

My using my cellmate's PIN? That was twisted into my trying to evade detection and get secret messages to my family. My conversation with my mother about the money in our shared account meant that I was trying to hide my wealth to appear poor, in the prosecutor's words. (Months later, Solari formally apologized in court to my mother for misrepresenting this conversation: "To the extent I may have misrepresented anything about the conversation between you and your daughter at the initial hearing, I apologize to you for that. That was certainly not my intent. My only job here is to present the facts as they are, and I never want to do otherwise. So, again, I want to apologize to you." Well, I was held in horrible jail conditions partly because of her misrepresentation. My mother refused to look at Solari when she gave her bullshit apology.)

The damage was done. Deep, deep damage. Hiding funds, studying Middle Eastern languages, writing down Taliban leaders' names, saying bad things about the US government—it all added up to my being, if not a terrorist, then certainly someone who wanted to become one if released.

Titus did his best, pointing out that it is murderers and rapists who are routinely released on bail who are "downright frightening," not someone plugging a flash drive into a computer. He said I had no history of violence and was not a demonstrated threat to anyone. He also pointed out that, um, "we have no evidence. In fact, the government went through a long litany explaining that they have no idea when they'll be able to release the evidence. All they have is what they found when my client was interrogated by ten law enforcement officers who were armed in her home." He did what he could to point out the absurdity of the government's worst-case assumptions about things they didn't know. "They've made several references to Tor, but they never said what she did with Tor because they have no idea," he pointed out.

Judge Epps could have granted me bond right then and there, but the framing by the prosecution and the testimony from the agents were all he'd needed to hear. "The government has said that publication of this information would put our country in grave danger," he said. "So I think the nature and circumstance of that type of offense militates in favor of detention, not in favor of release." He didn't say that the government had *proved* that the information's publication would put America in grave danger, just that they'd said it. He was concerned about all the blanks that the government had pointed to in my life. "Where is that thumb drive? If that information was downloaded from a top-secret computer, by its very nature that information would be—put our country in grave danger." What? *Can* information put the US in grave danger? Which information? Just information the government says needs to be kept secret? None of these considerations seemed to enter his mind.

He denied me bond.

I made history. "It marked the first time a civilian defendant in an Espionage Act media disclosure case was denied bail," Engelman and Shenkman wrote in *A Study of Repression*. And whatever the prosecutors said about me automatically became fact. They determined that at no point during my FBI interrogation had I been scared. That there was no way I'd known that any of the agents were armed. None of what they said added up, but once prosecutors said it, it became an immutable truth for Judge Epps. That was maybe the scariest feeling: the total lack of control, wherein truth, evidence, and argument were defenseless against the power of government. On Titus's advice, I entered a plea of not guilty, because we didn't know the evidence before us and he thought we could maybe escape unscathed.

But it seemed that the court had already determined that I was a dangerous, devious Taliban wannabe. Since this decision, several other people charged under section 793 of the Espionage Act have either had their bond revoked or been denied pretrial release from the outset. It took this one grotesque skewing of my character to set the legal precedent of keeping ever more Americans locked up before trial.

AFTER THE *INTERCEPT* PUBLISHED ITS STORY about the report I sent them, and uploaded a PDF of the report, distinguishing identifiers and all, they came in for major criticism across the board. "The court documents in the case raise questions as to how carefully the *Intercept* protected its source in pursuing the story," opined the *Washington Post*'s media critic. Wrote *New York* magazine: "The decision to publish the PDF with the tracker dots unobscured—especially considering the *Intercept* likely had no knowledge that Winner was the leaker, and she was already in custody—is a baffling unforced error from a site that hinges on being a secure place to send documents." The *New York Times* reported, "Veteran journalists did not hold back on Tuesday in criticizing *The Intercept*." The newspaper summarized the consensus among reporters and cybersecurity experts: "National-security reporting is specialized, but journalists in the field said Tuesday that *The Intercept* had appeared to ignore some basic tenets." WikiLeaks tweeted an offer for a $10,000 reward for whoever exposed and fired the reporter who had screwed up so badly.

For its part, the *Intercept* commenced an internal investigation and soon enough reached out to my lawyer to offer substantial financial support for my legal defense. It was now clear that we were going up against a United States government hell-bent on destroying me, and we needed all the help we could get. I was facing up to ten years in prison. My trial date was set for November, five months away. The battle for my freedom was on.

Sixteen

> But survival means more than simply being alive. It's not just the body that must survive a jail term: the spirit and the will and the heart have to make it through as well. If any one of them is broken or destroyed, the man whose living body walks through the gate, at the end of his sentence, can't be said to have survived it.
>
> —GREGORY DAVID ROBERTS, *Shantaram*

The night after the judge denied me bail, I called my mother to apologize. For existing. For being someone about whom their own government could say such disgraceful things. I told her that there were a few things I'd like to keep, but that she and my stepdad didn't need to save all my belongings, and that I didn't expect them to stay in Georgia and try to defend me. I offered them a way out of the shithole I'd just turned my life into. But Momface said she wasn't returning to Texas yet. She was going to wait a bit. Little did I know that she would never leave my side.

Within a week of the hearing, the government offered my lawyer a deal: if I pleaded guilty, I would receive five years in federal prison. One year for each page of the report I had leaked. That was probably just a coincidence, but it was no less arbitrary than any other explanation for the proposed sentence. The prosecutors were clearly confident after seeing that the magistrate was so partial to them.

You need to understand how cruel and punishing the offer was, and how powerful people are dealt with differently than people like me. Donald Trump, Joe Biden, Hillary Clinton, and Mike Pence all mishandled scores of classified materials. Trump had thirty-three fucking boxes of stuff that he was not entitled to, at his Mar-a-Lago compound, and shared it with anyone he felt like impressing. He was charged with thirty-one counts of violations of 793(e), the same law I was charged under, and yet there were no pretrial conditions for him. He was allowed to arrive at court on his own, get indicted for espionage, and then travel for his birthday that weekend. Pence had four boxes of classified documents. Biden had four "batches" of papers. Pence and Biden at least concede they screwed up. "Let me be clear: those classified documents should not have been in my personal residence," Pence admitted. "Mistakes were made, and I take full responsibility." But for Pence and others like him, responsibility didn't mean what it meant for me. For them, an apology sufficed. Trump didn't provide even that lip service, saying instead that there was a witch hunt against him. Well, I was no witch, but they sure treated me much more harshly than they did big-time politicians in Washington.

And not just them. Former CIA director and retired general David Petraeus shared entire notebooks' worth of classified information with his mistress. As a key architect of Washington's foreign policy for decades, he of course had access to far more secrets than I ever did. The stuff he handed over while cheating on his wife included, according to the government, "the identities of covert officers, war strategy, intelligence capabilities and mechanisms, diplomatic discussions, quotes and deliberative discussions from high-level National Security Council meetings, and defendant David Howell Petraeus's discussions with the President of the United States of America." Much more than anything I sent to the *Intercept*.

After pleading guilty, Petraeus got two years' probation and a $100,000 fine. The judge said he gave Petraeus a fine to "reflect the seriousness of the offense."

The list goes on. In 2016, General James Cartwright pleaded guilty to sharing secrets about the Stuxnet computer virus used to attack Iran's nuclear program with *New York Times* reporters—and then lying to investigators about it. His plea deal included up to six months in prison, but before he could be sentenced, President Obama pardoned him and restored his security clearance. George W. Bush and Dick Cheney both supported the pardon. That's who gets pardoned in Washington—people who are friends with the president.

If I insisted on going to trial, I faced ten years in prison and a $250,000 fine that I would likely never be able to pay off. But I told Titus that there was no way I would sign the government's deal. My parents were now speaking to the media, and support was beginning to come my way. My treatment was harsher than that of any whistle-blower in the nearly 250 years the United States had been around. We appealed the detention order, which meant delaying our trial. But I felt they couldn't keep me locked up when I was not even convicted of anything.

Because we decided to fight my charges, however, it was clear that I would not be leaving jail anytime soon. Once the hope of a quick resolution evaporated, I shifted into "doing time," simply living from day to day. That consisted of making character studies and watching people. After being in county jail for about a month, I had seen a few women come and go, but it was mainly the same seven or eight women there most of the time.

But then this new woman arrived. Everyone called her Red. She had been there before and knew the staff. She had two sons down the hall in the men's unit, but they were in different cellblocks because they were in opposing gangs. From the start, she pleaded with the guards to let her out: "I'm pregnant. Let me hurry up and take a pregnancy test.

Y'all can't do this, I gotta get out, I'm pregnant." The next morning, she approached me, since I was the only other person awake. "Hey, so before I got arrested, I did a nickel. It wasn't a lot. Do you think if they drug test me today, it's gonna show?" she asked.

I had no idea what a nickel was. I had no idea she was talking about dope. But when it finally dawned on me, I could only shake my head—she had just spent the last day saying she was pregnant. It was the saddest moment. It made me think of my mom's work, of the families she tried to help, and how hard, if not impossible, it was to reach certain people. In any event, I didn't know if that nickel would show up on her drug test.

Red would also be the inspiration for this entire memoir. There was a night when the group was reminiscing about life on the streets, and the drug business. Red had the funniest stories about being cheated by her own brother, who was also her dealer. She said he would take apart his scale and put pennies inside it so his dope would seem to weigh more than it actually did. "So you gotta bring your own motherfucking scale," she told me, finger in the air. "Police will call you a dealer if you have it on you, but you can't trust these motherfuckers out there so you gotta bring your own." Her brother used to keep the little packets in his mouth to hide them, or that's what he said. Red wasn't buying it. "Don't buy wet dope—it weighs more too!" What a life, getting scammed by your own brother.

I passed this information off to Titus as groundbreaking news. I was teaching him what I was learning about crack and dope, and he found the business of the scales interesting because prosecutors will automatically upgrade charges to distribution if you're caught with a scale too.

"And let me tell you about the wet dope," I said.

Titus leaned in. "The wet dope?"

"Yeah." I felt like an expert in that moment, so I lingered before saying, "Don't buy wet dope!"

Titus decided on the spot that when I wrote my book about all of this—*when*, not if, he said—the title would be *Don't Buy Wet Dope*.

But Red's words about always bringing her own scale also affected my understanding of my own situation. I suddenly understood how important it was not to let anyone else's measurements determine my own value. I knew Titus was right: I'd have to tell my own story.

One county inmate that I got to know was a dead ringer for the religious character Pennsatucky in *Orange Is the New Black*, a petite white woman with black teeth, stringy hair, and an off-the-wall accent. She couldn't kick meth and would come in every other year for about six weeks, she said, before returning to drug court. When she was in, she would often snatch the remote from the common room, turn off the television, and keep it off until we had all listened to whatever Bible verse she was trying to memorize. That was Pennsatucky.

And then there was Shannon, who was facing ten years on a meth conspiracy charge. Her specialties were money laundering and trafficking—she knew how to make meth, so she had a lot of money. Her husband, Rickey, was down the hall, an inmate on the men's side of the jail. The men went out in the yard before the women did, and he sometimes picked a flower and left it on the windowsill for her to grab as she came back in during our shift. Shannon was skinny when she arrived at jail but gained weight because she always slept and never exercised.

One morning, she told me, "I had a dream about the love of my life."

"Rickey? That's so sweet," I said.

"What? No. Dope." *That* was the love of her life.

Shannon's mother was also a methhead, and the FBI had not discovered all of their stash when raiding them. Sometimes I heard Shannon screaming in the phone booth at her mother to "leave the ice cream alone," a code term. She was one of the funniest people I have ever met, and it's a shame that she couldn't channel all her entrepreneurial energies toward something productive.

The best friend I made in jail was Kay-Kay. She arrived in October 2017 and looked exactly like Bhad Bhabie, the internet-infamous teenager who appeared on *Dr. Phil*, taunting the audience, in a ridiculous accent, to fight her, using the immortal words, "Cash me outside, howbow dah" (translation: "Catch me outside, how about that"). I was so excited, thinking a mini-celebrity had come through the jail doors, that I called my sister, giddy and starstruck, to tell her that Cash Me Outside Girl was here. My sister sent me a postcard with a still frame from the *Dr. Phil* episode.

Alas, Kay-Kay was no celebrity. She was a seventeen-year-old troubled but kind Hispanic girl from a rural area. She was the first person I met in jail from a similar background to mine; we had all the same cultural references. She had puppy-dog energy, and she would sing good morning to the guards and make up raps and songs. I could be my silly self with her. This was her first arrest, as it was mine. She had been arrested for domestic battery, after fighting with her mother, who wanted to teach her a lesson and scare her straight. It had not worked, and her mother bonded her out so she could make it back to work at McDonald's on time.

I next met Kay-Kay in the spring of 2018. She looked different. Her hair wasn't straightened, and she no longer had makeup or a tough attitude. Terrible things had happened to her since I'd seen her last. She was facing drug charges, and as an eighteen-year-old, she was on her own. I began to look out for her, making sure she had hygiene rituals and products, and food. I let her use my PIN.

We were wild together, and for the first time, I stopped taking everything deathly seriously. Everything became a game, every night a party. We stacked up empty Coke bottles in an unoccupied bunk and threw packages of maxi-pads at them like a carnival game. Toilet paper rolls became volleyballs. There wasn't a situation that we couldn't turn into a song. A couple of the others would join in, and we would be so loud, our ridiculous jail choir.

After six weeks, Kay-Kay was released on pretrial, since the police investigation was going nowhere. I was exhilarated for her, but I was that much lonelier without her. I asked my mom to look after her because she was just going to return to jail if left to her own devices. Mom met her and saw the same sweet, funny person that I did. She essentially adopted Kay-Kay, who became part of our family. She enrolled in a GED course and got her job back at McDonald's, and for a while it seemed she would be okay enough to receive probation as a first-time offender. As long as she stayed in contact with me and my family, we could be the gravity holding her down in a life of relative freedom.

Around this time, a nonprofit organization called Freedom of the Press Foundation, which, according to its mission statement, "protects, defends, and empowers public-interest journalism in the 21st century," generously offered to help with my defense, supplemented by funding from the *Intercept*. Joe Whitley, a lawyer from a firm called Baker Donelson, headed the team. He had been the first general counsel for the Department of Homeland Security under George W. Bush and was a hardcore conservative. We needed a guy like that in rural Georgia, someone who understood the playing field and environment. His colleague Matt Chester was also involved, and I spoke to him on the phone rather than Whitley. But Titus and his colleague John Bell assured me they were there to stay as local counsel and were still advising me as the new team onboarded. Even though I'd admitted my actions to the FBI, we wanted to signal to the government that we were prepared to go to trial, which might get me a better plea deal.

By far the hardest part of doing time for me was managing my eating disorder. People don't take bulimia seriously, but it can be deadly.

Even when it isn't, it consumes your life, vacuuming your energy while you obsess about food, fixating on exercise and calories and carbs. After figuring out what the jail's menu was, I jotted down on a legal pad what I ate, and how much exercise I needed to offset the calories. Running became even more of a lifeline for me on the inside than it had been before, because it was the only way I could burn off my pent-up anxiety, frustration, and sadness. Only when I was running could I imagine a future for myself, the sky being the only reminder of the outside world. The days we were prevented from going outside meant there was no future, which is to say that they seemed hopeless. Those thirty minutes each day on the mini basketball court saved me. With no clocks anywhere, I counted to 100 or 150 laps daily to track the time, running back and forth while the other inmates watched me and my obsessive routines.

A book cart that guards brought by the cell every other week (well, some guards were nice enough to do that—others refused, just to be jerks) offered some reprieve initially, but soon enough I never gave that pitiful cart of romance and young adult novels a second glance. Fortunately, my family sent me books, which I devoured and gave to the other inmates. They were less interested in my Latin textbooks, but I think they enjoyed the other stuff. I taught yoga in that small cell and pasted photos of Nelson Mandela and the pyramids of Egypt on the bottom of the bunk above me. It became my Sistine Chapel.

But the Lincoln County Detention Center is hellish, and there is only so much an individual can do to retain her sanity. As Morgan Freeman's character says in *The Shawshank Redemption*, "Every man has his breaking point." Sometimes you see movies or television shows where individuals thrive in jail or prison by finding themselves, finding God, or finding peace. Maybe they get their education or go off drugs. That was not my experience. I finally understood why inmates spend their time watching television and doing as many narcotics as they can, as often as they can. We had zero power over our lives. We fought over water because a person who "drank too much" was denying another person their share. Our cell was isolated except for the occasional yard call or when guards dropped off laundry, meals, and medication. Sometimes there were thirteen prisoners in our cell, so some women would be forced to sleep on the floor rather than make the perilous climb to the top bunk, which had no respite from the lights that never went out.

Jail educates you quickly. Some of that knowledge is about who is most threatening. For instance, I learned that the most dangerous person is one who was sentenced earlier that morning—because they have nothing to lose by acting out. They are headed to prison, freer than us, so they can do whatever they want, and the jail will just be eager to send them off.

In more literal ways, jail gives you an education too. My brain adapts to the dialects spoken by the people around me—I do a lot of what's called "linguistic convergence." If I'm around people from the Bronx, within a few weeks, I take on more of their vocal mannerisms. Same with a Minnesota accent, or a British one. In jail, I picked up a unique way of talking. Ever since military training, I'd sometimes had something of a potty mouth. But in jail, there was no filter, no interactions with polite society that would necessitate screening out curse words. Gradually, I became like my fellow inmates, swearing like a sailor in a Southern drawl. I arrived in that facility speaking English, Pashto, Arabic, and Farsi. I soon added Southern jailspeak to my vocabulary skills—that isn't something a person can obtain in college, but it cannot be placed on a résumé either, alas.

Something else I learned in jail: how I could use my hair to make a personal statement to the world. An inmate named Shelly, who had been featured on *Cops*, had one outstanding virtue: she had incredible dreadlocks. We were always trying to take care of them. We even convinced one of the guards to smuggle in hair supplies for her. Inspired by Shelly's beauties, and with the help of other inmates, I tried putting my own hair into locks for the first time, something I had thought about a lot over the years. For me, it was a private way of defying the people who had locked me up, a middle finger to respectability politics. The dreads didn't quite work the first time, but later, I would give it another shot.

But for all the fun we had with Shelly, she had paranoid schizophrenia and once had a psychotic episode in our cell, though she didn't hurt anyone. She received daily pills for her psychosis, as well as something tantamount to horse tranquilizers every Thursday, when she would go out in the morning and come back with just enough time to collapse in bed. She wouldn't open her eyes for two days, but I swear I once saw her reach her arm out from under her blanket, feel around on the bunk next to hers, and grab a honey bun to eat without ever opening her eyes. Shelly smuggled heroin into jail and got some of her friends high. Two other inmates wanted to bond out, so they snitched on Shelly and the drug users. The jail authorities drug tested them, and Shelly's charges tripled as a result. Once she received her prison sentence in late December, the jail figured that prison would be picking her up shortly—and so they didn't continue her psychiatric regimen. By the second week, all she could talk about was wanting to hurt someone. We warned the guards and medical staff daily that she was going to explode unless she got her medication, but they kept saying it was coming. She threatened a nurse the Monday of the third week, one of the few compassionate staffers. I had been keeping that nurse updated on how violent and disruptive Shelly was becoming; I'd told her I felt we were living in a sick version of Russian roulette. Then that Wednesday night, one of the women who had snitched on Shelly and been correspondingly released caught another charge and was placed back with us.

The snitch—I'll call her Steph—tried to make peace with Shelly by making fun of a third woman, Jasmine, who had left. When Shelly didn't laugh, Steph asked me why. I said it was because Jasmine had eaten Shelly's cootie (which was true but probably should have been kept to myself). Within half an hour my comment became public knowledge. When will I ever learn?

I was on the phone with my father and could hear Shelly screaming that she was going to kill someone. "I've been telling everyone I've been violent this whole time, I'm fixin' to do sumpthin'," she said.

My dad could hear too. "Is everything okay? What's going on?"

"I pissed someone off," I said. "It'll be all right."

When I returned to the cell, Shelly confronted me. "Why did you tell that to Steph?" she demanded.

"Because it's true," I said.

"It's my sex life, it ain't nobody's business. I'm an adult, I can do what I want."

"She wanted to know why you weren't talking crap about Jasmine, so I told her," I said. "Plus I thought it was funny."

"Oh, so you think it's funny?"

Shelly began hitting me. She pushed me between two bunks into the corner, where the cameras in the room had no visibility. I hadn't pleaded guilty yet, and a fight could get me in a lot of trouble. In jail, and in prison, self-defense is not recognized by authorities. It doesn't matter who starts a fight. You're both in shit. So I maneuvered back into the camera and put my hands in front of my face because she had long nails and I didn't want to lose an eyeball. I let her hit me in the face a few times until a guard saw it on the camera and arrived to pull her off me. I wasn't mad at Shelly—she had a severe mental illness. I was mad at the jail for depriving her of her meds. That's what I explained when I was asked if I wanted to sign a statement or press charges against Shelly. But there is no way for inmates to file charges against their jailers for being negligent and callous.

My attorney reassured me that I couldn't be held liable by the prosecution. All that happened was that the jail placed Shelly in solitary confinement, a barbarous form of torture. When we would go out for yard time, I would tell the staff that she should be allowed to come with us. The day the state came to take her to prison, two months after her sentence, we spoke through the door. There was nothing but love between us. The jail was essentially playing games with people's mental illness—it had been only a matter of time before she landed on someone, and that person happened to be me.

There were a few times—but only a few—when I was immobilized by despair. When winter rolled around, the heat broke down and our cell's temperature was freezing for days at a time. It was so cold that I always had to stay fully clothed and couldn't move much. On those days, I couldn't exercise, which meant I couldn't function.

But just when I felt I would succumb to misery, when depression seemed like it would give way to fatal hopelessness, people reached out to me. Strangers who had learned about me from the news, or sometimes just from word of mouth. Letters, cards, drawings—they came from all over the country, and soon from all over the world. At mail time, the guards would hand a stack over to me, while other inmates were lucky to get one item a month. Or the guard would stand there and read out each recipient's name while handing out the mail to the inmates:

"Winner."

"Winner."

"Winner. Goddamit, stay there. Winner."

"Winner."

"Jenkins."

"Winner."

"Winner."

It proceeded like that each day, embarrassing me but also buoying me up and making me feel deeply proud. I had not expected the gush of attention, even after Julian Assange's expression of solidarity. Overwhelmingly, the people contacting me were supportive. This surprised me. On the news, government spokespeople, intelligence officials, news anchors, pundits and associated talking heads, and ignorant armchair experts were trashing me. Actually, they were talking about me like I was toxic waste. On Fox News, Tucker Carlson compared my act of civil disobedience to robbing a liquor store and said I was part of a "ruling class" trying to "overthrow American democracy." His fellow Fox pundit Lisa Kennedy Montgomery said I was "intoxicated" by "a sense of power and control."

But these correspondents were mostly different. Some put money in my commissary, incredible acts of generosity that allowed me to buy things like coffee and creamers, the only solace I had in the mornings. One person put one hundred dollars in my account each month. A Vietnam vet from Chicago placed twenty-four dollars per week in my commissary. The first letter I received from him was like an electric shock—his handwriting, all capital letters, was identical to my father's. He was seventy-two, and my father had just passed, at age seventy-four. They seemed to have parallel lives: This man was drafted to Vietnam, but unlike my father, he served. Both were addicts, and alone. Both were Trump supporters. He was so surprised that I would write back to him, since Chelsea Manning hadn't. Eventually, his letters became too negative politically and unrelated to me, so I suggested that he was the one who needed help. He seemed to enjoy that and never stopped the support. I stay in touch with him today.

A CrossFit enthusiast wrote me, and I jumped at the chance to correspond about my passion. A photographer sent large, glossy prints, which I hung on our walls, as if we were a corporate office space. A woman in Florida named Wendy Collins wrote letters that were so kind and warm, and the letters just kept coming from her. At some point she began including photographs, which showed her carrying a picket sign that read, "FREE REALITY WINNER," or a sign bearing a photoshopped image of the Statue of Liberty holding a sign that said my name. In one photo, Wendy held a sign at a CVS. In another, she wielded it in front of a restaurant. In still another, she held a sign on the beach, raising awareness about me. And then one arrived of Wendy holding the sign in front of the Augusta courthouse.

Wendy, who was retired, amazingly devoted her life to me, a total stranger. She became a one-person public relations machine, starting a Twitter account to support me that swiftly amassed fifty thousand followers. Unlike most of the others, she asked what she could do to help me. She reached out to my mother, and they became fast friends. Somehow, this woman who had never met me and had no self-interest in supporting me became the head of my very unofficial, unpaid reputation-management campaign. Wendy spearheaded the effort to move the public opinion needle in the media, which up to that point had mostly slandered me. Trust me on this: when your existence is threatened, the only thing that makes life even semi-bearable is having people in your corner. Wendy's letters made me realize that my name was getting out there beyond my family, and in fact, through people like her, my understanding of the meaning of family was enlarged; indeed, my family is spiritually and emotionally better off now, and that we have only become stronger because of this experience demonstrates to me that we were meant to overcome everything the Department of Justice tried to throw my way.

Another group, calling themselves the Whistleblower Support Network, raised funds to have a billboard erected in Augusta, along a major route leading downtown. The court was furious. To this day, neither I nor my family has any knowledge of how the billboard came to be—the identities of our generous supporters remain a mystery. My first thought on seeing photos of it was that it looked like a missing person poster, my face in shades of gray, already a postmortem.

Not everyone was so kind, of course. Some people were bothered that I had violated my oath as an intelligence officer by leaking. "You should have known better," a typical letter read, the writer sounding like a disappointed father. Someone at Christmas sent me a season's greetings card. The note read:

Dear Reality,

Wishing You Were Sentenced to Life.

Sincerely,
A Trump Supporter

Much as I would have liked to send this person a card back, to thank them for the nice greeting card with its matching envelope, no return address was included. The big, loopy cursive made me think it was from somebody's grandma, and I tried to imagine who she was. Maybe a nice old lady who baked cookies and knitted and wrote notes to strangers in jail telling them they should suffer even more.

On August 30, 2017, we were back in court for a status conference to update everyone on the proceedings. My parents were in attendance—it was the first time I'd seen Brittany since my arrest. The same magistrate, Judge Epps, presided. One of my lawyers told him that the quick schedule he wanted for my hearings and eventual trial wasn't feasible because it would take time for our team to get security clearances and read everything the government was using as part of its case. It was simple: our legal team didn't know what evidence was being used against me, so we could not mount a defense. How could we continue to trial if we didn't know what the government believed I was guilty of?

Judge Epps wouldn't have it. He wasn't going to have endless delays, he said. Forget about security clearances and access to the evidence: what mattered to him was adhering to an arbitrary, predetermined timeline. I was the one suffering in jail, but he was the one insisting that we hurry up, even if it ruined my case. He pressed my lawyers for a date when they would be ready. My lawyer explained that he couldn't set a date because he didn't know how much evidence the team would be given to examine, when we would get it, or what it would contain. "What's hard for me is without knowing anything about those documents, it's hard for me to give the court this date. I know you want hard dates. I want—and I'm happy to work that out, but I am operating completely blind here," he said.

Judge Epps said he didn't care. "At the heart of this is just a fundamental disagreement about how you approach litigation. My approach and my requirement here is that we set specific deadlines." That outweighed my right to mount a serious defense, in his view. I was willing to remain in jail for longer if it meant that we could fairly review the government's materials for the case. Over and again, we said that we needed more time to access and review and understand the evidence and do other things that are supposed to be regular features of the American courtroom.

One month later, on September 29, 2017, the appeal hearing was held for my pretrial detention. The date was my deceased father's birthday, the first since his death, and I knew that I would be unstable if the government denied my appeal.

Solari returned, saying that the government's case to keep me detained was stronger than ever. She called Special Agent Garrick to the stand, as the government's first witness. He seemed so different from the kindly, fatherly fella who'd befriended me at my home on a sunny Saturday afternoon. "She is extremely dangerous," he told the court. The FBI's search of my home had turned up disturbing material, including those journals mentioning the Taliban and several cell phones. "We were on guard for anything, prepared for anything, but she is more dangerous than I even thought." That was why they'd had guns on them and were afraid of finding someone else in my house, he told the court.

Listening to him, I felt so afraid that my teeth began to hurt, and all the horror of my interrogation became clear. I suddenly understood just how much danger I had been in that day in my home. They had been prepared to kill me. That contradicted Garrick's argument that, while he was afraid of me, there was no way *I* could have been afraid of *him* and his partner that day. But he maintained that I was threatening, even after I had been so meek and accommodating and voluntarily spoke to him when he and his partner interrogated me without reading me my rights.

We had mentioned to the court my deteriorating condition in jail. It was clear that I was having an extraordinarily difficult time managing my eating disorder. But Garrick said that he had spoken with someone at the jail and that they were making special accommodations. "They said that they're making special trips to the grocery store for additional food," Garrick testified, adding that they gave me leftover breakfast grits with peanut butter instead of the white bread at lunch. "Fruit cups, various items," he said, though I had never seen a fruit cup at that jail. He quoted letters that I had written to people describing a good meal on a particular day to make it seem as though that were the norm and that I was being treated well and was flourishing. Had anyone asked me, I would have been happy to disabuse them of that notion.

My lawyer got a chance to question Garrick.

"Now you've been in counterintelligence for a long time, have you not?" he asked.

"Yes, sir," Garrick responded.

"Do you have any interest in knowing what it is that the bad guys are doing?"

"Yes."

"I bet you've spent hours and hours reading books, studies, maybe even online reading about the entities that might be posing a threat to the United States, have you not?" the lawyer asked.

"I have," Garrick said. But then he added, "I was on my work computer."

"Okay. Never at home?"

"No."

"Would it be anything wrong if you did it at home?"

"It may not be the best idea, but it's not illegal."

Strangely, Garrick was suggesting that being curious outside of work was an inherently nefarious thing. Reading about the history of the Middle East when you're a counterintelligence analyst—that's somehow bad!

My lawyer also asked Garrick about his alleged fear of me.

"Let me ask you, did she attempt to flee while you were there?"

"No."

"Did she show any desire to flee?"

"No."

"Were you ever fearful that she was going to flee?"

"She made no attempts. I wasn't fearful one way or the other."

"Were you fearful for your life that she was some dangerous person?"

"No."

"Have you any reason to think that Reality Winner is a dangerous person?"

"Physical danger, no."

Given all that, it seemed possible that I might be released before my trial. Some hope welled up inside me. From our side, my sister spoke. She talked about how excited I had been to get my plaque commending my exceptional military service. "She thought one of her life's missions—and it became one of her life's goals to go to Afghanistan and help, you know, with humanitarian aid. Now that she knew the languages, she felt that she was in a unique position to help people there, and that was something that she really wanted to do," Britty explained.

A freshly minted PhD by that point, *Dr.* Winner, with her poise and clarity, seemed to glow in that drab courtroom. She spoke directly, loudly, proudly, and with a smile when she mentioned me. She gave context to what the government had suggested was dangerous. I liked to study religion, she said. "She also read the Torah. She was interested in Judaism. She was interested in Buddhism. So she's kind of a yoga fanatic; so she's really into sort of the sayings, the philosophies, sort of the ethics of things, and then, of course, because of her connection to, you know, the language that she learned for her job, part of some of her training and the people that she interacted with were Muslims, and so she was introduced to the religion, the culture." I was hardly fixated on Islam, she pointed out—not that adoring Islam should even be a problem.

Britty explained my patriotism, my sometimes inappropriate sense of humor, my fierce moral nature (some might call it insufferable self-righteousness, but let's not split hairs here), and my military service. She contextualized my infamous quotation about hating America. "I didn't interpret her statement to mean that she actually hated America. Even though I clarified—even though I said, 'You don't actually hate America,' she was making a joke. She said, 'I mean, yeah, I do. It's literally the worst thing to happen to the planet.' It's something that if we were in person, she would be rolling her eyes."

Again, however, Judge Epps took the government's side, saying that I was too hazardous to be released since I was a flight risk. "One need look no further than Defendant's own writings to surmise that she hates the United States and has plotted against the government," he wrote. "The nature and seriousness of the danger she poses to our nation is high." He said that I wanted to burn down the White House, ignoring that I had written "ha ha" after it. John Mulaney would understand.

It would be a long week until the decision was made public by the court, and as I had anticipated, I was in no way stable enough to handle it when the government denied my appeal.

Seventeen

> If we were dealing with the person that Miss Winner's parents know and love, then there would be no question that she ought to be released.
>
> —The Honorable Brian K. Epps,
> in his decision denying me pretrial release

A guard approached our jail cell one day and said, "Winner: you're needed up front. Get your jumpsuit on." I figured it was a call from my attorney, but he led me into the captain's office, where I hadn't been before (in county jails, captains are akin to wardens). The room was probably fifteen by fifteen feet, with a few filing cabinets and the captain's community college diploma on the wall. The office was the one part of the jail where there were no cameras. Staff were always present, but normally that would include only the guards, medical personnel, and captain.

Waiting for me, alongside the captain and another staff member, was FBI Special Agent Garrick, in the same douchey polo and khakis he had worn when he'd interrogated me.

I stood in the doorway. He nodded at me. I glared at him. Just a week earlier, he had testified in court that I was extremely dangerous. Now he was willing to be just two feet away from where I stood, unshackled and detesting him.

The captain said, "Miss Winner, we're here because, obviously, you've been receiving a lot of hate mail. We wanted to make sure you read this particular piece in the presence of officers." He handed a letter to me. He and other staff watched my eyes pore over it. They could have let me read it privately, of course, but I believe that Garrick enjoyed watching me encounter such a violent threat.

An anonymous correspondent had written to tell me that I was a traitor for whom the death penalty was not enough. Instead, I should be raped in jail by a "bull dyke." The note was nasty and disgusting, but I was most taken aback that the writer had identified himself as an air force veteran.

Garrick spoke. "Miss Winner, I know the letter doesn't have his information on it, but we found out who wrote it, we found his information. Do you believe you are safe here? Do you feel threatened by him? Would you like us to go interview him?"

The room was cramped with the four men standing there, as if we were squeezed in an elevator, with three of them watching my reaction. I wasn't going to give them the satisfaction of getting a rise out of me.

I looked Garrick in the eye and said, "No, it wasn't that bad a letter. It's not a third as bad as what the court said about me."

Badass line. I'm happy I said it. I was unwilling to let FBI agents fuck up another person's life in my name. After that meeting, the jail just funneled the hate mail to me directly.

One wholesome task that preoccupied me was making gifts for my family. Cards, letters, and drawings were invariably screened and often confiscated by jail authorities. But the jail encouraged me to get rid of my books by giving them to my family. If I inserted the cards and letters into the books, if I wrote in the margins of the pages or on the inside of the book covers—history books and language-instruction books, mostly—they might not check those. And they wouldn't dare to confiscate Bibles. So I placed journal entries, drawings, and notes inside those books, highlighting different parts that were important for Britty and me to discuss. A guard flipped through one of the books and saw my detailed sketch of a corner of the jail cell, complete with leaks dripping from the ceiling—it was literally the only thing I could see in front of me—and confiscated it, saying the drawings were maps and diagrams of the jail that could be used for an escape or something. And he took about four other books and some cards with him. I was devastated—this was the last chance I had to interact with the outside world that wasn't monitored in some way and that wasn't about my legal case.

Soon after, the guards brought me into the captain's office to speak with my attorneys. But when an inmate on the men's side began banging his head against the wall, the staff left the office and rushed over. Alone in the room, I looked around and noticed the books and would-be presents that had been taken from me. I stole them right back from the office and returned them to my cell. I held on to them for months before releasing them again to my family, this time successfully. It's one of my proudest achievements from my time in jail, that little act of disobedience.

Otherwise, the days were dark. Suicide entered my head as an urgent possibility. But I knew that jail, like the military, will put you in a turtle suit and stick you in a room with padded walls if you admit that you are thinking of hurting yourself. That's their idea of mental health support. And I didn't want to be more of a burden to my family than I already was. So I kept it all to myself and considered ways I might end my life. Should I leave a suicide note? The jail would probably just confiscate it before it went out. For two weeks after the court denied my bond appeal, I practiced the act, taking into account supplies and timing. I did dry runs and calculated when on certain weekdays I would have enough unsupervised time, when the staff was most busy, and who was most likely to be working.

What originally kept me alive was timing. My mother stayed in Georgia instead of moving back to Texas, as I had insisted. She made a life for herself in the home I rented, befriended Kathy from the dog rescue where I'd gotten Mickey, and volunteered helping parolees reintegrate into the free world. A documentary team led by Sonia Kennebeck was now filming my family's every move, beginning a five-year process that became the film, *Reality Winner*. All that complicated my suicidal ideation. I was determined that Momface wouldn't learn that I had died in a city where she was living alone without my dad (they were still very much together but he'd had to return to Texas for work), and where there were a bunch of reporters camped out. I wanted her to have distance and emotional support, which she would get only in Texas. But it turned out that she was never alone. Even after that terrible hearing, another person in the film and theater industry, Tina Satter, reached out to her to make a play and movie about my story. Collaborating with a theater director and the film crew gave my mother a community and purpose. I'll say again: my mom is the only reason I'm here. She was later asked, on *60 Minutes*, in 2021, why she didn't leave Georgia and return to Texas. She simply couldn't, she told them. She couldn't leave, so I couldn't either. I had to survive.

And right when I was ready to give up, I spoke to Matt Chester, the attorney from the law firm hired by Freedom of the Press Foundation to defend me in court. Because the government was trying to make everything about my defense complicated and inefficient, we would discuss the details of my legal defense only in a small supply closet at the Augusta courthouse, which was converted into what's called an SCIF—a sensitive compartmented information facility—a secure room where people with the appropriate classifications can review information the government has deemed secret. One day, without warning, I was told to get dressed, and they shackled me up and drove me to the courthouse, where we had a meeting. When I returned to the jail, the guard told me I had missed the yard time for the day. Exercise was the only thing keeping my mental health even semi-intact, and I went ballistic. I told Matt over the phone that I was bulimic and couldn't function without exercise, figuring he would brush it off like the jail and court had, but he didn't. He understood the seriousness of my state. Even though I knew that I was on a jail phone and that I could be placed in a turtle suit, I told him that I wasn't doing okay. I was, in fact, drowning in pain. He said, "This isn't okay. We are getting you a doctor." Hearing myself confide to this man I barely knew more than I had confided in my family, just verbalizing my pain, helped me immensely. It released a pressure valve in me. It changed everything, knowing that while medical care would be minimal at best, they *knew* I wasn't okay. I was medicated with the antidepressant Zoloft from October 2017 until I arrived in federal prison a year later.

It was during this time that my jail days became smoother, more regulated. I felt as if I were in a sort of survival machine, where all I had to do was the bare minimum—keep going every day. And I could accomplish that. I could hear, through the cinder-block walls, the squeak of the cart carrying our breakfast trays. So I would get up to see if the TV power had been switched on, since they cut power to the TVs from about 1:00 a.m. to 6:00 a.m. Breakfast usually began between 6:11 and 6:16. We would watch the weather on TV, and while everyone else went back to bed after eating, I would make an iced coffee with the ice water left over from the previous night. Sometimes I would have to get up really early, by instinct, to get enough ice even to fill my cup. I would start dissolving the hard instant coffee crystals before we ate, and by the time everyone was asleep, I would have a perfect iced coffee (by jail standards) to drink while watching CNN. Some mornings, we got a random channel that would show the German Bundesliga soccer matches. I would wait until about 8:30, when the nurse came by for the morning med call, and then get ready to exercise. My daily workouts consisted of strength, cardio, yoga, and what I lived for, those golden thirty minutes outside, running in a small circle. I would also do ladder training, meaning that I would incrementally increase and then decrease my reps, so many days would look like this:

    1, 2, 3, 4, 5, 6, 7, 8, 9, 10, 10, 9, 8, 7, 6, 5, 4, 3, 2, 1
    handstand push-ups, alternated with
    10, 20, 30 . . . 90, 100, 100, 90 . . . 30, 20, 10
    single-leg or "pistol" squats.

On Sundays, when Ms. Piggy was in the kitchen cooking, I would do extra reps and sets. We didn't go outside on weekends or holidays, so I would have to go crazy with burpees. Ms. Piggy was not a derogatory name, by the way, or at least we didn't consider it one; she was known to those who loved her and those who hated her alike by that name. On Sundays she would cook soul food that was so good she would sell plates to the community straight from the jail. If it sounds like she was skimming from the jail budget, she was, but we also would never have gotten that quality of home cooking if wasn't for that little extra incentive. Those days, my workout would be much longer and more painful.

My Sunday routine consisted of ten rounds of thirty lunges on each leg plus fifty burpees. Some days I would add regular push-ups. Every day, I would leave the floor soaked with my sweat and the windows of the phone booth steamed up.

I worked out until they brought lunch. Lunch came at a different time every day, so I always stored my food until I'd worked out "enough to eat." And I never ate lunch before yard call, which, again, was at a different time each day, or never. Jail is waiting to live; I spent my days waiting to exercise and waiting to eat. I spent considerable time honing my yoga practice, doing the ashtanga primary sequence from memory. Each time, I articulated the poses and cues in my mind. I imagined teaching, in my favorite sunny studio in downtown Baltimore, or in a dusty wooden-floored studio I dreamed of opening in my hometown; teaching a full class was less lonely than practicing in solitude.

On the days when I finished my exercise early, I would have the afternoon to study Latin. At the chow table, I would crack open *Wheelock's Latin* and study one straight hour, or draw, with the textbook out. Most afternoons on weekdays we would be joined by church ladies until dinner. One, Miss Addie, was a relic of the Billy Graham days. I didn't have to agree with her to appreciate her mission and her kindness. Another group came from Augusta. Ms. Joyce became a beacon of light in a time of distress. She is one of those people who find connections in things and see signs. For instance, she had once seen a billboard with a picture of a butterfly on it, and then she met someone going through a difficult time who really liked butterflies; for Ms. Joyce, that was no coincidence but a divine signal for her to step in and help that person out. I enjoyed her presence immensely and even had her meet my family when they came to Augusta for a court hearing. I hoped that Ms. Joyce's ability to ease my pain in jail would mean that she could also ease my family's pain in Augusta. It did, and we formed a lifelong bond. The people who go into our county jails week in and week out to bring *some message, any message* of hope, peace, joy, or purpose—those are special people.

Eventually, dinner came, and then the mop bucket. Part of my coping strategy was to clean the cellblock the way I *needed* it to be cleaned, especially my workout space. That meant sweeping and mopping in a specific order, or else some idiot would mop the toilet and shower area first, soil the mop water, and then do the bed area, and lastly my workout space by the door. *Fuck no.* An inmate named Sparrow and I were the only two energetic enough to properly scrub the shower to fight the daily advance of black mold. Usually, cleaning the toilet and the sink was assigned to whoever had control of the remote that day.

But I was a control freak who didn't want someone to go through the motions simply because it was their TV day. I took over that task soon enough. People got the remote because it was fair or because they had good taste, and I cleaned the way I wanted. After the mop bucket was the nightly medicine call. By then, we had settled into a phone call rotation, and depending on the night, and the TV series, we started the nightly marathon. Certain shows, *America's Got Talent*, *Animal Kingdom*, *Wild 'N Out*, and others, were required watching regardless of the remote assignment. After that, it was usually a Lifetime or BET movie. We did this until about midnight every night. During this time, mail would be passed, or the orderlies would do our laundry. This was when I tried to write to people, but to be honest, we would mostly be too hyped up. To say I was locked in a room and *still* couldn't sit still long enough to write coherent letters would be an understatement.

A letter from a federal prison in Jesup, Georgia, written by a man named Drew, arrived around then. He had decided to reach out to me because he had seen me on the nightly news and recognized my neighborhood. He was from the very same part of Augusta and wanted to know two things. First, why had I been living in that neighborhood? (If you are *not* from Augusta, you do not move to the bottom half of Battle Row, just across the tracks from Section 8 housing.) Second, what was my side of the story about what had happened? What he'd seen on the news was incriminating, he said, but he knew better than to trust that account. He wanted to know why the government highlighted the phone call with Britty in which our deadpan sarcasm was taken for entitled belief in preferential treatment by the system.

Drew's letter was so sharp, curious, and intelligent that it stood out. Nearly every letter writer had already decided their opinion of me, about who I was, what I did, and why I did it. Lawyers warned me against speaking to the public and media, but in the meantime my actions, background, and worldview were being twisted out of all recognition. With Drew, I felt that I might have at least one person who truly cared to understand where I was coming from. It was my first chance since my arrest to explain myself. Most importantly, Drew had the ability to understand me the first time I explained something. He had been sentenced years earlier for armed robbery in that very same courthouse by the same judge who would later sentence me. Of everyone in my life trying to help me in those early months, he was probably the only one who knew what I was actually up against.

Drew and I began a regular back-and-forth, sending two or three letters a week, and even started a book club. We talked about dreadlocks, and how they had long been a symbol of rebellion, dating back thousands of years to ancient civilizations. We coordinated so that we watched *Animal Kingdom* together on TNT on Tuesday nights. Then, in our letters, we would break down the episodes. A few months in, photos arrived from him, taken at his prison. These weren't the first photos to have arrived from another prison, but we usually laughed at those. My mail was usually a group event; we pored over the pictures, articles, and strange letters I received. These were different. Drew was a normal person. And by normal, I mean covered in tattoos and with the longest dreadlocks I had ever seen on a person. When he squatted in the "prison photo" stance, with his elbows on his forearms, they pretty much swept the floor. The ladies gathered around.

"That's a keeper," Shannon said.

"Mr. Haaandsome," an inmate named Sarah cooed.

And he was handsome, and a keeper.

At the same time, we began working on my trial defense. Titus was as sharp as they get, but he was a thirty-year-old thrown on the case as a public defender and retained as pro bono counsel. The lawyers paid by the *Intercept* were experienced and expensive—the company behind the magazine ultimately paid over $2 million for my defense. Joe Whitley visited me in jail for the first time, along with Titus, John

Bell, and some other lawyers from Baker Donelson. We met in the drunk tank, the only room available—there was still vomit on the walls and not enough space on the cinder-block benches for us to sit properly.

After we introduced ourselves, I decided to give Whitley some of my trademark humor that had served me so well in the courtroom. I looked him in the eye and asked him, "Hey, so what's the plan to get me out so I can go to Cuba?"

Exasperated, Titus just put his head in his hands at my wisecrack. Poor guy.

Despite my downright uncivilized appearance and punch-line flop, Whitley proved to be a compassionate, dedicated lawyer. He knew something that neither Titus nor I had initially understood: the odds were overwhelmingly, fatally against us. For a lot of reasons, sadly. First, we would have to go before a jury in small-town Georgia. A bunch of hypernationalistic rednecks—his word for them—wouldn't be sympathetic to some left-wing, vegan, hippieish, weight-lifting, Trump-hating girl the government said was a traitor to the United States. "It's good to be back in Redneckistan," Whitley joked to me once.

Second, the Espionage Act is so broad that it sweeps up all sorts of things well below the level of spying. And it excludes any defense on public-interest grounds. That meant that I wouldn't be able to say to the court that while, yes, I had leaked something, I had been justified in doing so because the contents were of public importance and should never have been kept secret in the first place. If we wanted to say that the report I leaked contained information that was already public knowledge, or was part of a larger problem with overclassification, or anything like that, we couldn't, because we were not allowed to determine if that was true. Such an argument would have no standing, the way the law is written. The head of the nonpartisan Freedom of the Press Foundation, which promotes the First Amendment, has said that "basically any information the whistleblower or source would want to bring up at trial to show that they are not guilty of violating the Espionage Act the jury would never hear. It's almost a certainty that because the law is so broadly written that they would be convicted no matter what." We couldn't present a word about the nature of the information retained and disclosed, or the tangible effects of the disclosure on the nation's security. The courts wouldn't care if my actions damaged anyone or anything, and the government had no burden to prove it either. An old saying has it that a good lawyer knows the law, but a great lawyer knows the judge. Well, my new lawyers, being from larger cities around the country, including Atlanta, while savvy about the law, were forever at the disadvantage of being outsiders simply because they didn't know the judge. Plus, by associating themselves with me, they were marginalizing themselves. I was radioactive politically, and they put themselves on the boundaries of acceptability by helping with my defense.

But there *was* some good news, mercifully: Whitley knew someone with connections to the Federal Bureau of Prisons and arranged a meeting for me with someone from their board. I met with the guy at the courthouse. They posited the meeting as an evidentiary review, so we were allowed a private boardroom away from the marshals, but not in the cramped top-secret room, since we weren't discussing classified information. I showed up in my orange jumpsuit and shackles, and the man in the wrinkled gray suit from the board of the BOP showed me his binder with photographs of the different federal prisons and what they offered. Although my lack of any criminal record suggested I could be placed in minimum-security facilities, which have more freedom and amenities and (relatively) fewer human rights violations, the government insisted I be placed in low-security, a grade higher. So, no "prison camp" for me, the phrase used to describe places like the facility in *Orange Is the New Black*. Even if I was a model inmate, I wouldn't get there. Ever. By then, though, even the low-security compounds looked better than the jail I was in.

I said I wanted to be in Texas with my parents. I wanted to go home—or at least be as near to home as possible. He said, "Carswell, in Texas: they send a lot of administrative prisoners there, it has all levels and good medical. If we can prove you have psychological medical needs, which you do, you'll be taken care of. This is probably gonna be the best place for you." He showed me Carswell's commissary list and described their rec center. He said it was the only "open" compound in the Bureau of Prisons, which meant you could go from point A to point B without having to go through locked gates everywhere. Plus, it wasn't known to be violent. Everyone in there did their time quietly. Maybe I could even take college courses and finish my bachelor's degree.

This guy said one more thing. He knew I was looking for a facility that would honor the Jewish faith, unlike my current residency, and that I had a reputation for being, um, outspoken. He said, "By the way, Miss Winner, I just want you to be aware of the people around you and try not to stir up trouble. There's going to be a lot of white supremacists there due to its geographical location."

I looked straight at him and said, *Inglourious Basterds*-style, "It's like the great Davy Crockett once said: 'You can all go to hell. I'm hunting Nazis.'" However, he wasn't from Texas, so again, my joke fell flat to the floor. I have this line tattooed on my leg now (another prison relic: we used a fan motor and bread ties for the needle, and graphite for the ink), but at the time it was cocky and brazen. But I didn't give a fuck anymore. For one thing, I had gradually learned in jail that other women saw me as imposing. It made sense once I thought about it. The US government hated me, I read all the time, I got tons of mail and was on the news, not to mention that I did push-ups standing on my head. I wasn't afraid to be loud or outlandish to get us attention.

One time we were begging for toilet paper. A woman was stuck on the toilet waiting, and I had to pee, too, but they ignored our pleas for hours. So I jumped on the picnic table and started stripping for the security camera. That got someone to our door. He was mad, but he brought us the tissue. It taught me that the only way to have my needs met was to be as disruptive as possible.

But also, as I said, the most dangerous person in jail is a person who has just gotten sentenced, because they are leaving jail for prison. My sentence was impending.

In the spring of 2018, we decided on a last-ditch effort to challenge the Espionage Act of 1917. We filed forty-some subpoenas, trying to glean as much information as we could about the document I had leaked. We wanted to prove it wasn't closely held, and that the results of the leak were not as damaging as the prosecution had alleged, without proof, back at my detention hearing. We had an in-person hearing that lasted for hours, arguing back and forth with the prosecution on how crucial this information was to my defense should we take this to a trial. Essentially, if the government was going to allege that the release of national defense information was gravely damaging to national security, the least they could do was show the hard data in court to a jury. Judge Epps denied thirty-nine of the subpoenas, calling them a "fishing expedition." The Sunday after that hearing, Matt Chester called me. The offer from the prosecution was now sixty-three months. Up three months from the last offer because of the months taken to prepare for the hearing against the subpoenas we had filed. The message was clear: the harder we fought this charge, the higher the price they'd try to make us pay.

"SHE'S NOT PLAYING, MATT," I yelled into the captain's desk phone.

"No, they're done. We can go to trial and get ten years and risk you going to the wrong prison, or we can end this now."

All I had ever wanted to do was take responsibility for what I had done. No more, and no less.

I had come clean to the FBI. We never denied my actions in court. All we had held out for was the historical chance to say, yes, I violated the Espionage Act, but here's *why*. I had wanted my own words to go on the record; I'd wanted to say that I had released information that never should have been classified in the first place, that of course my motives were not to harm America. The Espionage Act is one of the only laws where mens rea, or criminal intent, does not have to be established for a guilty verdict. This means that the prosecution can allege that a defendant has a criminal state of mind, as they had done by depicting me as some sort of terrorist and forever damaging my reputation. However, because it isn't *necessary* for a conviction to establish intent, it is therefore completely irrelevant for a defense team to counter such statements. We were not allowed to deny the allegations of the government, because the characterizations they made of me weren't necessary in the first place under the Espionage Act. They could say whatever they wanted, without burden of proof, but the moment we pushed back, the argument was no longer relevant. To this date, that aspect of the law has not been sustained in a court, and I would have liked to challenge it.

I would not be heard in front of a jury, would not be allowed to explain my actions to twelve of my peers, as I once had hoped to do. So I chose to expedite the process of taking responsibility. Having already served so much time, I was ready to face the rest of the consequences and accept everything that would happen from there on out.

IN JUNE 2018, I changed my plea to guilty. I was ready to move on. The conditions in the federal system were much better than in state and local facilities. And I knew I wouldn't make it in jail forever.

Eventually, I would give in to my despair. I needed to exercise every day, which everyone said was easier in prison because there is more outdoor space and facilities like basketball courts and free weights. That was all I was living for. My lawyers agreed that pleading guilty was the right thing to do because there was no way we would win the case. If we went to trial, the jury would decide against us, no matter what evidence we presented.

Even after I changed my plea I still had to wait nearly the entire summer to be sentenced. Even that process wasn't guaranteed. Yes, I had signed the guilty plea and accepted the plea deal that the prosecution was obviously also in agreement with. But the judge? If he had felt that I wasn't sentenced to enough time, he could have rejected the deal. That's how nerve-racking everything was: *You cannot even go to prison yet because someone may still believe you deserve worse.*

In August, I officially signed a plea bargain with the federal government. They gave me sixty-three months, to be followed by a three-year term of supervised release. It was the longest sentence ever handed down for an unauthorized disclosure of information to the media, or to a whistle-blower, in all American history. As part of the deal, I swore to always accept responsibility for my criminal actions and refrain from appealing my sentence. The government agreed not to oppose my choice of prison, provided that it wasn't a minimum-security facility.

For the last time, I went to the courthouse in my orange jumpsuit. The DOJ had sent an entire army of men and women in nice suits to sit in on the proceedings. I felt like a prize fish they'd caught. But I had my own crew, and it was much more impressive: Momface, Gary, Britty, Wendy Collins, Kathy Ellis from the dog rescue, Sonia Kennebeck and her team as they made a documentary about my case, the journalist Kerry Howley, and Kay-Kay. I stood in front of them (they were literally behind me) and read my statement:

"I would like to begin by expressing my gratitude toward this court, the Department of Justice, the FBI, and our government, and sincerely apologize and take full responsibility for my action.

"To say my father was unique would be an understatement. A psychology and theology major, he expected us to engage in intellectual discourse by the time we were out of diapers. He taught me some of the most profound and influential insights into our world that undeniably led me to my chosen career. Language became a topic of sincere interest to me.

"I would like to apologize profusely for my actions which have resulted in the damages caused and resources expended by the government and this court, and in particular, I want to apologize to my family. My actions were a crucial betrayal of my nation's trust."

This wasn't the moment or the place to justify my action or say I'd been trying to help. Sometimes you just hang your head and accept that you were in the deadass wrong. The judge begrudgingly accepted the plea deal. He agreed to recommend that I complete my sentence in Carswell.

His decision was a relief, and surprisingly fraught. It hasn't been reported anywhere, I don't think, but on the night that I was sentenced, Judge Epps's house and car were trashed. The vandals threw eggs at his home, broke his windows, keyed his car in his driveway, and spray-painted on his garage the words "FREE REALITY WINNER."

Authorities didn't tell my legal team or my family about the crime. I found out after being reunited with Kay-Kay in the weeks following my sentencing. She had been arrested again, for drug possession, and showed up back in jail with me. Shortly after I was sentenced, she was called to meet with someone from the sheriff's office, the man in charge of her pretrial bond conditions. He then told her about the vandalism and explained that she had been a suspect but was cleared after he confirmed she had been with my parents that night. But he warned her to stay away from me and my family, as we would only hurt her legal opportunities in the future. As if we were the bad influences! When Kay-Kay told me this, I was livid—the last thing I wanted was to hurt anyone, let alone a judge so crucial to my future. What if I had to go in front of Judge Epps again? If someone had wanted to jeopardize my case, they could not have done anything more. The whole thing was awful and bizarre and remains unsolved, as far as I know. I rushed to the phone and called Matt, not caring that it was a recorded line. I demanded details about the damage. Matt was unaware of what had happened, but he promised to ask the government if there was anything our team could do to help the investigation and offer condolences.

"What do we do, Matt?" I was hysterical. "Can we send, like, an apology fruit basket? You know we [my family and I] had nothing to do with this!"

Send a fucking fruit basket, yeah, okay. Probably not the best way to apologize for someone else's crime.

Kay-Kay told me something else: when she was being booked in, she'd overheard administrators saying that I would be heading out the next day. I spent the rest of the day transferring my property to her and preparing to mail stuff to my family. At two in the morning, the same officer who'd booked me in fifteen months earlier came to tell me I would be leaving.

"I know," I said. "I just need ten minutes to get ready."

"How did you know?" he asked. Normally prisoners take hours to collect all their belongings.

"I'm a spy," I said, smiling. Same old Reality. Always a wiseass. He told me I had thirty minutes to pack up. I had assumed I would be traveling in my orange jumpsuit. Instead, I learned, I'd have to be transported in the clothes I'd worn when I'd arrived. David, the corrections officer, and I stood in the little supply closet where inmate property was kept. He pulled out my denim cutoff shorts and stretched them between his hands, as if that would somehow make them fit on my body once again. But they didn't. Despite all my exercise, I'd gained a bunch of weight in jail. David told me that I couldn't leave the jail in their orange federal pants, so I raced back to my cell and put on thermal underwear. I walked out of jail wearing only white boxer shorts, thermal underwear, and the white T-shirt and button-up I'd been wearing when arrested. I looked ridiculous, but my entire life seemed ridiculous by that point.

Four hours later, they put me into a van. After fifteen months of sharing a shoebox with a dozen other women, I was off to federal prison. Compared to where I'd been, federal prison would be a vacation, filled with activities and amenities. I began to feel something that felt like hope.

But we had two stops on the way to Texas. Everyone who knows the federal prisoner transit system knows about "diesel therapy." Diesel therapy is the use of the transfer process from one facility to another in an exceptionally punitive way. During the transfer, access to water and restrooms is not required. I was quite lucky. The first leg of the journey was driven by the captain of the Lincoln County Detention Center himself, in the jail van I was accustomed to. And then the luck ran out. Our first destination was an Immigration and Customs Enforcement detention center in Florida. It wasn't a bad-looking place. I was placed alone in a holding cell and offered lunch. Because I thought I would be there only a short time, I refused the meal; I didn't want to explain my diet if I wasn't going to be there long.

But as it turned out, they stuck me in solitary confinement. For eight. Fucking. Days. By the next morning I requested kosher meals, and for the first time, I received milk every day, with lettuce salads and microwaved kosher meals from Jacksonville. I picked out the meat, grateful for anything fresh. I kept believing I would be getting out and transported to Texas any minute, but time dragged on. In solitary confinement, the one light source in the cell never turns off. You are allowed to leave the cell to use a phone once every other day, and to shower every third night, usually around midnight, when the staff isn't busy. Not that time had any relevance anymore. I didn't know if I was being punished, so I only asked for a Bible for reading material. I read it twice, mostly while doing step-ups on the cinder-block bench in the cell. I was so lonely. Kind officers would pull back the curtain over the observation windows so I could look out at the dozens of immigrant men who were detained, booked, and then deported all in one night, every night.

Finally, on the eighth day, I couldn't stop crying and having panic attacks. I demanded to see the jail captain and was honestly shocked when he agreed to meet with me. I asked him what I'd done to deserve to be placed in solitary. And for more than a week! It was inhumane.

The captain said, "Well, you're pretty high-profile. You were on the news." He believed he was isolating me for my own protection—with no thought to how solitary confinement warps a person!

I explained to him that the average person didn't know who I was, and certainly not people in jail. "I'm not in danger," I told him. This was an ICE unit where few people were US citizens or spoke English, let alone kept up with the news about national security whistle-blowers. I had been in jails for more than sixteen months and had emerged with only a few scratches on my face from someone with paranoid schizophrenia. Solitary was far worse than anything another inmate would do to me. It feels like torture because it is. "America's prison isolation regime is not unusual, but it is cruel," according to Amnesty International. "The United Nations' top expert on torture and other cruel, inhuman or degrading treatment has called for solitary confinement to be used only in very exceptional circumstances, as a last resort, and for as short a time as possible." But my experience shows how easily and arbitrarily jail and prison authorities inflict solitary torture on inmates.

The captain agreed to send me to general population. And then, what do you know, I was transferred out—but not yet to Texas. I was sent to Grady County Jail, in Chickasha, Oklahoma. They call it Shady Grady because it's just a warehouse, with conditions somehow even worse than in Lincoln. Think a light fixture gleaming over one hundred beds in a single room. The toilets were one foot apart, and a single shower was used for all those women. Though the shower had several showerheads, because of federal regulations, only one inmate at a time could be in there. Of all the federal regulations to follow, they chose the one that resulted in a twenty-four-seven line for the shower. You would ask the next person standing outside the restroom who was behind them, and then find that person, and then the next person, and so on, until the thirtieth person in line shrugged and said you could be next. While I was there, the overcrowding was so intense that a woman announced on the intercom that we, the Ladies of Grady, were allowed to shower up to four at a time. We cheered and made innuendos about a giant orgy, but really all that happened was no more shower drama. The warehouse was filthy. I bullied my way into being in charge of the mop bucket and went to work. The frequent fliers of the jail said I had that building cleaner than it had ever been. Cleaning was my outlet. It was my violence and my zen.

But Shady Grady had one thing going for it: anyone could email inmates; they didn't have to request to be placed on a list and be approved by the jail authorities. Someone at the *Intercept* had offered to put me in touch with Chelsea Manning, so I emailed her through the BOP's email system.

She responded right away and couldn't have been nicer. I'd read that she'd done time at Carswell and asked for advice that might make my bid easier. She told me her prison name was Jefe. That was a funny thing about people like Manning and me: even though we were aliens to this environment, we assimilated well. Despite our vague yet menacing legal disposition, the people around us trusted us. When you are incarcerated and the majority of abuse comes not from the criminals around you but from the uniforms of the government, you understand how to build a real community of mutual respect and trust that can transcend most individual disputes.

The Oklahoma shithole jail had another quirk: it was possible to do video calls there. I had already been in Shady Grady too long and was losing whatever mental stability I had. I couldn't wait anymore. So I thought, *Fuck it, I'm going to do a live video interview with a journalist so the public can see what the conditions are like here. And maybe the lady who refuses to wear clothes will be out and about and will make a cameo appearance!* I started making arrangements for the call, and lo and behold, suddenly they put me on a bus at 2:00 a.m. to federal prison. When they called my bunk number, no one could believe it. I had basically line-jumped people by a month!

Paradise awaited. I just wanted to do my time with my head down, work out, maybe take some college courses, and eat healthfully.

Of course, things wouldn't be that simple.

Eighteen

The degree of civilization in a society can be judged by entering its prisons.

—Commonly attributed to Fyodor Dostoyevsky

Federal Medical Center, Carswell holds approximately 1,600 women for all security levels and sits on a naval air station joint reserve base in Fort Worth, Texas. In 2009, a prisoners' rights group told Congress that Carswell was "clearly the 'gold standard' in terms of what BOP facilities can achieve in providing medical care," calling their care "excellent . . . sometimes for extremely complex medical needs." It sounded great.

It looked beautiful when I got there, expansive and free-ish, with the autumn leaves covering the ground and people running in the massive yard. The track wasn't perfectly round; a meandering sidewalk oval wove between the trees (trees!), which were prohibited on all other federal prison compounds.

I can see how going from freedom to Carswell, where everything is dirty and horrible compared to the outside world, would be a depressing shock. It is prison, after all. But I was coming from much worse places. Carswell was so big that as I looked around, I thought, *This is huge! I'm never gonna find my way around.* My senses had been diminished. Those sixteen months spent in one room in county jails gave me an unlikely appreciation for the comforts of federal prison. It was like going from a studio apartment to a mansion. It didn't feel like prison initially; it felt more like university. One of my first letters home, on a tiny strip of paper, read: "Mom this summer camp is the worst—there aren't even bears."

The housing unit was one giant room with two tiers, white cinder-block walls, dark grayish-brown cement floors, and metal-grate stairwells, like in the movies. Along with a few other new prisoners, I was put inside a "bus stop," one of two temporary cells at the end of the hall on the second floor. There were eight bunk beds in each of those cells, with large windows, and the entire unit had a view to the inside. It should have been called "the aquarium." The regular four-person cells were about eight by eleven feet each, which provided far more space per person than any of the jails I had endured. There were metal lockers at the end of each bunk bed, stacked one on top of the other. Compared to the jails I had been in since being arrested, these were luxury suites.

When they walked us through the chow hall, I saw that the meals had vegetables. Honest-to-God vegetables, sometimes canned, sometimes fresh in a vegetable soup. I was nervous about walking the line, asking for the no-flesh or vegetarian option, never quite knowing what it would be, but simply knowing that the option existed would be an improvement. They showed us that rooms existed for religious purposes, including for the practice of Judaism, Islam, and Nation of Islam. Going to services would be of great comfort to me, I was sure. I felt I could make the best of my time in Carswell's accommodations.

Being famous has its perks in prison—people avoid fucking with you because they think you're some big shot. But there are drawbacks too. Chelsea Manning had told me about SIS, which stands for Special Investigative Services. She said, "They're gonna come talk to you. They are *not* your friends." If normal prison guards are like city cops, SIS is like the FBI. They don't handle the petty arguments and grievances; they handle drugs and cell phones being smuggled into prison, hate crimes, and the like.

Sure enough, on my first day at Carswell, someone from SIS picked me up on my way to chow. She looked like anyone else, wearing a prison-guard uniform, but she brought me back to an unmarked office in that labyrinthine section where the higher-ups had their personal offices.

"I'm surprised you're not back in admin," she said, beginning the conversation with that casually implicit threat—nobody wants to live in the administrative section, which is a de facto supermax prison, one hallway lined on both sides with single-person cells. In admin, exercise time consists of a half hour in an outdoor cage. There's no prison yard access, no email, and you're surrounded by the most dangerous and violent offenders. This is where the SIS agent was suggesting I belonged. She explained that they knew I had a plea deal, and reporters were going to reach out to me. If I had questions about what I was permitted to say to the press, everything must go through SIS. They didn't want their bosses in DC asking questions about me. She said, "Your mail, including your email, is going to be checked directly by SIS. If you ever feel like your outgoing or incoming mail is taking too long, you can come see us, because it all comes through us." Veiled within what sounded like helpful information was a message: SIS was watching me.

SIS would become my frequent, unwanted companions. Whenever a journalist filed a formal interview request, I had to sign and acknowledge the request, and SIS could accept or reject it. The paper trail of Carswell repeatedly denying my access to journalists began to grow. SIS made their displeasure at my notoriety known by making sure that I had to sign those requests at the worst possible times. My name was always being called on the prison-wide intercom with instructions to report to the lieutenant's bench, which was the prison equivalent of sitting outside the principal's office; everybody thought I was always in trouble because I got called down there so frequently. The SIS officers would essentially fish for potential wrongdoing. They'd tell me, "You're going to the SHU under investigation. We have six months to do it, until you explain what you said in this email." (The SHU is the special housing unit, which is a much more confined area.) Or, "We think you're talking to journalists, and you know you can't do interviews without us knowing." These junior wannabe FBI agents applied constant pressure to me, and I took their threats seriously. If there is one thing the nearly two million Americans in jails and prisons lack, it's power. If there's one thing the security staff and administrators have, it's virtually unlimited control over their prisoners.

On day two at Carswell, orientation was held in the visitation room for the fifty or so of us newbies—we were mostly Latino with a few white and Black people sprinkled in. Chairs were lined up in rows, facing a screen. A Black woman in her late fifties or early sixties, with a big smile and tight ponytail, introduced herself as Ms. LeBlanc. She went around the room giving people nicknames. She looked me up and down and saw my braids. "You're Pippi Longstocking," she said, satisfied with her creation. She walked and talked like she had been running this prison for thirty years already. She was intimidating, but I liked her immediately.

As part of the orientation process, Ms. LeBlanc delivered a thirty-minute presentation on romantic and sexual relationships in prison. Because she used a lot of slang and graphic terms, it was the most unintentionally funny thing I had ever heard. I remember thinking, *There is no way the federal government is paying someone to come into a prison and use the term "booty hole."* But it happened! Her number one rule? Don't put your mouth on something when you don't know where it's been, and vice versa with mouths you allow on your body parts.

Lesbians, not women who were "gay for the stay," she explained, were her favorite, because they were picky. The rest were just trying to get off however they could, which was actually a serious infraction. In prison, you see, nobody can give consent. If you have sex with someone, even if you're in what you define as a relationship, you are legally sexually assaulting them, and they are doing the same to you. Them's the rules. The presentation seemed unnecessary—from where I sat in that depressing, sterile room, having a relationship with another inmate seemed unthinkable. There was no privacy, tension was everywhere, people were assholes—prison is the least romantic place imaginable.

But loneliness and isolation will change a person. I did a lot of things there that pre-prison Reality wouldn't have done. When the choice was between losing my sanity and breaking the rules, I broke a few rules, and I let go of some sanity in the process.

Not that I began as a rule breaker. After two weeks in the bus stop, I was placed in the first of the nine prison cells that I would pinball among during my Carswell years, moved around for seemingly arbitrary reasons, without explanation. I was on a top bunk, lying over a woman in her late forties or early fifties named Miss Jones, who reminded me of people at the Georgia jail because drugs had fried her brain. She had childish tantrums whenever she didn't get her way. On the top bunk across from me was a young white woman named Brianna. She was always getting into trouble. That was something I noticed about the younger inmates—if they'd been sentenced to less than two years, there wasn't much incentive for them to be well-behaved, since if they were released early for being model inmates, that meant maybe two weeks early. They weren't angling for the best jobs, or really any privileges. They just wanted to make their time bearable by having some fun where, when, and how they could.

Below Brianna was someone with multiple nicknames: Dixon, Sassy, No Shine Like Bo'Shine, or, as people who respected her called her,

Mrs. Dixon. She was a rapper who had committed a small white-collar crime—she hadn't bilked millions out of people or anything—but she was housed with us instead of in the minimum-security facility because she had an autoimmune disorder that required constant medical attention, which only our part of the institution could provide. They upgraded her entire security level because it was more convenient for them, even though it meant she had much less space, privacy, and comfort than her sentencing court had determined she deserved. Dixon was Black, but because of her disorder, she had sprinkles of white on her face and body where her skin had lost pigment, and it looked like the Milky Way galaxy. She was intelligent, spiritual, and lovable, traits that served her well when COVID emerged and people with medical conditions for whom COVID would be a death sentence were vying to be released under a law Congress passed in 2020 called the CARES Act. It took half the prison staff lobbying for her release to convince the Bureau of Prisons that she deserved to be protected from the virus.

Dixon had a job in education. As with an ant colony, everybody in prison has a job. Newbies are supposed to do six to eight weeks in the kitchen washing dishes before getting a better gig, but I knew there was a work-around: I informed both the education and inside recreation centers that I wanted to be an instructor, either in fitness or in GED classes, thus staying two steps ahead of the job-assignment process. Fortunately, I was accepted right away in the education department. Boss move. Or so I thought.

Soon after I started that job, I made my first good prison friend. You have to remember that I had always had trouble making friends in regular life. I never valued other people as much as I did my next workout or yoga class, and exercise became the wall around me. But at Carswell, where I didn't have complete control over my workout schedule, I met the best friends I've ever had. Some of them had done unspeakable things. Almost all of them had endured horrific circumstances or gotten themselves hopelessly addicted to drugs. In other words, they were the type of people whom American society chooses to discard and declare unworthy of love. But these weirdos, outcasts, and criminals loved me, and I loved them back.

Ashleigh came up to me randomly when I was in the bus stop—she was a pretty white girl, the kind of skinny that's a sure sign of someone addicted to meth—and offered me a special kind of shampoo. "Hey, they don't sell this kind out anymore, but I have a little left." She gave me a gray exercise T-shirt that was too big for her. She told me where to obtain shower shoes and a coffee mug—these and other essentials of prison life that authorities don't care if you figure out on your own. Ashleigh did all that and walked away, helping a newbie out for no other reason than that she was a decent person.

A few days later, I went outside to the track and found her there by herself. We started walking and talking. Another girl appeared across the field, and Ashleigh said, "This is my favorite part of the day." The girl proceeded to dance, and Ashleigh got out her radio and tried to figure out which song on which radio frequency the girl was moving to—the girl would stop and start at commercial breaks. It was a ridiculous, silly thing to do, and I loved it. Soon I was spending as much time with her as I could.

I realized that friends would be precious, because being a GED tutor wasn't the right fit for me. Despite never having graduated from college and not having a high amount of formal education, I have an academic bent. Although I'd wanted to teach social studies or something similar, I was pushed to explain math and science simply because I had the knowledge. In that GED classroom, I was trying to teach the algebraic concepts I'd learned in middle school, but my students were struggling horribly with it, and they resented me. I didn't know how to speak their language. There and elsewhere, inmates tended to project their insecurities onto me by suggesting I was being condescending, but I wasn't looking down on them—I just wasn't skilled at communicating. Some students complained about me to the department head's office, and I got reprimanded. Even when a student threatened me, I was in the wrong. This was an introduction into prison politics for me: anyone who creates more work for the staff members is, by definition, a problem inmate, even if that person hasn't done anything. Rather than get myself into any more trouble, I resigned.

Or at least I tried to. In prison, a job is mandatory. Resigning requires sign-off from a counselor, and mine wouldn't agree. In my second week of trying to resign, a voice came on the prison intercom calling me to see Ms. LeBlanc, whose office was in a part of the prison that was formerly a hospital. I hadn't seen her since orientation but hustled up five floors and into a hallway with a line of older, sick women waiting outside a door. I eventually made it to the front of the line and into the office, which was so warm and inviting it could have been anywhere in the country. It was a portal to normalcy.

"Sit down," she snapped at me. She gruffly told the inmate who was directing me into her office to close the door behind her as she was leaving. I was ready to die at that point. How had I managed to piss her off so badly already?

"Do you know why you're here?" she asked.

"No, ma'am," I said.

"Don't call me 'ma'am,'" she interjected. "It's rude." That was news to me. She continued: "You were in the military, so I'm giving you a break. You can say 'yes, sir' and 'yes, ma'am' to other people, but not to me. Got it?"

"Yes, ma—" I bit my lip as her eyes flashed back up at me. I was shaking.

Ms. LeBlanc offered me a new job, though she didn't say what it was. And I didn't ask any questions before accepting it. I would have taken anything. She then turned her attention to my air force career and, lastly, my conviction on espionage charges. I was floored and slightly shaken as she expressed her gratitude for what I had done and said she would personally look out for my well-being.

"I bet you didn't know you had a Black mother, but you do. I am your mama, and you are my last child," she told me. It was a line out of a storybook: at a moment of great despair, some magical being, a deity or djinn, appears out of thin air and provides the protagonist with unconditional support. Ms. LeBlanc, I would come to understand, was the rare prison authority figure who wielded her considerable power to save lives. People called her a modern-day Harriet Tubman, because she could find any loophole to release ailing and elderly inmates early to die at home with dignity. Ms. LeBlanc did indeed have my back until her retirement. They said she left for medical reasons, but I felt it was out of disappointment. There was a change in wardens, and at every turn, it seemed the administration managed to subvert her ability to lead sick and dying women to Exodus.

The job she gave me was cleaning the bathrooms for the inmates on the ward where she worked, often referred to as the nursing home. This probably doesn't sound like a huge favor, but cleaning that chronic care unit and working directly for Ms. LeBlanc was not a job that was advertised openly, nor was it available to any inmate; she handselected for the gig. Up on the fifth floor of the old hospital building turned prison, there was relative shelter from the drama of the prison compound. Don't get me wrong—there was still plenty of chaos to be had. Women using wheelchairs and oxygen tanks would fight hard and often. Duels were conducted with walkers. There was so much screaming at one another, often by angry grandmothers in their seventies and eighties, with actual body counts to back up their bullshit.

During that first month in prison, I met my second friend. We were standing at the bathroom sinks in the morning, both trying to get ready. She was tall and had a massive tattoo on her neck of a circle with an eagle in it, and the words "America's Most Wanted." I wasn't gonna ask what it meant. We wound up having a brief but intense conversation about the education system in the United States. Mercedes was a Puerto Rican woman who had grown up going back and forth between group homes, foster care, and juvenile detention centers. It was almost inevitable that she would end up at a place like Carswell. She had a killer sense of humor: when she reported to prison, she wore an *Orange Is the New Black* T-shirt. She actually did that. All the staff thought it was hilarious.

Mercedes was a conspiracy buff, like my late father. She knew everything, or thought she knew everything, about aliens, UFOs, government malfeasance—the works. She was a great storyteller, and I loved that she was fascinated by things in the world that she believed, truly believed, were covered up at the highest levels.

Of course, alongside this capacity for wonder was a pervasive sadness. She explained that her brother had been trespassing once and got shot in the back by police. The officers had lied about it and gotten away with their crime. The unending pain it caused her was buried deep inside her.

I lived next door to Mercedes for about seven months in 2019, and it was one of the most memorable summers of my life. Long days in the sun, and nights spent sitting on the floor outside our two cells, talking about aliens and demons. In prison, I was amazed and delighted to see, you could integrate the people you met into one big friend group, introducing disparate people and accumulating new friends as you were shifted between cells.

After six months of cleaning the shittiest toilets you have ever seen, I finally got a job as a full-time fitness instructor. This proved miraculous; I had never enjoyed a job so much, even if the clients were difficult and downright intimidating. One young woman would attend the warm-up of my 5:30 p.m. circuit training class, and by that I mean she only stayed for the warm-up. She had "Bitch, Don't Kill My Vibe" (the name of a Kendrick Lamar track) tattooed in sprawling cursive across her forehead, just along the hairline. I never passed the vibe check, so she left.

To my intense surprise, I found that I enjoyed these classes more than anything I had done in my career as a fitness instructor on the outside—much more than instructing physical therapy failures from the various branches of the military or teaching yoga for bougie people. Here, I was learning how to work with underserved communities. I taught a classroom-based course from the BOP's approved curriculum, known as Fit for LIFE. The handouts I was supposed to teach from were a lot of overgeneralized .gov bullshit, which never once addressed the chow hall food or options on commissary. Even in the free world, "fitness" is a loaded term that often leaves out impoverished urban neighborhoods and poor rural regions. In prisons, where there were truly finite nutrition and exercise options, looking at pictures of dinner plates heaped with salads and fresh vegetables or pictures of women exercising with equipment we never had was discouraging, even to me. I had to find a way to relate to our current circumstance, lest we all simply be waiting to improve our health after our release.

So I scrapped the government curriculum and began to teach *prison* fitness and nutrition, as well as to offer information on how to shop and eat on a budget when released from prison. I was learning how to teach nutrition to people who would get out and live at the poverty line, in stark contrast to my previous clientele of people with disposable income living in gated suburban communities with private chefs. Knowing that so many of these women would find themselves in food deserts, where fresh fruits and vegetables were scarce commodities, I had to figure out how to teach somebody to shop for their family with only food stamps at a local convenience store, or how to teach someone who was facing ten, fifteen, or twenty years at Carswell and didn't want to be obese anymore.

"Does anyone know what this is?" I held up the MyPlate.gov poster of a circle divided into fruits, grains, vegetables, and protein that so many inmates had passed by on their way to the chow hall. A few nodded, not sure where I was going with it, only certain that being in this classroom was an utter waste of their time.

"Has anyone seen a tray from the chow hall with even close to this many vegetables?" I threw the poster behind me and pulled out Michael Moss's book *Sugar Salt Fat: How the Food Giants Hooked Us*. The US government had subsidized the obesity epidemic in the country, I explained, and these were the same people who had given us the MyPlate poster with one hand, and shitty trays with tablespoons of canned vegetables, if any, with the other.

I once thought I might coach athletes and advise on nutrition for performance. But I was on a completely different course now, where I had to make health and nutrition a matter of equity. Amazingly, I found my dream job in prison.

The best solution I've ever found for my bulimia is making a habit of days that I don't binge and purge. I take a day when I didn't have problems with my relationship with food and make that day a template for myself by trying to replicate my routine. By doing that, I can build up a record of consecutive good days. At Carswell, that's what I did every day of the week. Strict eating and exercise. And luckily, prison has a set food schedule, sort of. We often joked that every morning the captain (who was in charge with operations) would pull out a binder that said "How to Run a Federal Prison" on the spine and go through the steps again as if for the first time. Much like in the military, *nothing* was ever on schedule, and the slightest security infraction would mean delays for the remaining 1,600 women and officers on the compound. If insanity is doing the same thing over and over while expecting different results, I don't know what prison is, in which we did the same thing over and over, and yet the results were nearly always different from the day or week before. But the food was mostly predictable. I knew that on Wednesdays, the chow hall would always serve burgers, so I could have a small lunch of a burger and three fries or something. So Wednesdays were always safe lunches, which I could count on, and that helped my brain relax for the morning. Holidays were always hard and confusing, because I never knew what the kitchen would make, and it would invariably be too much food. But any other day, I could structure my eating, much as I had my food shopping in the real world. And when I wasn't working out, I was teaching classes, which were very demonstration-based, so even my primary job assignment involved working out again. This was my biggest hustle.

And then when I could, I was out on the track, walking while listening to NPR. For me, that was super cathartic. I would time how long I spent walking, and whenever I had to stop to talk to somebody or use the restroom, I would pause the stopwatch. That's how obsessive I am. I wanted to walk eight hours a week, and I had to do seven hours of cardio per week and five hours of strength training. I recorded everything I did. If I didn't write down everything I accomplished, it was as if it didn't happen. Comparing my diet and exercise from one week to the next gave me a model to follow: if I didn't want to throw up, if I didn't want to be obsessed to the point of distraction, if I didn't want to go through immense pain, I could look at my record and see how I'd constructed a strong week. And if I just did that every single day, my condition would be manageable. I was always running to stay two steps away from slipping up, so I could never slow down. But I could stay sane.

Another perk of my inside recreation job was that I was eventually trusted enough to paint the bulletin boards that hung outside the chow hall. My grand debut was a Christmas village, complete with a giant golden retriever in a Santa hat. That assignment complete, I was commissioned to paint a Valentine's Day board for February. *Valentine's Day? On* this *compound, with all the child molesters? Hell fucking no.* I couldn't think of anything more inappropriate. I insisted on pitching an idea for Black History Month instead. I had my fairy godmother, Wendy, send me TouchNote postcards of the most iconic photographs from the civil rights movement: John Lewis on the Edmund Pettus Bridge. Dr. King kneeling in prayer. Hell, I even threw in the activist James Reeb, a white preacher who marched at Selma with King—and was murdered by the KKK for doing so. I designed it to look like Polaroid black-and-white photos scattered on a tablecloth. Appropriately, we painted it on a prison bedsheet issued to us by laundry. And each photo had an accompanying quote, reflecting themes of oppression, resilience, and nonviolence.

During this period, my spin class, my favorite class to teach, was threatened because our bikes were continually breaking. People were breaking them by being stupid, so I put up signs: "DO NOT PEDAL WITH ONLY ONE LEG. THIS BREAKS OUR BIKES." Yet sure enough, from where I was painting in my little classroom in the back of the inside recreation center, I could see that a large woman had her entire body weight on just one of our delicate, precious pedals. I lost my shit. I came out of that office roaring like I was a sergeant in BMT and told her to read the motherfucking sign. I walked off and went back to my painting. Suddenly, I heard a booming thud. The woman was punching the plexiglass window between us; her arm was tattooed with an iron cross. *You picked the craaaaazzzyyy one*, she mouthed at me through the glass. I was ready to fight, even if she had me by sixty or seventy pounds. In prison, you don't have to win the fight, per se, you just have to fight back to be respected. And not snitch. She was heading around to the classroom door, and I knew there were no cameras in our room. I was trusted to be there.

As I turned away from my painting, one of the quotes leapt out at me. "We will meet your physical force with soul force. Do to us what you will. And we shall continue to love you."

Everything in me stopped. The anger. The pettiness. The righteousness in me to protect the bikes, even my joy. I had been ready for violence over a spin bike in a system in which scarcity was their means of control over us. It pitted us against one another at every turn. How could I paint words that were meant to unify us and yet still fight? I was so immediately shamed by those words from the postcard that I knew that if she came through the door, I would be ethically unable to defend myself. *I was so fucked.*

The woman never came in. But later that day, she complained to her girlfriend, who at the time was my bunkmate's best friend from the streets before prison. (Prison is a small world.) All our friends happened to be there, and they told the woman how stressed and angry I'd been over those bikes, which had been breaking every week and no one would pay to fix them. They told her how much my spin class meant to me and to the women I was coaching. Now she felt bad, even if I was the asshole.

The next day when I was working out, she walked by, squeezed my shoulder, and smiled. She didn't say anything because the feeling was mutual. We never tangled with each other again.

That was how prison people got on: with drama, and sometimes with friendship. At some point in 2019, I met Zantana, who was bunking with a friend of mine. She had outrageously large red hair, was crazy smart and well educated, from an upper-middle-class background, and had a Midwestern accent. That was all unusual: brilliant Midwestern women with perfect hair were rare in federal prison.

Zantana and I had the same pop culture reference points. We liked the same movies, books, and television shows. She adored *Across the Universe*, the movie scored with songs by the Beatles, and she knew every word to *The Phantom of the Opera*—just like me. More impressively, she had read every word Lewis Carroll had written, not just *Alice in Wonderland,* and could quote many passages by heart. She made intelligent references but then also acted out entire scenes from *SpongeBob SquarePants.* One of the best memories I have from prison is of Zantana walking on her hands in our cell, back and forth; that always impressed me.

And so I persistently wondered how this highly educated, talented woman from a great background had ended up in prison. The answer was addiction. Zantana had already done a three-year stint for selling fentanyl. When I met her, she was in for a DWI, which, combined with her previous record, was enough to send her to Carswell for the remainder of her probation. She confessed to me that she was profoundly ashamed of selling her body for heroin. I never did find out what had gotten her hooked on Xanax and heroin in the first place. Whatever it was, it was deeply traumatic, and she wouldn't discuss it. Zantana believed that if she wasn't high and let people get to know the real her, they wouldn't like her. She hated herself so much, for reasons I could never fathom, because I loved her. When she got out, I knew she could do great things if she could stay sober.

But that became difficult for her, and for many people, when COVID hit. Of course, the virus and lockdowns affected everyone in the country, to one degree or another. But for those of us locked inside in small cages with other human beings, where social distancing was impossible and even soap was rationed out, as bureaucracy perverted common sense and basic public health measures, it was disastrous. As conditions in the world deteriorated that first year of the pandemic, prisons and jails became microcosms of deprivation and empathy erosion.

In mid-March 2020, the BOP decided to mirror the rest of the country, shutting down areas where people would gather. Unlike in most other parts of society, real physical distancing wasn't possible because American incarceration is designed to stuff as many people as can fit into the smallest possible spaces while still delivering lip service to human rights. But Carswell tried. They paused chapel services and broke up the education courses into even smaller groups. The inside recreation center, where I worked, was closed until they could figure it out. None of this helped much, of course, because we weren't isolated from one another in our cells, where the disease could run rampant should an officer or other staff member bring the virus into the compound.

With my anger growing, I needed an outlet. Unlike in jail, decent hair products were available in prison. So I worked with some inmates to fashion my dreadlocks. It felt desperately important to assert some degree of independence, and there were not many other ways I could defy the authorities who had locked me up unjustly or express my opposition to the daily human rights violations that were occurring before my eyes. By forging dreadlocks, I was tapping into a long, storied tradition of using hair as a form of protest. It was a reminder, if only to myself, that I was human. And that my morals didn't have to be defined by who the government said I was. My dreadlocks immediately felt like a vital part of me, and I have had them ever since.

Nineteen

> Prison is a second-by-second assault on the soul, a day-to-day degradation of the self, an oppressive steel and brick umbrella that transforms seconds into hours and hours into days.
>
> —Mumia Abu-Jamal,
> *Live from Death Row*

By June 2020, our COVID lockdown collided with a national Bureau of Prisons lockdown. The thing was, they didn't tell us at first why they were putting us all in full lockdown. We assumed it was in response to the civil rights protests in the wake of George Floyd's murder—they thought we would riot. On an NPR report on Donald Trump's infamous Lafayette Square photo op—he'd had protesters cleared from the DC park so he could hold up a Bible in front of an Episcopal church—I heard that task force officers from the Bureau of Prisons were among the unmarked, un-name-tagged police officers dressed in black, like storm troopers, pepper-spraying nonviolent protesters. It occurred to me that one of the reasons why that anonymous police force was so brutal and effective in suppressing civilians was that they were accustomed to using that level of force on inmates. I made the connection that the Bureau of Prisons had sent out their riot task force from various prisons across the country to maintain order in the streets.

I had to wonder how many of our officers at Carswell were among them, reinforcing the federal response to the riots—and was this why the prisons were so critically undermanned, thus necessitating a lockdown? Beyond any concern about staffing, now that these officers had the chance to tear-gas, beat, and brutalize civilians in broad daylight with no repercussions—people who weren't in prison uniforms, people who weren't just a number—how would they behave once they returned to the vacuum of their prison job? They must have felt like they could do anything they wanted. I began to taunt the officers remaining in the prison with us, asking them if they'd applied to go to DC to beat up civilians, trying to get someone to slip up and admit which staff members from our own prison were out there among the storm troopers.

I had been trying to do the right things. I was serving other people. I was coping with my sickness. But now we couldn't leave our cells. Now a cellblock of 220 women had to wait at their cell openings, waving rolls of toilet paper, for permission to walk thirty feet to the restroom, eight at a time, twenty-four hours a day. Some women shat and pissed themselves, or pissed in their trash cans while waiting for the bathroom. A defiant woman actually dumped her urine out into the main area. As I stood in line watching grown women forced to go to the bathroom on themselves in front of their cellmates and other prisoners, my anger boiled like water. Why were they coming at *us* because people were protesting George Floyd's death and what had happened outside that church? When the counselors and higher-ups would try to announce new lockdown "policy," I would disrupt them, yelling that they were the murderers.

Everything I had endured since my arrest and incarceration seemed now to become a crescendo of fury. Sometimes people ask me how I didn't have a complete breakdown, killing myself or becoming catatonic in jail and prison. The answer is that I was in a constant state of low-level anger. But the realization that cops could kill someone in the streets and punish *us* by revoking our dignity and our few basic privileges—it was too much. The truth is, I cracked. The country cracked that summer.

I would talk to some of the officers, telling them, "You're on Derek Chauvin's side. You don't even know why we're locked down. You don't know why you're treating us as less than human when last week we were able to go use the bathroom on our own. Last week we could go talk to our families on our own. Why did you just decide to cut us off from the world? And you can't tell me you're just obeying orders because that's what the Nazis said."

A few days before the Lafayette Square protest, I'd had an incident that I just couldn't stop thinking about. The warden was away, and the acting warden that day was Chaplain Clark. We had a respectful relationship, and we would level with each other. And so I asked him, "Why are you all doing this to us? The police killed George Floyd. We didn't. We're not rioting. We're not causing riots. And I'm willing to bet there isn't a riot risk in other prisons. Why then is the entire BOP under lockdown? This has got to be a message. Are we being used to send a message?"

And Chaplain Clark looked at me and said, "Man, nobody gives a fuck about you all in here." And then he walked away.

Give him points for honesty.

And then there was COVID. How bad was it to be in a US prison when COVID hit? "Former NSA contractor Reality Winner, who was convicted of leaking classified documents to a news website, has tested positive for the coronavirus at a federal medical prison in Texas where more than 500 other inmates have come down with COVID-19," read one Associated Press story from July 2020. "The number of confirmed cases at the Federal Medical Center-Carswell in Fort Worth jumped to

510 on Tuesday, only two days after the Bureau of Prisons reported that 200 women there had tested positive for the virus. Only the [men's] federal prison in Seagoville, also located in the Dallas-Fort Worth area, had more infected inmates."

Carswell's reputation as a federal medical center plummeted when it became one of the worst of all federal prisons, with the most outbreaks and the highest infection rates. The Bureau of Prisons was supposed to release individuals who were at risk because of illness if they didn't threaten the community, but few got out of Carswell. Dixon, with her autoimmune disease, was one of the lucky ones. Everyone loved her for her faith and service to the other inmates, and staff pushed for her to be released under the CARES Act. But several others like her—low-risk to the community because they were considered nonviolent, but high-risk should they get sick in prison from COVID—died waiting.

When lockdown hit, I was sharing a bunk with a woman around my age named Flee, who we used to joke became my prison wife because we were tight. Like almost everyone in prison and jail, Felicia came from horrible circumstances: she'd dropped out of her Oklahoma high school in eighth grade and was raped repeatedly as a child. She got into meth, and she said that the only people who ever gave her a chance and a feeling of safety were Aryan Nations gang members.

Flee was doing federal time on a drug charge, but she had been transferred from an Oklahoma state prison for a horrific crime: she'd taken part in a hit on a rival gang member. She and five friends had gone to his house and killed him. Her job was to make the body disappear. So my sweet and caring cellmate, a woman I am still in touch with, dismembered the corpse with a hatchet and sank it in concrete. Authorities never found the body, and every few years, they approach her and ask for the location. But she won't reveal it. She can be unimaginably ruthless—I won't sugarcoat that or pretend otherwise.

And yet, even while Flee was capable of horrendous things, she equally had the capacity to be a wonderful friend to me. I often think of lawyer-activist Bryan Stevenson's mantra that an individual shouldn't be defined by the worst thing they have done in their life. Flee was the most honest person in Carswell—she never denied what she had done. And she wasn't trying to pick up any more charges, so she was clear that she wanted to stay out of trouble. In prison, the rule is: unless a person is a child molester, you judge them by their behavior while they are in prison, not by what they did on the outside. And on the inside, Flee was a good person, hard as that might be to believe.

Shortly before I made my move into the room with Flee and another inmate, taking Ashleigh's old bunk while she was in the SHU because her husband had shown too much of himself during a video visit, another woman had been moved into the room, in the bunk below Flee—a child molester (known as a "chomo"). Because the prison rules on hazing protected chomos more than any other group (since they would be the first to get hazed, brutally), we had to step on eggshells while trying to push her to move out of our cell. She tried to defend her awful actions to us once. I was downstairs when I was told that Flee was about to lose her shit, so I ran back up, even though I wasn't sure if I wanted to intervene or have a front-row seat. As I stepped into the cell, Flee got in this woman's face and said, "You ruined your child forever. When I was a kid, I was raped, and my parents didn't care. So I joined a gang and I did drugs, and when my friends killed a guy, I cut him up and put his body in the river. And I just want you to know that your daughter is going to turn out just like me. Because of you." That's who Flee could be too. She didn't get violent, aggressive, or unintelligent with the woman. She just shut her up using the truth. That was how I learned to respect, and love, my wifey.

Of course, I follow the Jewish faith and shouldn't have gotten along with any Aryan Nations members. But I didn't know about her gang connections until I moved into the cell with her, and in that prison, it wasn't reason enough to find another cell. Also, I looked at Flee as a challenge: I spent a semester doing correspondence courses, writing essay after essay about gangs, why people join them and how they get out. I never ran out of source material, despite having no internet connection, as I needed only to email my mother or Wendy with book titles or genres and the books would flow in from supporters following updates about me on Twitter. *Healing from Hate* by Michael Kimmel became a well-worn and dog-eared resource. I'd leave Ibram X. Kendi's *How to Be an Antiracist* on my bed or locker for my cellmates, hoping to inspire them.

My breakthrough came not from studying hatred, however, but from another book that had been sent to me. Earlier that summer of 2020, I was down a rabbit hole reading books on World War II and military history. Someone had sent me *The Rise and Fall of the Third Reich* by William L. Shirer. Flee took the book to read herself, and that was how I found out that she had no idea about Nazi Germany. People like her had dropped out of school early and knew nothing about history or politics. And I mean *nothing*.

"That's some really fucked-up stuff in there," she said to me. "I didn't know about any of that shit." She didn't know about the Holocaust, she didn't know about World War II, she didn't know anything. And she wanted to be in a gang ostensibly devoted to Nazi beliefs! But largely, people who join gangs are in them for a sense of belonging, safety, and maybe even purpose. Not for the ideology. Did I hear them use racial slurs? Yes. By that point I knew better than to fight fire with fire and used facts instead, giving lectures on the dark history of the worst words imaginable, until they were used less in my presence.

Another book passed around Carswell would introduce me to my first girlfriend in prison, Taylor. The guy Flee's group had killed was nicknamed Tripwire. Interestingly enough, there was a Lee Child paperback thriller by the same name. Taylor made a point to find that book wherever it was thrown or hidden and leave it on Flee's bed, or in her laundry bag. It was a running gag. Flee and Taylor had been friends on the streets. After the murder, Flee fled to Texas, where she hooked up with Taylor, another young woman addicted to meth and heroin, and therefore connected to the drug-trafficking gangs. Together, wearing ski masks they'd decorate with glitter, they broke into hotel rooms and stole credit cards and money from safes. They both ended up at Carswell, and Taylor came by our cell often. She was beautiful, with jet-black hair and huge blue eyes. She was witty and compelling. She had the distinct ability to inject flirtatious hints into every comment she made to everyone; she just oozed sexuality. People started telling me she liked me. But she was uncaring and unfeeling, sociopathic in a way that Flee wasn't at all.

I had imagined I could never be involved with another inmate, but once COVID hit, they took exercise and access to the yard away completely. While I could teach a secret exercise group at night, upstairs and out of the camera's view in a blind spot by the trash cans, during the long days I needed a diversion. Taylor provided that. During various lockdowns throughout the year, they implemented full control over the unit. July 2020, in which we all fell ill at one point or another, pushed me to the edge. We couldn't leave our cells except to use the bathroom or send an email in a five-minute window, so we passed notes back and forth between our cells when we walked by one another, like we were in elementary school again. We sent food back and forth too. There was no more hot food, because there were no inmates left who didn't have COVID to prepare it, so the guards would bring us sack lunches three times a day.

One night, after three weeks of COVID lockdown, everyone just left their cells, refusing to stay confined any longer. Brown Bear, which was what I called the officer on duty, gave up and chilled in his office all night. Unable to handle the growing sexual tension any longer, Taylor and I sneaked off and got intimate. And by that, I mean that we built a tent out of a bedsheet and ate each other out. We started doing that whenever possible. And despite our practically putting on a show for the entire unit, there were never any consequences for us.

But things got toxic quickly. Taylor was possessive and didn't want me talking with other people, even with my own cellmates. Whenever I ate with someone or walked with them, she demanded to know what we discussed. Taylor talked badly about me to other inmates, and to me about other inmates. The sex was great, though! And I didn't want to end it, because I needed something, anything, to make me feel good at that point. While we weren't the least bit secretive about our antics, we were never messy, either. Other couples were often caught in common areas, or in the bathrooms. What we did in the privacy of the tent we hung from the ceiling over a top bunk was our own business. For a while, we were the prison version of a celebrity couple, like Brangelina or Bennifer, a pairing all the other inmates gossiped about because we were always squabbling and loud and sexy. Our drama was like a solar panel for me, energizing me at a time when I needed something to be pissed off about. I could punch Taylor in the arm for repeatedly jumping out from behind my locker and scaring me to the point of anger, but I couldn't lash out at the state of our society. Alas, we were randomly tossed into another unit, one where the guards were stricter and wouldn't let anyone out of their cells. And that's what ended the relationship. And, to be honest, some of my sanity.

Conditions for doing my time well were deteriorating. Prison is not just some mindless routine that you muddle through. It is a constant mental battle. I had SIS on my back. I had barriers that prevented me from taking care of my physical self. During the June 2020 total BOP lockdown, something in me became unhinged. And in prison, there is only one thing guaranteed to make you feel better right away.

One of the ladies who lived in a cell nearby was the wife of the head of a Colombian drug cartel. This isn't bullshit. Sylvana, as she presented herself, was an enigma, having grown up in Saudi Arabia and lived in Colombia at one point. She was arrested getting off a flight in Miami. Right off the runway. Although she was most certainly in on some major conspiracy on the outside, the authorities had only been able to get her on a white-collar crime, just as they'd put away Al Capone on a tax-evasion charge. This woman was selling drugs to my neighbors, so we would pass stuff from cell to cell.

One day, as Sylvana was walking back and forth past my cell, my bunkmate Mercedes, who was high on something, said, "Hey, do you want something? Because you are not okay."

My other bunkie, City, was high on something else. She agreed. "Yeah, you're not okay," she said.

They were right. Lockdown meant we couldn't exercise. We couldn't leave our cells, which were so small that only one person could stand up at a time. There was no vegetarian food—they kept "forgetting" to bring it to the housing unit—which meant that I barely ate but then some days would have access to large amounts of peanut butter: perfect for bingeing and purging cycles. For the first time after almost a year of stability, I was throwing up again. I was becoming unbalanced, snapping at guards and taunting them as killers. I would voluntarily relinquish my phone calls, as a way of asserting control and exercising my will. This was, of course, ridiculous—they didn't give a fuck if I made a phone call! And to be fair, I couldn't make the calls anyway. See, in federal prison, you have to use voice recognition alongside your PIN to use the phone, but in our unit, only two of the six phones recognized my voice and authorized a call. During the lockdown, you were brought to whatever phone was open, and if you were caught trying to sneak around and switch phones, they treated you like . . . a criminal! Even if I lucked into a phone I could use, it was impossible to talk, because we were manned by administrative officers who had never run a housing unit before. They would stand by the phones yelling non-stop, wondering why we were all taking so long to make a five-minute phone call. I screamed at one but then decided I would boycott the phones during the day. Instead, I'd come down at night to call home while sitting in a giant cardboard toilet paper box as a noise barrier.

"Are you in a box tonight?" my mother would ask.

"Yes, Mom, but it's a nice box. I think I live here now." We would laugh.

In prison, battles against authority are won by the authorities. But pushing back against things was the only way to assert that I was still a person. Still, I resisted the lure of drugs. Instead, I resorted to what I referred to as "marking." Every binge, every purge, every day I couldn't exercise, I put it on my body with a razor blade. Of course we were allowed to shave, and routine locker and cell checks would have revealed the broken razors. But lockdown after lockdown meant that searches were becoming few and far between. I had a nice collection of blades stashed away and was beginning to form a collection of lines on parts of my body, invisible under clothes, but a constant reminder of every time my disease killed a little piece of me inside.

Until a friend outside my cell said she could get me some "bumblebees." Benzodiazepines, which are legal pills if they're prescribed by your doctor. And so I began buying pills. I needed something to help me survive because I wasn't going to make it otherwise. I had never smoked a cigarette or drunk much on the outside, let alone done "actual" drugs. But in prison, you'll do almost anything to make it through.

And I'll admit: I loved it. That's why people in pain flock to drugs—they make you feel better when you feel so bad you want to die. In prison, I felt like nothing mattered. And then suddenly—and I mean within minutes of popping a capsule—I would be laughing and joking again. My silliness reasserted itself. Sharpie markers are hard to come by on the inside, but I always had a stash because I would buy more on commissary every time someone stole them from the education department. I began drawing on my eyebrows in Sharpie. First, I would draw great big caterpillar eyebrows. And when a certain officer would walk by our cell, I would poke my head out, just the upper half of my face peering around the cinder blocks, and show him my new brows. Handily, Sharpies are not permanent if your skin is as oily as mine is—so I would wipe off the caterpillar markings and then draw big McDonald's arches to replace them. Again, I stuck my head into the walkway when this particular guard walked by. Each time he made his rounds, I had a new identity. My silly behavior made me laugh hysterically. People nearby thought I had lost my mind, but I was euphoric, elated to be released from my rage and anxiety.

Does this sound crazy? Yes, it sounds crazy. Prison plus drugs will do that to you. It's a toxic combination. Soon I was taking the pills regularly.

And once lockdown eased, I didn't stop taking them. I integrated them into my routine. I would balance my workouts with the pills, because after coming down from them, you crash hard. Everything would be very funny for an hour, and then I would need to sleep, at any time of the day. Because I didn't want my friend who'd gotten me into the pills to know how often I was taking them, I now bought them directly from the Colombian woman. And she sold me on a different drug called K2, a synthetic cannabinoid that, in some forms, is in a legal no-man's-land because it hasn't yet been declared illegal in all states. People who did K2 would walk around Carswell looking like zombies. Though I'd never thought I'd do it, I did—and I loved it far too much. I loved the roller coaster of it all. Waiting to ascend, and then laughing until I cried and crying until I laughed. Sometimes I would hallucinate—I thought I was being pulled toward the rails around the top-floor tier, and my biggest fear was falling over that tier. I would wrap my arms and legs around one of the bunks and scream, "It's coming for me! It's coming for me!" I felt as though someone, or something, was dragging me on the floor. One night, I became a cat and was rubbing against my wifey's legs and meowing. The best time was when a new Marshmello remix came out and I wanted to listen to it high. I fumbled around for my MP3 player so I could see the colors of the song. I heard and saw the most amazing music—until I realized that my MP3 player was still off. When I turned it on, the music filled my ears, until I noticed that my earbuds were not even plugged into my MP3 player. I never heard that song again.

Everyone knew I was getting fucked up. Even some of the officers. One found me alone on my bunk, with a do-rag on my head, sunglasses, two face masks hanging from the sunglasses down to my neck, wrapped in a bedsheet, rapping, "COVID dreams, COVID COVID dreams," instead of Common's "Ghetto Dreams."

I even tried meth once, because I mildly overdosed on pills in June 2020.

One Sunday morning, I thought it would be nice to get high and eat lunch; the tiny, dry pancakes with sugar-free syrup and peanut butter tasted like heaven when I had the munchies, instead of the sad, cold meal they actually were. I crushed up my Zoloft and mixed it with three bumblebees in a hot mug of coffee so it would hit harder and faster, but instead I got sick and began heaving. I was on my knees on the filthy bathroom floor with the emptiest yet most painful stomach. That was when they called chow. Needless to say, inmates don't get to negotiate mealtimes. You eat when they call you, or you don't eat. Although my stomach felt like battery acid was eating through it, I thought food would absorb whatever it was that was making me sick. Somehow, I managed to get dressed and crawl to the chow hall. Drugs are of course a direct ticket to solitary confinement and an extended sentence, so I was terrified people would see that I was high. But then I realized that when they saw me slumped over and dead-eyed, they'd just assume I had COVID (the irony is that when I actually got COVID a few weeks later, I was totally lucid for it).

While I was waiting in line, this bitch in front of me was yelling at someone behind me. My ears were ringing like an alarm. As anyone who has ever suffered a migraine or been hungover can imagine, each of her many decibels was stabbing through my eardrums.

"Excuse me, can you not yell?" I asked.

"What?" she said, annoyed at my request. "You don't want me to fucking talk?"

As a matter of fact, I would have loved it if she didn't talk. But that would have been unreasonable. I just wanted her to let me endure my excruciating pain in peace. "It's not you, but I can't do this," I said, more than once. Guards get pissed off when inmates trade spots in line, but I was tempted to offer to switch with this woman's friend so they could stand closer and wouldn't have to scream in my face. Instead, they kept yelling back and forth, and my panic spiked.

I felt faint. And the guard on duty was a sadistic prick named Lieutenant Anthony. He liked to intimidate everyone. *If you faint in front of Anthony, you're going to wish you died*, I thought. I felt I would rather die than have the guards find out I was high and send me to solitary. *You are either going to die on this floor or you're going to make it back to your unit. If you fall, you'd better die.*

I remained stable enough to get my food in a Styrofoam tray and began walking back toward my cell at the pace of an elderly person. My clothes were soaked with sweat and my body shook with chills. A friend spotted me and asked if I was okay. "No," I answered honestly. "I don't feel good. I need to get back to my cell." She helped me back to my unit. I left the food on my bunk, waddled to the bathroom at the end of the hall, and dry-heaved into the toilet until my body stopped convulsing. Back in the cell, I slammed my food down my throat and then passed out, without the meticulous toothbrushing of a well-practiced bulimic. I'd never done that before, but I couldn't move, and I prayed that the food in my stomach would soak up the pills I had taken. I woke up two hours later from the best nap of my life.

At my lowest, while looking for something to take that wasn't going to put me in a panic-filled, nauseated situation again, I was offered some of the strongest psych meds given on the compound. These pills were strictly monitored, and mouths were searched with flashlights to ensure they were swallowed. I don't know how far down someone's throat the pill that was brought to me had made it, but paper towel was stuck to it in places where spit had eroded the delayed-release shell. Ms. LeBlanc's voice from that first prison day echoed in my head. I had never believed her before that people would take pills and medicines that had been thrown up or hidden in gums or mouths—*you don't want to know where they been.* I bought the wet dope, took it, and felt nothing. Felt embarrassed, really.

Meth was similar for me. It just wasn't fun. I found myself inside the face of my G-Shock watch, mesmerized by the seconds display. Except that as each second took a full minute to pass, I was stuck watching for twenty minutes of perceived time. I was looking for something to help *pass* the time, not slow it down.

Doing drugs, unfortunately enough, never had actual consequences for me. But consequences for things I didn't do certainly came fast and furious. Earlier in 2020, a prison guard had touched me while I was in bed. I had woken up in the middle of the night to find a female correctional officer named Gilmore in my cell, rubbing me up and down. I hadn't reported it and had been stewing over it ever since; generally, if you report things, the victims are the ones who are punished. I didn't want to be pulled out of my unit. I didn't want to be ostracized. But when I spoke to a fellow inmate about my predicament, she assured me that Gilmore was notorious and had many sexual complaints against her. She would ogle people in the shower and was disallowed from certain units as a result. So I worked up the courage and submitted a complaint under the Prison Rape Elimination Act, a law Congress had passed in 2003 to deter sexual assault inside jails, detention centers, and prisons. In my complaint, I described what Gilmore had done. Then I waited for a response. Nothing happened. But Gilmore stayed away from me, so I thought maybe something had changed.

Then, in December 2020, Gilmore was reassigned to our unit five nights a week and began terrorizing the entire unit. The reason for her reassignment: the week prior, when she was in the unit downstairs from us, she had taken off her officer's belt, with her radio and keys, and told an inmate to come fight her. That's what they do in Texas state prisons—the officers often assault the inmates or challenge them to fights that can't be won. Gilmore believed it was her prerogative to change the culture of Carswell to be more like the harsh conditions of state prisons, because we didn't deserve federal standards. She changed the rules every night. She decided that we couldn't take showers after 11:15 p.m., already a highly arbitrary rule. She wanted everything shut down by then. But when a woman left the shower at 11:05, Gilmore chased her down, ripped her shower bag out of her hand, threw it across the room, and then proceeded to tear apart her locker, destroying everything inside. Other inmates were protesting, yelling from their cells, screaming out the time. "It's not 11:15! You said 11:15!"

Gilmore settled the issue by declaring, "I can change the fucking rules if I want."

That was just one incident of many. But she exerted her control most forcefully in the bathroom. She would tell us, "I know y'all are nasty, but I need to be able to use these restrooms when I want." Then she would head into the stalls. While guards can announce their presence when entering restrooms to monitor anything that might be going on, they cannot—*by federal law*—commandeer our restrooms for their personal use. It was Sex Offender 101: you prime your victims to be used to seeing you where you're not supposed to be. Gilmore spoke freely about our bodies, our hygiene, our sexual appetites. And she treated our property as if it were garbage she could paw through at her leisure. We felt completely undone by her.

But, like most tyrants, she overplayed her hand. Gilmore's shift started at 4:00 p.m., and so by 6:00 p.m., most women in the unit were just over it with her. One day, for those two hours, she had everyone, all 250 in our unit, going into our rooms and then coming back out, going into our rooms and then coming back out, all because she was looking for the flat iron that we shared on the unit. The flat iron was broken and had been locked in a drawer by the day officer so that people would stop trying to check out damaged equipment. Gilmore didn't believe us and was getting angry. She threatened every one of us that she would go from room to room and confiscate our property at her discretion. And so women started waving at the cameras hanging from the ceilings, holding up signs for help. A lieutenant announced over the PA system that he was on his way.

Gilmore realized she had screwed up and launched into a speech along the lines of, "Oh, but when y'all had COVID, I was taking care of you. Who let you use the restroom? Who let you take a shower? Who fought for this unit to be allowed to use the phone?"

When the lieutenant arrived, everyone was trying to get his attention, to relate the content of Gilmore's threats. I was already sleep-deprived and on edge, and having to listen to her irrelevant moaning about how we were just trying to get one up on her made me snap. I stepped out to the rail and yelled down to the lieutenant.

"What about the PREAs?" I bellowed, referring to the complaints that other inmates and I had filed under the Prison Rape Elimination Act.

Gilmore looked up at me, her eyes bugging out from her head. "You're a liar!" she said.

"I'm not a liar! There are three women in here with PREAs against you. You should not be allowed in this unit."

I looked at the lieutenant and said, "Lieutenant, where are the reports? Why are you covering them up?"

Gilmore shouted again, calling me a liar.

I shouted back, "You touched me in my bed." The whole unit nearly lost its shit. Everyone started screaming and jumping up and down. I was worried there would be a riot. I hoped there would be a riot. I was in a state beyond fear, consequences, pain.

Gilmore leveled her voice and said, so everyone could hear, "You're lying on me. I'm coming for your blood."

I never cared about an ass whooping, but my stuff meant everything to me. I ran back to my room and gathered my things—photos, anything that had been custom-made for me, my picture board, a siddur (prayer book) that Wendy had sent years earlier, everything that held me together. I needed to smuggle them out of my room pronto. If she came to my room that night, she would destroy everything I owned. We began moving my things to nearby rooms and eventually down to my girlfriend Taylor's room.

The lieutenant left, and Gilmore returned to her office and didn't come out until 11:00 p.m. But when she did, she hit up everyone's cell, doing exactly what she had promised, harassing inmates and destroying property. She started upstairs, in the bus stop. Everyone had to put their shoes, with receipts in them, out in the hall for inspection. Receipts for items were no small thing to come by. Many people couldn't afford shoes from commissary anyway, so they were often scavenged from the trash, and therefore considered contraband. Gilmore left many of the inmates barefoot that night, and thus ineligible to go to chow. From one cell to the next, she came closer to mine. Then, at

11:56 p.m., she stopped at the cell right next to mine and said, "I'm done for tonight, but we're starting over tomorrow."

I guess immediate retaliation would have been hard to explain away. Plus, she got to keep me in suspense.

I had sixteen hours, or two staff shifts, to right the situation. I was wired, frantic. In the morning, I demanded to see the captain, or anybody who would discuss the status of my PREA report. But it was New Year's Eve, and we were on holiday schedule. I sent a Hail Mary message to SIS, who were not my friends, and an SIS officer arrived within the hour. That was when I learned that the special investigative agent (SIA) would investigate my report, if I chose to make another, though it would have to wait until January 2. I was told not to worry about the officer in the meantime. When I finally met with the SIA, I told him about the complaint I had filed. I said, "I filed this complaint on March 23, 2020. This same officer has now threatened physical violence against me in front of a lieutenant, and nothing has been done. I am considering a lawsuit."

The SIA replied, "Your report was never read here at this prison. You sent it to DC, where they have a backlog of cases." There were posters everywhere in Carswell—by the water fountains, the phones, the computers—for DOJ Prison Rape Elimination Act procedures. The posters told us to call a designated number or a secure hotline, send an email or forward a report to the email address listed, or send a letter to the given secure address. I had followed the procedures. But now I learned that my report was never read and that it was my fault.

"Do you feel like you have been victimized?" the investigator asked. I understood his implication: *Do you want to go to the SHU? Or maybe admin? That's where troublemakers go.*

"Well, I mean, no, but she also threatened me, and I have witnesses." I recounted my unit's week of hell. The grooming for sexual abuse. The threat. I listed forty-two witnesses from the unit. That was about as many people there whose government name I knew. The investigator left, and we were given almost a week's respite from Gilmore.

January 6, 2021, was an unhinged day on two levels. We watched the violence at the Capitol unfold, every TV in the dayroom landing on a different live news network for the afternoon. Everyone was waiting for the lockdown to be called—if anyone was to be punished for this riot, it would certainly be us. But no. We racked up for count, and everyone's favorite officer walked in at 4:00 p.m. I started packing my stuff away again. I would take my family photos downstairs with me and stay in the safety of the atrium, where she was less likely to confront me in front of everyone.

The evening proceeded very quietly. Gilmore refused to leave the office. When she came out, she went to one of the TV rooms, and a commotion ensued. We were called back into our cells as yelling was heard from that hallway. Several officers from the compound and nearby units rushed in for backup. Gilmore was escorted out.

Long story short: Gilmore had called two inmates into our unit, even though we were on a twenty-one-day quarantine after COVID cases had been found on the unit. She didn't know which one of them it was, because they had the same nickname, but told them that one of them had a girlfriend who was in the shower with another stud and said they could go across the unit to find out if it was true. It wasn't. The woman Gilmore lied about confronted the officer in that small hallway by the TV room.

"Why you gotta pull this ho-ass shit? What did I ever do to you?"

"You're cheating, your knees are wet, you were just in that shower," Gilmore replied. However, she didn't appreciate being yelled at, so she pulled out her pepper spray and hit the panic button on the radio. Women in the area rushed the officers who came in to assist and told them what had really happened before the woman was accused of assaulting an officer.

That was it. That's what it took to get her off our unit for good. Just kidding. Gilmore was put on administrative leave for almost a week. Everyone on the compound soon heard an account that she had tried to call the captain to ask to be allowed back to work. Instead, she'd dialed the wrong extension and left a voicemail in which she was heard being on a first-name basis with the captain, trying to explain that her children were driving her insane at the house, and begging to be allowed to come back to work. She was assigned to her favorite unit, the mental health ward, in which most of the inmates were too incompetent to file complaints about her harassment and assault. The investigation into my claim was picked up about a month before I was transferred to the halfway house where I would transition into my term of supervised release. Many of my witnesses had already left the prison, and many more were too complacent to testify and were just relieved that she was no longer our unit's problem. Not five months after my release, Gilmore was back on that unit, and she presumably works at Carswell to this day.

Such was the impropriety at the prison. Many of the offenses were petty, scoffable. An awkward male officer was known to bring in cosmetics not available on commissary for the prettiest inmates who flirted with him, though I never heard that he took things further to assault. He invited me to his house after my release, because he "had a bar in [his] living room." But there was a lieutenant who walked off for being caught having sex with an inmate, and shortly after my release, another lieutenant was caught for the same thing, and his victim was pregnant. Each time, the victims were sent to the SHU for months to await transfer. This is why so many assaults go unreported. You weigh the benefits of your current location, proximity to family, and safety in your current community of inmate peers against any benefit of making a claim of sexual harassment or assault. It almost never pays off.

Around this time, Carswell tasked some of us with digging holes in the yard. For almost a year, we had been prohibited from using the volleyball courts and the softball field, and grass had grown over everything. To get rid of it, we had to dig two feet down to unearth it. Turn the dirt over, let it dry, rake the grass out of it, and then push the soil back down. This raw physical work was wonderful. Getting our hands dirty and employing underused muscles felt delicious.

Throughout this time, I desperately sought to kick my dependency on getting high. What got me clean was partly the fear of being caught. I admit that. I would rather have died than be caught. We were aware that the staff was coming closer to busting the drug ring. Rumor had it that a woman on our unit had the whole ring's organization chart written in her notebook—and she lived with a snitch. The woman with the notebook got taken down. I had bought from someone who'd bought from her. I felt I was just one step away from going down too.

The other reason I stopped drugs was more bizarre: an awful prison guard inspired me to resist her with my spirit. In November 2020, about eight months before I got out, they started shuffling around the units, trying to figure out how to do programming with COVID still underway. They put me in a north unit, where, for whatever reason, all the white supremacists lived. The inmates had tattoos of swastikas and other Nazi symbols, and graffiti with that shit was written in the bathrooms. There was one counselor who liked to put Black inmates in cells with white supremacists; that was her idea of a fun time, even though she herself was Black and would probably not have enjoyed living in the same neighborhood as the Klan in her own life. She spoke more with her eyes than her mouth, and her glare was worse than a physical assault. Everyone feared her.

Since we were banned from going outside because of COVID, I would work out in the corner upstairs by the unit trash cans. But this counselor told me that I could not exercise in her unit. I said that I would find a way to do it, or else I would find a way to leave the unit. I went to the psychiatrist, got formally diagnosed with bulimia, and asked to be prescribed the only thing that kept my disorder in check: exercise. But the doctor said that because of COVID restrictions, they couldn't accommodate my needs. The counselor kept harassing me every time I sneaked a push-up, crunch, or lunge, chastising me and threatening to write me up for being insubordinate. That was no idle threat: she could throw me in solitary confinement for the crime of trying to exercise to prevent myself from getting sick. She would ask people to snitch on me if they saw me exercising, and she reviewed security camera footage to track my activities. Finally, I tried the strategy of writing to the prison chaplain, saying that I didn't feel comfortable in this unit.

One afternoon, this same counselor called me into her office and asked about my stealing secret workouts. She told me she had heard about my "little note" to the chaplain. "You are never getting off this unit, Winner," she said. "You know, I was in the air force too. I did twenty years on the flight line," she said. And she threw some jargon at me about bases where she had been, travel she had done, and promotions she had earned. It all meant nothing to a former linguist who didn't even know what a "flight line" was.

Standing there before her in my inmate uniform, I felt an unexpected surge of pride. The air force had taught me the importance of integrity, service, humanitarianism. That was what had appealed to me about the military. And here was this cruel former servicewoman using that uniform to denigrate helpless people, to humiliate and oppress and assert unnecessary authority.

Until that moment, I had always felt ashamed that I had gone from a camouflage uniform to the khaki one we wore at Carswell. But for the first time in my years incarcerated, I realized that I possessed some innate dignity and decency that couldn't be conferred—or denied—by any uniform. None of the letters calling me a hero, or the public declarations of solidarity from activists and celebrities, or the interviews with big-time journalists, or the knowledge that a movie about me was in the works, none of it erased my self-hatred like that brief conversation did. I would rather have been me in my prison uniform than that woman in her prison guard uniform, because I was still a person with morals and integrity, and she was not, and that made all the difference. This woman inadvertently gave me some purpose, and I went off drugs.

During my last six months of prison, I ended up sharing a room with a guy who became something like a baby brother, a trans man with a mohawk, named Yoshii. In federal prison, of course, men and women are segregated, but all trans people are vulnerable to violence on the inside and so are housed with women, who are less violent (but not nonviolent, which is why trans people are vulnerable there too—yet another thing *Orange Is the New Black* got right). Yoshii was a light-skinned Mexican with black hair and gray eyes—once you saw him, you never forgot him. He was in for smuggling drugs over the border.

Yoshii and I vibed together immediately. We loved the same rave music and the same stupid jokes. Sometimes I would be on my bunk and whisper to him, "Fuck yeah, man."

He would respond from his bunk, "Fuck yeah, man." And we'd go back and forth saying those three words for minutes until someone else in the cell couldn't take it anymore and told us to shut up. Somehow this cracked us up. You had to be there, I guess.

Yoshii was one of those people without much time on their sentence, and so he didn't mind creating drama. He hooked up with half the girls on our unit; he was shameless. He was always down for whatever fun could be had, and I am into people like that since I go back and forth between being ultra-intense and mega-silly.

Yoshii, one of his girlfriends, Anika, and their friend Megan shared a table downstairs in front of the TV, where they watched *RuPaul's Drag*

Race every Friday night. During the long days in which we were kept inside, not allowed to go to work, attend our programming, exercise, or do anything that might make us better suited for society, we would scrapbook, do avant-garde makeup on one another, and carve soap. And there I discovered maybe the most clichéd thing I ever learned in prison: I had an affinity for carving bars of soap.

I never meant it to become a thing. Yoshii decided he wanted a Ouija board, and so I carved out of soap the little triangular slider with the circle cut out, which was essential to communicating with the dead. All it lacked was the glass lens. Security was a joke by this point, after a year of COVID lockdowns; as long as someone didn't flip out violently, or try to exercise in the housing unit, they'd stopped caring, so I used the blade of a deconstructed toenail clipper to establish the clean geometric edges. The only officer who protested was, in fact, my boss from the outside recreation department. He didn't see a security violation, but he repeatedly warned us about the Ouija board, saying, "You can call whoever you want on that thing, but you don't know who's gonna pick up the phone." Words to live by.

A dog, a statue for my brother, a bouquet of roses, and a Salad Fingers action figurine for a girl I had a crush on—these became my artistic projects. I don't know how it happened, but we took some fuzz from my dreadlocks and glued it to the Salad Fingers head so that it looked like the former British Prime Minister Boris Johnson. Salad Fingers Johnson.

This had become my prison life under COVID. I went from having a great fitness job, working, walking, and taking college classes to wasting my time on soap and girls. Toward the last six months of my incarceration at Carswell, I used my position as a recreation worker to try to get as much outside time as possible. I would find excuses to clean inside the rec center, only to sneak off and cycle on a spin bike for as long as I could. A new supervisor there caught on and confronted me—I think she was most upset that I didn't stutter when I replied that that was exactly what I was doing. Again, no one knew the bulimia I was fighting. I was a high-profile inmate with regular mentions in the media. Every time I angled for more opportunities like exercising when others couldn't, I was assigned a superiority complex; I thought I was better, more important than others. But I was just trying to keep my food down so I wouldn't carve another line into my body.

This officer assumed the worst of me in another way. Her counterpart was a young male CO. Handsome. He also did not give a fuck about COVID. He'd tell stories of working the men's prisons, and the violence there, and then ask us how to use the coffeepot in the office. His supervisor colleague would accuse us of ho-ing ourselves out to him, often under her breath as she walked by. She would be sideways and particularly nasty to me, though anyone who witnessed it swore it was because my locks, which were starting to mat up at the scalp, were better than hers.

What I didn't know was that she was right all along. Within three months of my release, that officer was arrested and charged with assault at Carswell. I never would have guessed. Sometimes, I am ridiculously oblivious; my only focus was escaping the monotony of the lockdowns.

I should have learned at Grady County Jail never to use the words "rock bottom." You can always sink lower. Having survived three lockdowns, COVID *twice*, the officer from hell, and personal harassment for exercising, by February 2021 I foolishly thought that I had seen it all. And then hell froze over. Our housing building lost heat that week, but worse yet, on February 14, in the early morning hours, we lost all water in the building. It was a Sunday, Valentine's Day, and I was trying to kick it with a new chick from our friend group. Salad Fingers Johnson girl. By midday, not having any form of running water had changed from a minor inconvenience to a sanitation crisis. The toilets were overflowing by noon. Women were desperate to use the bathroom, to bathe. The hot-water spouts for beverages soon burned out with women using that water—the only water in the building—for everything. By the evening medication call, the entire unit left to see if there was water in the building across the compound. There was, and heat. We stole trash bags of water, slinging them over our shoulders and making the trek back over iced sidewalks. We scooped shit from the toilets and used that water to flush what remained. We would be without water for drinking or bathing for two days.

The solution for lack of heat? It felt like a scene from a movie. A cart was wheeled in Monday afternoon with old woolen blankets heaped on it. One older lady approached the cart, grabbed a blanket, and shook it out. A comically large cloud of dirt came off that blanket. She accepted it, but no one else approached the cart. What upset me most was not the idea that we had it worse than other people; millions of other Texans were suffering in the cold. It was the fact that just one building over, there was heat and running water, and there were hundreds of us willing to carry the gallons of water needed to keep the toilets flushing, to keep the shit from piling up on the floor. They made the deliberate choice to keep us in that filth. Those officers on duty those two days made the conscious decision to deprive hundreds of women of basic sanitary conditions, because that choice was more convenient for them.

But I was done. Four months later, in June 2021, I left federal prison, sober and semi-sane. I had made it. More time than any whistleblower in American history.

The system didn't break me, no matter how hard it tried.

Twenty

I want you to feel what I felt. I want you to know why story-truth is truer sometimes than happening-truth.

—Tim O'Brien,
The Things They Carried

Red BOP photo card; dead leaves; a pressed flower (an Indian paintbrush); a list of books from my friend Shawn, who thought I could move heaven and earth to bring any book into the compound; a crumpled review of Salman Rushdie's *Quichotte* (it was not a favorable review, but the photo of him in the article was the closest thing I'd ever had to an image of my own father in the prison); a scrap of paper with my favorite last-resort workout scribbled on it; a print of a black-and-white photo of Archbishop Desmond Tutu walking through tear gas; and so much more, including a laminated wind phone calling card I made, inspired by the wind phone in Ōtsuchi, Japan, a grief device that is an unconnected phone booth where people who lost their loved ones in a tsunami can enter and speak one-way to those who passed. My prison ID card holder was a small plastic sleeve filled to the brim.

By the time I walked out of that prison, I was definitely not okay. Despite finding a regular schedule of intervals in which I could escape the housing unit to dig holes in the softball field outside, and the fact that the prison had decided to benevolently allow each unit three hours per week outside to exercise, there was a final hurdle to being released. Quarantine. We were told that we had to be vaccinated to leave, so I jumped in line when the shots were brought to the prison. Yet we still had to go to the hospital building of the prison, seven to nine women in rooms designed for two patients, and not leave that room for a minimum of twenty-one days before we left for the transition housing. My original release date was May 27, 2021, but I never spoke of it or believed it was real. I was wise not to do so, because in mid-April, I was called into my caseworker's office, where she explained that because my halfway house in Corpus Christi accepted new inmates only on Wednesdays, my release was being pushed from that Thursday to June 2. An extra week in prison. In my mindset at the time, it wasn't just six days; it was an entire disciplinary write-up, a loss of good time. I could have earned that handily in a fight or by cussing out a cop, and instead, when I had done neither, the time was still taken from me. Furthermore, they took inmates to quarantine only on Mondays, and so I spent twenty-three days in that room, during which time I lost my absolute shit.

We stayed up all night, every night, playing strip Monopoly. It was my idea. I made this girl pay the rent on Park Place with a hotel with her shirt. Two nights later, when my own luck ran out, I was in my underwear, buying houses, when the officer did his check. He was pissed, and my extended hand, showing him the houses I was buying, didn't help. Another day, after two of the women in the room with us were casually told that they weren't being released on the CARES Act but then were denied use of the phone to tell their families not to come to the prison to pick them up (they had skipped our phone day the prior day as well), I snapped. I put my shoes on and kicked the door until one of us was going to break. When a counselor came to the door, I roared one word: "LIEUTENANT."

Not only did that bully walk away, so that we were ignored until the night shift came in, but she doubled down the next morning. She knew who was coming in the next day: Anthony, the cruel guard. She opened the door and sweetly said, "Winner, the lieutenant is here to speak with you, as you requested."

I was on the top bunk when he walked in, and I jumped down, snatching my face mask.

"Winner, you don't need to come over here, you're not leaving this room." He'd recoiled at the speed with which I had crossed the room.

"Yeah, but we're gonna have a conversation," I said far too loudly, matching his accent. "I'm not about to yell across the room while they're sleeping."

He said that there was a lot going on for him to be here dealing with me. I calmly replied that I was aware that the day prior there had been two fights, and I listed the units. *You are speaking to a professional spy*, my eyes told him over my mask. I explained that we had been denied the phones, while we could see the room on the other side of the hall being given the phone every single day. I explained how the officers were disrespectful when we asked when our turn would be. I gestured to the two women sleeping.

"My family's gonna be here whether I call them or not. These two were just told they're not going home, and no further effort has been made to give them a chance to call home and tell their families. This ain't for me, *sir*." I didn't start the conversation respectfully, and it only went downhill from there.

The counselor stood against the wall, aghast. Anthony was a cruel jerk who would have tear-gassed anyone for less. But I wasn't afraid of anything at that point. There are twenty-three scars on my body, one for each mind-numbing day of quarantine in which I couldn't do anything but become more and more disruptive and wild. It had been a long year leading up to that point, and I was desperate for someone to hurt me, at least as badly as I had hurt myself.

A week later, I walked out into the sunlight, shaken and desperate. They released me over two hours late, knowing my family was in the parking lot with no idea what was going on. They had to hurt my family one last time. I was expecting to see my parents and Alison, my genius attorney and friend, waiting for me. But Brittany was there, too, with my baby niece, Indigo. As thrilled as I was to see them, though, I couldn't enjoy that day in the car. After being released two hours late, I was still expected to make the seven-hour trip down to Corpus Christi, to check into custody by 5:00 p.m. *You are not free until you are free, and even once you are free, you are still not free.*

Once I was at the halfway house, the arbitrary, petty rules didn't end. Carswell refused to send my vaccination records, so I had to quarantine again. Quarantine continued to apply when we went outside for smoke breaks or, for me, exercise. There were only certain hours of the day when I could go outside, and even then, for only one hour at a time. The men's area had two tables, dumbbells, a pull-up bar, and other exercise equipment. The women's area was a picnic table on the other side of the parking lot, with no shade. If a single man went outside, I could not use the exercise equipment. I jogged in place on the sidewalk for two hours every day, inhaling cigarette smoke and looking at the dumbbells as if they were the long-lost love of my life. I was there for seven days before I was given an ankle monitor and allowed to go home.

Home confinement is so stressful and limiting that I would recommend people stay in prison rather than suffer through it. That might sound insane—*what could be worse than prison?*—but the term "home confinement" does not adequately convey the experience of it. "Retraumatization" is a better word. It is a real process, and our government is really fucking good at it.

The Tuesday afternoon before I went home, I was given a condition: if, and only if, someone picked me up at 8:30 the next morning, I could go home. I called my dad, and we decided to surprise my mom. It had been a fight to be released from the halfway house. When I'd first arrived, authorities told me that as long as my probation officer had approved my release address (which he had, months earlier), I could go home. The next day, of course, they realized who I was, and they took home confinement off the table. Alison started asking questions, and they realized they couldn't keep me there. Of course, when Gary picked me up, I felt elated. But when we got home and immediately phoned the halfway house, as required, they told me that my ankle monitor wasn't picking up a signal. My dad sent them the exact coordinates of the house. The halfway house person asked us to restart the monitor. We did. They asked us to charge it. We did. They then said that we could always come back for a working monitor, but we were already fifty miles away, and I did not want to give them an opportunity to hold me another day while they fixed the equipment. For two hours, the monitor vibrated on my ankle, indicating that they were looking for me. Finally, they made the thing work, and I could relax.

Sort of. I realized that this was how my life would be until they removed the monitor. I left my bag packed in my closet in case I needed to return to the halfway house at a moment's notice. If someone from the halfway house called my phone, I had to pick it up within two rings, or they could mark me as an escapee and call the police! If I was in the shower, if my phone broke, or if I was just on the other line, I could be rearrested. Once, I was running sprints in the front yard and doing lunges, and my phone was just over the fifty-meter Bluetooth distance away, so I couldn't answer it with my watch (I had bought a smartwatch to make it easier never to miss their calls). Fumbling with sweaty hands, I called them back less than a minute later. Too embarrassed to say I was doing something as self-indulgent as exercise, I said

I was doing chores outside and my hands were too filthy to pick the phone up right away. At least the wind blowing across the receiver did confirm that I was outside. The lady on the line chuckled and said that if I had taken one minute longer, she would have marked me as "escape status." *It wasn't a joke.*

My family noticed the change in me. Of course they did. "It was like dealing with a rebellious teenager," my mom says of those early days. "I felt like I was the target of all your anger, and I wasn't ready for that. It was extremely hard." Gary was the mediator between us, but I chafed at any rule or restriction—in my mind, any authority, even the greatest mother imaginable, was stifling, unjust, and oppressive. My behavior was traumatizing for them. I was secretive and kept to myself, eyeing them suspiciously. I tried to manipulate them and was ruthless. When Momface offered me advice or guidance, I resented it. "You're one of them," I spat at my mother when she told me she'd taken a job at a jail. I had never talked back or spoken harshly to my mother, or to any other family member. But now I was like an abused dog, ready to strike at anyone who came near me.

But I was determined to find joy now that I was home. I sat on my parents' back porch with their dog, Domino, removed my shoes, and felt the Texas sun lean onto my face. That glorious experience felt heavenly. I took a selfie to capture the moment, and it's now my digital avatar, so I can see it every day and feel it endlessly. And simply having a cell phone, being able to call anyone I loved at any time, was a luxury I hadn't realized I'd missed so deeply. In retrospect, it's so obvious: connecting with other people is one of the great joys in life, and you're deprived of it in prison. But it surprised me.

And the bananas! So many bananas, which are a scarce fruit in prison. I began cooking for everyone, a delight. But I used too many spices, since my favorite stolen spice, bought from the contraband market, was cayenne. It took me a while to unlearn that. What they don't tell people who are about to leave prison—well, they don't tell you anything besides your probation conditions—is that you will experience sensory overload. The walls have color. Walking in and out of the door unrestricted is possible. That first night, Domino curled up with me in bed, but I did not sleep. Without another person in the room, I just couldn't. No security was watching over me. In just under five years, I had become what Morgan Freeman's character in *The Shawshank Redemption* calls "institutionalized." For a while, I couldn't go outside alone in the dark. Where we live in small-town Texas, there are no streetlights or neon lights on signs. Evening here is as black as the FBI's heart. And in horror movies, the people who venture outside when it's dangerous are always the first to die. So for a long time, I didn't leave the house. I stayed to be near the phone. To be near light. To be safe. And I hated the silence. In prison, you wear earplugs and have an MP3 player in one ear at all times to block out the constant static of hundreds of people talking. On home confinement, I couldn't escape the quiet.

There was a social pass program. I needed the exact address of, say, Walmart, the local store's phone number, and the precise three-hour window in which I wanted to go there. I had to call before leaving, upon arrival, before leaving the store, and once I was home. The ankle monitor buzzed no matter what—there was no turning it off. At various stages of my home confinement, social passes would be taken away, as a COVID measure, but I would not be notified. My family would get dressed up to go to a restaurant, for instance, only to call the authorities and be told that our pass was not available. Sometimes it wasn't in their computer system, for God knows what reason. When that happened, I just shut down. My mother could not believe they could still do this to me, to *us*, and she called my caseworker. I was horrified. I was sure I would now be harassed even more, called twice a week for drug tests instead of the weekly tests. My mother has always been my greatest advocate, and she gave the caseworker a piece of her mind. But nothing ever got through to those people. I was supposed to be grateful, answer the phone, and stay quiet for six months.

Carlos, my old high school boyfriend, began bringing his four-year-old daughter over to visit me. Our relationship seemed to rekindle exactly where it had left off when we were teenagers. We bonded intensely. But he had been charged with a DUI and resisting arrest, a felony. And, of course, I had a felony conviction. Two felons are prohibited from interacting unless they are married. Plus, he was having a custody dispute with his daughter's mother, who could gain sole custody if she told the court that he was spending time with me. So after one month of dating, Carlos and I got married. This was a strategy I had learned in prison: whatever you do, formulate a legal plan to anticipate the authorities ruining your activities. My mom didn't like Carlos and warned me against my decision. She was right, and not for the first or last time.

The marriage didn't last long. I bought Christmas gifts for his daughter and tried to see them over the holiday, but he was drunk and high. I managed to see her, though, on the porch of the house where they were staying, and said my goodbyes, going through all the gifts I had bought her, telling her to be smart and brave and kind. That relationship was a wedge between me and my family from the start—but it was my escape from being, well, *me*. I wasn't famous with Carlos. He didn't give a shit about what I had done. To him, I was special because of our history together. In a life where I could count on one hand the people I had retained a friendship with from before the felony, this was the last shred of authenticity I had left. I didn't have to be intelligent, or a courageous "whistle-blower," or whatever else the people of the world who knew me only from my felony wanted me to be. All I had to do was love him, and his daughter. And I did, until I wasn't as fun or interesting as alcohol and delta-8. My last instinct of self-preservation kicked in, and I jumped off that ship. I was done being manipulated by the hope of having a family and a life completely unrelated to what I had done. I divorced him, seventy-four days after we got married. Mom, I should have listened to you from the start, but once again, I needed to make my own mistake. I'm sorry.

Despite all the drama and mess, though, home confinement is a privilege. To get it, you need a job, even though getting a job with a criminal record is difficult. Fortunately, I had arranged for work. It came about, like many good things in my life, from a supporter who found out about me from the news and wrote me a letter while I was in prison. It was part-time administrative work for a documentary film producer. Any work was wonderful, but if I had a work call and the halfway house contacted me, my phone would crash and drop both calls. Calling the halfway house back first, and getting off escape status, was my only priority in those situations. The producer understandably didn't take kindly to that, but I am eternally grateful he gave me a job.

Not that my first probation officer understood that. I first met him at the federal courthouse in Corpus Christi. It was my first time seeing the Gulf of Mexico in so many years—and it was one of the worst mornings of my life. I nervously navigated the courthouse to the probation office and checked in with him. I had to take a drug test, but there were no females in the office—I was given about a minute to fill the cup while he stood outside. We then sat at the table directly in front of the restrooms, and he went over my conditions. He tried to read my charge but could not pronounce the word "espionage." He stumbled on it twice, then said, "You know what it is. Whatever it's called." The government had given me the longest sentence of any leaker in American history, and my probation supervisor couldn't even pronounce the name of the crime they said I'd committed!

"Do you have a job?" he asked me.

I told him about my work helping the documentary producer.

"As long as the documentaries aren't about you."

"No, they're definitely not."

"What are your future plans?"

"Would it be possible for my income to be from my GI Bill? I could go back to school full-time," I said.

"I don't see why not. We'd just have to approve your field of study." The officer explained that it would be difficult for someone with manslaughter to study heart surgery, for instance.

"Oh, well I was thinking of studying kinesiology."

"Well, I don't know if that's realistic," he told me, "because you can't be in schools and around kids."

It took me a moment to understand. The guy thought I was a goddamned *chomo*. He saw that I had a curfew and more post-release restrictions than most murderers and armed robbers get, and because he couldn't read the word "espionage," he concluded that I had committed the worst crime imaginable. In prison, if someone says something like that to you, you flip over the table between the two of you and charge them, because the worst thing to be known as on the inside is a child molester. You don't call anyone that unless you know they are, in fact, one.

I froze up in that room. I wanted to be as agreeable as possible. I didn't push back. I said, "Um, I'm also a certified CrossFit coach, and I think it would help me start my own gym. Like to be a better coach. I've always been a personal trainer and a fitness instructor."

That seemed okay to him.

What's the best thing about being out of prison? Maybe having space and privacy. I built a CrossFit gym near the house, investing in a shed we also needed for the rescue horse my dad signed up the family to take care of. I have a spin bike with all the music in the world that I could possibly want. I have weights. Using all these helped me regain some mental and physical strength.

Only once, since I've been home, have I ever been so depressed that I could not exercise. That was in October 2021, when I heard that Zantana—my brilliant, red-haired, Lewis Carroll–quoting friend—had died. She was one of those friends in Carswell I wanted to reach out to after the halfway house. After she got out, before I did, she'd sent Yoshii pictures and letters and messages for the two of us. Once I was released to the halfway house, I could not contact her, because they have an app in your phone, and even on federal supervised release (probation), you are prohibited from talking with anyone with a criminal record. I knew from the few months of communications she'd kept up with us while I was in prison that she was using again, and I wanted to wait until November, when I would have less supervision, to find her. She didn't live that long. Her death came before I had the chance to express to her how much she meant to me, and to offer the possibility of a podcast together. She was so clever and funny; her life was a performance that ended prematurely.

Three weeks after she died, my home confinement ended, mercifully. As of November 2024, I am no longer on federal supervised release. I am no longer under house arrest, nor do I have a curfew anymore. I simply need to abide by the terms of my plea deal. That means not discussing classified information or anything related to classified information; not making money off my name or life story as it pertains to my criminal offense; and I have a lifelong ban on working for the federal government. Those are restrictions I can abide by.

My world now consists of my family—my parents, our five rescue dogs (Domino, Daisy, Dobby, Outlaw Babyface Nelson, and Dulce "Doosie"), and my own gorgeous puppy, Frannie—and my coaching job. We live in the same double-wide. It's cozy and comfortable and safe, and always has just enough room for everyone. I have a boyfriend even, another rescue that I brought to live with us because, well, he's just too handy to live without. He's another relic of my life pre-felony, a bond that's been tried and tested over time. I am a CrossFit coach in Kingsville, and I work six days a week and sometimes clean on the seventh. My job is everything to me. I don't know if I would have started driving again if there wasn't a CrossFit gym waiting for me to be there. Strict physical routines are essential, and looking after my animals gives me great joy, as well as great heartache sometimes. They don't always get along.

Dreams? Yes. I have those again. Hopes for the future took a while to reappear, because for so long just getting through the day seemed a nearly insurmountable struggle. Sometimes I think people in prison imagine that once they're out, they'll spend all day bettering themselves: reading, exercising, taking classes, writing, or whatever else they think counts as self-improvement. But the truth is that maintaining emotional and psychological stability once you get out is difficult, so difficult that you have no energy for anything else. Managing day to day without having a breakdown is now my overriding priority, so much so that it's impossible to look further ahead by weeks, let alone months or years. Envisioning your future is painful while you're locked in a cell. It's like focusing on a drink of water while you're wandering in the desert. Since it doesn't, in fact, exist anywhere near on the horizon, it just makes you even thirstier. It's nearly impossible to fantasize about the future without having your soul smolder with envy, bitterness, and frustration. Accepting that your life is within prison walls, and finding the best way to live within them, is the only way to get through. But now, at last, I have started to dream again.

These new ideas about what I want to do with my life came about while I was locked up, I admit. Leading people through downward dog poses and push-ups in fitness classes like the ones I taught in prison now appears more attainable for me than solving social crises in rural Herat or building wells in Kabul. The harsh truth is that traveling to those countries in any capacity is out of my reach for a long time. The US government would sooner revoke my passport than allow me to visit South Asia. Even getting a job at an organization that works overseas, the kind of job I used to dream of, is probably lost to me forever. But I can visit a gym or yoga studio.

I can even start one, in fact. My dream is to found a nonprofit organization that provides intense, high-quality sports and fitness programs to vulnerable people: people who are struggling with addictions or facing other obstacles that put them at risk of incarceration. It needs to be a nonprofit because financial barriers prevent people from making fitness a critical component of their lifestyles. But fitness can be, and for some of us must be, a major part of life. Exercise was important to me before I got locked up, but while incarcerated I realized how crucial it is to my well-being. My own cure can be my story, my future, and my gift to others.

The strangest thing about being out of prison is that far more people are interested in me out here than they ever were on the inside or before I went in. No one has recognized me on the street, thankfully. But whenever one of the many people leaking national security information gets caught, a flood of journalists reach out to me (unless, of course, the leaker is a senior military official or politician, since nobody cares about *their* criminal behavior). After being burned by some reporters, I have become more selective about whom I talk to, when, and why. I went on *60 Minutes* and NBC's *Nightly News*. I spoke to Kerry Howley for her excellent book, *Bottoms Up and the Devil Laughs: A Journey through the Deep State*. My first interview following my release was for Sonia Kennebeck's documentary *Reality Winner*, which remains the most comprehensive coverage of my story from start to finish. They were there, film crew and all, waiting with my family when the prison vehicle dropped me off at the meeting point. But mostly, I don't respond to requests for comment (especially not from *Inside Edition*).

As I write this, a twenty-one-year-old member of the Massachusetts Air National Guard, Jack Teixeira, is being charged under the Espionage Act for allegedly leaking a bunch of classified documents to a private group on Discord, a social media platform mostly used by video game geeks. Everyone and their mom wanted to know my opinion. But I wouldn't offer it. Here's why: *if* this guy did anything illegal, he deserves a fair trial. And that is not possible when he is tried in the court of public opinion. Among the worst aspects of my ordeal was seeing myself portrayed wrongly in the media. Since I have never met Teixeira, I know no more about him and his motivations than anyone else reading the news. And I know how badly that portrayal can be botched. In addition, the Espionage Act is a law that is deeply unfair, selectively used, and designed primarily to incarcerate people the government dislikes. I will not be a party to that.

Also, I have to be careful about what I say. My plea bargain is stricter than the rules under which I lived within barbed wire. Before I went on *60 Minutes*, I reached out to my old friends at the NSA to understand how the prepublication process I would have to follow works, since they have the right to review everything I publish, including this book. It turns out that the rules are extremely vague, with sweeping language like "anything related to classified information." To my surprise, the NSA agents were friendly and helpful. We went back and forth over a document of about thirty talking points that ranged from my career in the air force to my brief time as a contractor. One of the statements was something like, "There was a war in Afghanistan. The United States was involved." They cleared that.

The NSA prepublication review agent called me several times and finally requested—should I be willing and have the time—that I meet with her and an associate with the NSA, "to discuss the matter" (my felony).

I wasn't sure if this was a genuine ask that I could reject or if it was basically an order. My knees got weak. I feared that this was a replay of what had happened five years earlier, when the FBI showed up at my house. Those guys were all friendly too.

"Is this about the redacted document?" I asked. I hadn't leaked anything since I'd left prison except a lot of tears and anger.

"Yeah, and also the incident."

That's what they called my felony. It sounded like a minor traffic accident. I got five years for an "incident"?

I immediately said I wouldn't meet without my attorney (fool me once!). The NSA agent said that would be fine, even though Alison didn't have a security clearance; she explained that they were not interested in discussing the classified report itself but wouldn't say exactly what they wanted to talk to me about. She declined to offer an office for us to meet in, though I thought that would have been the logical place to meet, instead suggesting several times that we conduct the interview at my house. We eventually settled on a conference room in a hotel where my attorney was staying—after my trauma with the FBI years earlier, I didn't want any government agents near my property again.

We agreed to meet at the Hampton Inn off Highway 77, in Kingsville. I showed up looking as neutral as I could, in a CrossFit Kingsville T-shirt over my boot-cut Levis and worn Nanos. My attorney wore a nondescript black dress. We both arrived a few minutes early and were waiting outside the hotel when a fit white man walked by, looking conspicuously out of place. He wore high-water pants, a baseball cap pulled low, and a polo. He had everything but an NSA logo on his shirt. That particular hotel had a sign posted on the door saying that no guns were permitted inside. When he saw it, the guy turned around and walked from the lobby right past us to put his gun box in the trunk of his car. Then he returned to the lobby and took a seat in a chair right next to the hotel's sliding doors. My attorney finally went up to the man and asked him if he was there to meet someone at 9:00 a.m. He said he wasn't, and we left it alone.

Soon, two women showed up in business-casual clothing and approached us, introducing themselves as a special agent and an agency psychologist. We made our way to the world's smallest conference room and spent some time debating how to arrange the tables and chairs. They asked me to tell them my full life story, from childhood right up to "the incident." The psychologist informed me that she wouldn't record the conversation, but that she would have to report me to law enforcement if I confessed to a crime, if I expressed intent to hurt myself, or if I expressed intent to hurt others.

I was so relieved to have my attorney with me but was still terrified of saying the wrong thing. *What if they take something the wrong way? Are they trying to improve their agency or get me in trouble again?* The agent asked me to talk about the leak from start to finish, why I made the choices I made. I told them everything. I even talked about my misuse of quasi-legal substances in prison. Besides that, there really wasn't much I could confess to. I've been a law-abiding person, save for "the incident." They already knew about the eighth-grade food fight.

It wasn't fun. It was uncomfortable. They asked about my sex life in great detail. But they weren't looking for evidence of another felony. I think they were trying to build a profile of a leaker. They wanted to know if I had any feedback for *them*. What would have prevented my action?

I was torn. On one hand, here was an opportunity to make it known that I regretted betraying my nondisclosure contract with the United States government. On the other, I don't talk to cops. And during this interview, they sure felt like cops. I didn't want to make it easier for them to destroy the next conscientious leaker's life.

I took a deep breath and, yet again, just as I'd done five years previously in that small room with Special Agents Garrick and Taylor, chose truth.

"The NSA has some of the brightest minds in the country," I began. "They're honestly there to make a difference. Yet there's no outlet for people who no longer feel like they're on the right side. You're requesting blind loyalty from some of the most nuanced and analytical individuals—individuals, not soldiers—to process your intelligence and make predictions. Furthermore, in 2017, and likely until 2021—you know more than I do about those four years—you had a unique situation in which the NSA was completely ignored. So now these *individuals* who already wondered if they were doing any good were left wondering if they were doing anything at all. The culture of the NSA doesn't allow for *anyone* to question that aloud, or at least not without FBI agents showing up at their house. Your analysts need an outlet, and the director owes it to the agency to address historically unprecedented times, like those four years in which the NSA was completely disparaged publicly. We felt like we were alone in 2017, and it left me trying to single-handedly fix something far above my pay grade."

Five and a half hours later, my attorney and I were standing outside the hotel again, discussing where to eat. We went to our separate cars, and I turned my phone on. Alison sent me a text. "Don't look now," she wrote, "but our friend is walking out of the lobby carrying what looks like recording equipment." I looked over, and the polo-wearing guy was carrying a box with wires sticking out of it, fifteen minutes after my interview had ended. Maybe they can help me better remember what was said when I turn this manuscript in, since they have the audio. Cowards. They should have recorded our conversation in the open.

There are other things I would have liked to tell the NSA. For one thing, they should know that if I had been aware that I was basically being interrogated by FBI agents that fateful day in preparation for an arrest, I would have asked for a lawyer. And if I had done that, they wouldn't have been able to intimidate me into confessing to a crime under national security laws that are so hostile to civil rights. The law says that I was entitled to a lawyer, even with the Espionage Act's restrictions, and if I had asked for one, the FBI's questioning of me would have had to cease right away. I would have gotten a lawyer appointed to me, and they would have told me to shut up, or helped me answer strategically. And if all that had happened, the case against me would have been much, much weaker than it became. My life would have been much different, and better, if I had known all that. And the country's national security wouldn't have been any worse off for that.

But of course, I didn't know any of my rights in that situation, which is what the government was counting on. They knew that if they could pressure me by having armed FBI agents all over my house and isolating me, I would probably be so scared that I would admit to violating a tyrannical law, even though a judge reading the transcript wouldn't see the pressure that had been placed on me. And I'm sure prosecutors were aware that the FBI's de facto interrogation of me that day, while legally questionable because of their subtle pressure tactics, would probably pass muster with courts designed to protect the government's insanely broad definitions of national security.

I would have liked to say these things to the NSA, and to anyone else in the US government who had authority over me. But I knew they wouldn't care.

I was glad to return home. There's another reason that staying near home makes more sense for me than traveling to the far-flung parts of the world that I used to imagine myself saving. The only reason I am still alive is the love and devotion of my family, particularly my mother. Momface and Britty, Gary, Wendy and her partner, Deb, my parents' animals—they were all that kept me from self-destructing. At the time, in jail and in prison, it felt like a simple cost-benefit analysis, and the costs of continuing to live—extreme physical and mental suffering, feeling hunted and hated by the country I had sworn to serve—outweighed the few small benefits. It didn't seem that would ever change, even if I got to leave prison. People far more inspirational than I, who endured far worse, write of finding something deep inside, hope or faith as a source of resilience. Maybe that works for some people, but it didn't work for me, and I don't think it works for many people who struggle with their mental health. Instead, what caused me to continue functioning was the agonizing thought of my mother hearing I had killed myself. That was it. She chose to stay, alone, by my side during those bleakest of days. Only my love of my family, and their love for me, added enough to the life/death balance sheet to make sure life came out on the winning side. And I am so glad it did. As Tony Bourdain once predicted about his own death, "I will decidedly *not* be regretting missed opportunities for a good time. My regrets will be more along the lines of a sad list of people hurt, people let down, assets wasted and advantages squandered." I couldn't let those people down.

But I would be lying if I said I was not angry. Angry about how the government treated me, how they're still treating me. I'm still angry at the *Intercept* for telling the NSA who I was and where to find me, with little concern for my well-being. Hell, I am angry about the same things that I was angry about when I leaked the report, plus now the Espionage Act in particular and the revolting state of the American criminal justice system generally. I am trying to forgive and forget. But I am not there yet. The industry of mass incarceration in the United States is contradictory and bleak at best, and cruel and unusual at worst. Our experiment with rehabilitation and reform, or simply criminal intervention and prevention, has given way to profit and commodification of bodies behind bars. It's a world where money is made even without an individual's unpaid labor. It's the final form of capitalism, in which individuals need only *exist* in a confined space for larger corporations, subsidized by the government selling us, the public, the myth of public safety, to make a huge profit—off our own tax dollars. We are paying to do this to our own communities.

I did not do *hard time*. I will never claim that. The time I served was difficult, for me, for my family, for many reasons. I experienced violence, albeit mild compared to how badly things could have gone. I lived through a global pandemic behind bars, was infected with COVID-19 twice in one year. But as I write this, inmates in Texas state prisons are roasting alive in unair-conditioned cells, and people are still cruel enough to say, "You should see the jails in Mexico, or Thailand, or . . ."—insert the name of a developing nation. I am, however, alive. That's a big thing. Not everyone is glad about my strict policy of continuing to survive. When I was in jail and prison, people who believed the government's lies about me sometimes took the time to write and purchase postage to mail me letters wishing a slow, painful death upon me. I try to forgive and forget those people too.

I am not there yet either, though.

But I am still *here*. And sometimes in jail, when I felt my soul and mind rotting like months-old milk, that didn't seem like it would be the case. For my almost-freedom, for my family and pets, for my supporters, I am grateful.

And I am not your enemy.

Acknowledgments

This entire journey would not be possible without my family, born and chosen. Billie "Momface" and Gary, my parents, you stayed by my side when I was at my worst, and you continue to be my strongest advocates today. Your love for me is unconditional, and I strive every day to be worthy of it. Brittany, "my Seestre," you are my favorite person in the world, and I am so sorry I ruined your life. Sarah Nicole, my sister, I cannot thank you enough for having been there for our father during his last years and then for me when I was in jail. Auntie Kim and Uncle Rod, you never gave up on me. Mike and Annie DeMasi, the Quays, Conti, and the rest of my air force family, I cannot express my joy when you stood by me. Keith Golden, you're the best friend anyone could ask for. Nice bee story. Wendy, "FGM—the Fairy God Mother," we are connected in this world and the next. Deb and Drew Pollard, I can't say I would have ever made this decision again, but I also cannot live without you now; my biggest mistake also brought irreplaceable individuals into my life. I learned the art of beekeeping one letter at a time through my neighbor Jim.

ACKNOWLEDGMENTS

And Mr. Stengel, I adopted you, despite all protests to the contrary; thank you for being you. I cannot end this without mentioning my father, Ronald Winner, who taught me how to think.

I owe a world of gratitude to my legal teams, who put their careers on the line for this case. Titus, you were always my favorite. John Bell, your compassion for me and your wit in the courtroom never ceased to amaze me. Joe Whitley, I am sorry for being the most difficult person you have ever met. Thank you for the metaphors and letting me make terrible jokes. Holly, even when you threatened to take me over your knee and spank me, I lived for the days you would visit me in jail. You were my lifeline. Matt Chester, I can't say I miss those phone calls, but I am here because you saved me. Alison Grinter, you are the most intelligent and comedic human rights defender this side of the Milky Way. You are the calm before, during, and after the storm. Everyone needs an Alison in their life.

Chris Wittenbrink, you kept my passion for CrossFit going during tough prison times, but you also helped me get back on my feet and moving toward my goals post-release. Sonia Kennebeck, when the world fell out from under our feet, you documented everything, and our truth is preserved in a large way through your dedication. Stephanie Turner, Bob Fassbender, Eric and Nelma, Toby, Marti Lew, Dia Winograd, Lisa Runner, the Kent-Whites, Marc and Justice Ronnell . . . the list goes on to include everyone who wrote to me and remained my friend as the years stretched on. Your friendship was unconditional and steadfast when all I could do was send the occasional letter in return. Lisa Ling, the veteran's advocate I never knew I needed. Keri Blakinger, you're a good friend to have in low places. Thanks for giving me a chance when I was an absolute mess. Kerry Howley, I'll never forget the jail visit where they kicked you out after four minutes. Your tenacity in following this case is one of the wonders of the world. Susanna Fogel, Amanda Phillips, Emilia,

ACKNOWLEDGMENTS

Scott Budnick—the Winner crew—thank you for being the most sincere and genuine humans I have ever met. Kristina Satter and Dori Berinstein, when really powerful men wanted this story to go away, you two kept telling it. Rosie, thank you for speaking out every chance you get. People who have moved mountains for me: Michael, Jordan, Pierre Hollis, and countless others, you were like stars on a dark night. Mrs. Joyce, Miss Addie, and the other volunteers who visit jails and prisons, I appreciate you.

I will never forget you, the women who shared cells with me: my dearest Ivette, Shelly, Sparrow, Shannon, Sarah, Kay-Kay, Stephanie, Ashleigh, Mercedes, Felicia ("Wifey"), Brandy, Taylor, Krisa, Miss Nasty Nancy, Miss Peppers, Yozhii, Mrs. Dixon ("Sassy"), Stevie, Tovah, K, Mrs. Howard, Margo, Raven, Rita, Danielle, Martha Evanoff, Z, City, Diana, Anika, Baldeagle, Dee—I'm still trying to pay you for doing my laundry this past month—and Solo. Every single life I encountered is worthy of a memoir of its own, and I wish I could have taken your stories with me.

Lastly, this is for Daniel Ellsberg, who made me believe in myself once again. Rest in peace.

REALITY WINNER, a former linguist and intelligence analyst, was arrested in 2017 for leaking classified documents regarding national security. Born in Texas in 1991, Winner served in the United States Air Force and worked as an NSA contractor before her arrest. Her disclosure of top-secret information ignited debates surrounding government transparency, the use of the Espionage Act against whistleblowers, and the media's protection of sources. Winner was subsequently sentenced to more than five years in prison under the Espionage Act, the longest sentence ever for a single count of violating that law. She currently lives in Texas with her family and her dogs.